·

A Very Civil People

·

Hebridean Folk, History and Tradition

·

I am not ignorant that Foreigners, sailing thro the Western Isles, have been tempted, from the sight of so many wild Hills, that seem to be cover'd all over with Heath, and fac'd with high Rocks, to imagine that the Inhabitants, as well as the Places of their Residence, are barbarous; and to this Opinion, their Habit, as well as their Language, have contributed. The like is suppos'd by many, that live in the South of Scotland, who know no more of the Western Isles than the natives of Italy: but the Lion is not so fierce as he is painted, neither are the people describ'd here so barbarous as the World imagines: it is not the Habit that makes the Monk, nor doth the Garb in fashion qualify him that wears it to be virtuous. The Inhabitants have Humanity, and use Strangers hospitably and charitably.

Martin Martin, A Description of the Western Islands of Scotland,
1716 edition, p. 345

One half of the time, since I left you, has been spent in places quite remote from all correspondence, among the Hebrides, and other highlands of Scotland, with whom their neighbours seem to have less commerce than they have with either of the Indies. They are nothing so barbarous as the Lowlanders and English commonly represent them; but are for what I could find a very hospitable and civil people: and the main reasons for the contrary character I take to be for their adhering too much to their ancient custom, habit [dress] and language; whereby they distinguish themselves from all their neighbours; and distinctions always create mutual reflections.

Edward Lhuyd in letter to Henry Rowland,
12th March 1700

Is minig a theireadh nach robh dìchioll as a' Ghàidheal. Bu ghasda leam a dh' éiginn a thighinn air an fheadhainn as truim' air an càineadh a bhith air an caibhleachadh greis ann an eilein mara 's gun seòl beatha aca ach na bheireadh iad le 'n dìchioll fhéin a's a chuan ri sìde mar a tha an dràsd ann. Is mór m'eagal nach fhàgte beo dhiubh fear innse-sgeoil fo cheann seachdainn.

Mgr Ailein Domhnallach, Leabhar-latha,
1st March 1898
(for translation, see page 81)

We take a deal of killing, or we would have been killed out long ago.

Iochdar (South Uist) Crofter to Alexander Carmichael,
Report of the Crofters' Commission, 1886

.

A Very Civil People

.

Hebridean Folk, History and Tradition

.

John Lorne Campbell

Edited by Hugh Cheape

Birlinn

First published in 2000 by
Birlinn Limited
West Newington House
10 Newington Road
Edinburgh
EH9 1QS

www.birlinn.co.uk

Reprinted 2004

ISBN 1 84158 015 5

British Library Cataloguing-in-Publication Data
A catalogue record for this book is available from the British Library

The publisher acknowledges subsidy from the

Scottish
Arts Council

towards the publication of this book

Typeset by Trinity Typesetting Services, Edinburgh
Printed and bound by Antony Rowe Ltd, Chippenham

Contents

Notes and References follow each Section

Illustrations

1. Dr John Lorne Campbell of Canna, scholar, folklorist and farmer.
2. Map from Martin Martin's *Late Voyage to St Kilda* of 1698.
3. Peigi and Mairi MacRae, North Glendale, South Uist, shearing oats on their croft.
4. Seonaidh Caimbeul (1859–1944), South Lochboisdale, South Uist, bard and storyteller.
5. Father Allan McDonald (1859–1905), poet and folklorist, and parish priest of South Uist and Eriskay.
6. *Bannal* or group of women fulling cloth on the 'walking board' in Eriskay, 1898. This work was the occasion for the complex work- or chorus-song, the *òran luadhaidh*.
7. Stone cell of the early Christian monastic settlement of Sceilg Mhichíl, Co. Kerry, similar to beehive dwelling structures surviving on Eileacha Naomha, the 'Holy Rocks' of the Garvellachs, and in Canna.
8. Aonghas Beag, Angus MacLellan (1869–1965), South Uist. His vast store of traditional stories, ballads and personal reminiscences was recored by John Lorne Campbell and Calum MacLean.
9. Kelp burning at Gribune Head, Mull.
10. 'Kyloe' or Highland cow from the Hebrides, drawn in the early 19th century by the Scottish artist, James Howe.
11. Course-woolled blackfaced sheep of the Scottish Borders, drawn about 1798, of the improved breed whose introduction into the Highlands and Islands heralded the Clearances and drew the vituperative protests of the poets against '*na caoraich cheannriabhach*'.

Maps

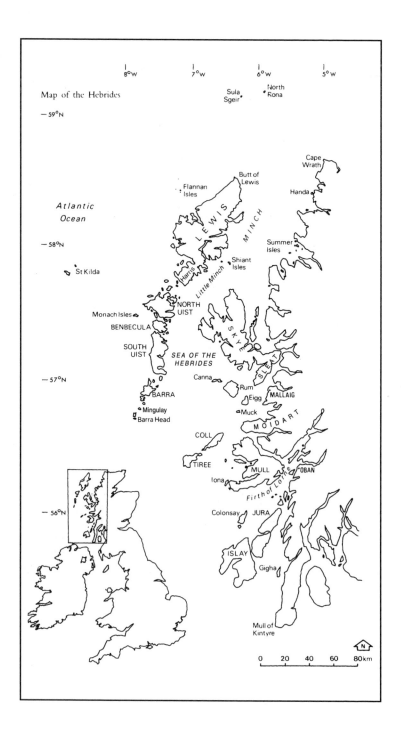

Map of the Hebrides

8°W   7°W   6°W   5°W

Sula Sgeir   North Rona

59°N

Cape Wrath

Flannan Isles   Butt of Lewis   Handa

Atlantic Ocean

L E W I S   M I N C H

58°N

St Kilda   Harris   Little Minch   Shiant Isles   Summer Isles

NORTH UIST   S K Y E

Monach Isles   BENBECULA

SOUTH UIST   SEA OF THE HEBRIDES   S L E A T

57°N   Canna   Rum   MALLAIG

BARRA   Eigg

Mingulay   Muck   M O I D A R T
Barra Head

COLL

TIREE   MULL   OBAN

Iona   Firth of Lorne

56°N   Colonsay   JURA

ISLAY

Gigha

Mull of Kintyre

0 20 40 60 80 km

viii

Introduction

'A Very Civil People'

The title of John Lorne Campbell's book of essays adopts the words of the Welsh polymath, Edward Lhuyd (1660–1709), the Keeper of the Ashmolean Museum who toured the Celtic countries of the British Isles between 1697 and 1701. This important collection of articles on Hebridean history and literature amply demonstrates that Lhuyd's was a fitting judgement on a civilisation of which John Lorne Campbell himself became a lifelong student and recorder and in which he shared to the full, especially as the owner and farmer of the island of Canna.

The present selection, which includes verbatim translations from the original Gaelic, reflects the seminal contribution of John Lorne Campbell (1906–1996) to the study of the literature, folklore and history of the Hebrides. Though written for the most part between 1935 and 1975, some of the articles and all of the translations are hitherto unpublished and have a freshness and originality as well as the scholarly rigour which characterised the author's work and allows them a continuing relevance for our own day. He studiously avoids the clichés of Scottish history such as clan battles and endemic internecine strife to concentrate on the deeper levels of everyday life of the widest spectrum of society, elucidating complexities of social interaction and offering penetrating insights into beliefs and attitudes.

The essays deal essentially with the Hebrides, but provide important inferences and conclusions for the wider study of Highland and Scottish history. Their focus moves from a conventional travelogue view of the island chain of the Outer Hebrides on their longitudinal axis to a regional study laid on a more latitudinal axis between the Outer and the Inner Hebrides. The author begins with St Kilda, which continues to have the power to attract, in the belief that there are still significant points to be made about this particular and much-studied island group. He continues with the Uists and Barra, their satellite islands and long and largely unwritten histories, and moves towards the mainland in looking at the Small Isles of Rum, Eigg and

Canna. The part-visible historical thread that holds this theme together is the traditional ownership and leadership of the MacDonalds of Clanranald who championed Gaelic culture and the inheritance of the Lordship of the Isles and whose territories stretched west to east across these islands. The essays continue with the scholarly investigation of the surviving corpus of the eighteenth-century Gaelic poet, Alexander MacDonald (Alasdair mac Mhaighstir Alasdair). Fittingly, the essays close with a selection of studies and insights into the Clearances, the period mainly in the nineteenth century whose catastrophic processes and consequences continue to reverberate today. Condemnation is all too easy and John Lorne Campbell does not overtly condemn; but neither does he condone. He provides analysis of the ways in which many estates became burdened by debt, particularly by the crippling financial obligations of marriage settlements and testamentary dispositions. Heirs of landed property were legally bound to meet such obligations and lawyers, often Edinburgh-based, would push them into clearing tenants and substituting sheep to this end. Typically, settlements were made in good times, for example when the kelp industry paid well, and had to be met in bad times, as brought down, for example, the MacNeils of Barra after 1822.

The traditional Gaelic material within the essays is drawn from recordings made by John Lorne Campbell in the Hebrides between the years 1937 and 1968. In translating the recorded Gaelic, he wrote:

> I have been glad to have the opportunity to give Gaelic-speaking Hebrideans a chance to have their own say, in translations of some of their memories recorded in their own language. Fortunately the invention of disc, wire and tape recorders came just in time to allow these to be recovered from the generation that was born in the 1860s and 1870s.

He was the pioneer of collecting the Gaelic oral tradition using mechanical recorders. The results of this work are testimony to his outstanding achievements as a collector and recorder and are preserved in the internationally important sound archive in Canna House. This achievement will be more thoroughly researched and documented in the future but it is worth noting in outline here in order to establish the chronology of this early work in the field. He acquired a clockwork Ediphone wax-cylinder recorder in January 1937, used it in Barra and Uist and, in September and October of the same year, in Cape Breton, Nova Scotia. In autumn 1937 he obtained a Presto J Disc Recorder in New York, and with this machine made the first electrical recordings in the field in the Hebrides, in

March 1938 in Barra. This was a difficult machine to use, since it required heavy-duty batteries and a rotary converter; the speed of records made with it were more like 72 or 73 rpm than 78 rpm. Recordings made with it, however, are extremely important since they serve to preserve and enhance the contribution to Gaelic literature and the personalities of individuals such as Roderick MacKinnon, Northbay (Ruari Iain Bhàin), and Mrs MacDougall, Castlebay (Anna Raghnaill Eachainn), first-class traditional singers who died before the arrival of wire and electronic tape recorders. The Presto Disc recordings were used to make a set of five 12-inch 78 rpm discs and a booklet, *Gaelic Folksongs from the Isle of Barra*, published by Linguaphone in 1950. At John Lorne Campbell's instigation, some studio disc recordings were made of the late Calum Johnston (Calum Aonghais Chaluim) of Barra in Edinburgh in 1948.

John Lorne Campbell bought a Webster wire recorder in the USA in 1948 but was frustrated in his efforts when the machine was detained by the British Customs for six months. The Webster was used extensively from 1949 to 1951 and, working with the aid of a Leverhulme Foundation expense grant, over 1200 items were recorded. These included stories from the outstanding Duncan MacDonald (1883–1954), Peninerine, South Uist, and probably the last waulking held in South Uist, at Gerinish on 29 March 1951, when, with nine women at the *clèith-luathaidh* or waulking board, twenty-five songs in all were sung by four different soloists and three rolls of newly woven cloth were waulked. Campbell began working with magnetic tape in 1956 with a Grundig Recorder. He recorded Angus MacLellan (Aonghas Beag) and his sister, Mrs Neil Campbell (Mòr Bean Nill), whom he had met first in 1948 and were then both in their 90s and living at Frobost where electricity was then being introduced. From 1962, tape recordings were made in the field on a battery-powered Phillips portable recorder.

In his long scholarly career, John Lorne Campbell was not only the recorder of traditions but also the author of a considerable number of books and articles and has been for recent generations a prominent historian of the social and economic conditions of the Hebrides. Working outside the institutional framework of the universities, he maintained preceptive principles of challenge and response in the face of what he regarded as suffocating orthodoxies in Highland history, moulded in the Whig thesis of Scottish history with its Calvinist rigidity and devotion to the unequal incorporating union of Scotland with England. This he consistently challenged, engaging in lengthy debates in print based on the solid ground of exhaustive research in primary sources. Some of the essays here are the by-products of such debates.

Rationalising his decision to stay independent of the universities, he contended that the systematic study of the popular culture and traditions of the British Isles had rarely found a place in the universities, and certainly not until very recently. But while the wealth of these resources in Scotland has always been well known, they had tended to be ignored by academics imbued with the romanticism generated by James 'Ossian' Macpherson and Sir Walter Scott. It was of cardinal importance to him that he was not a closet scholar but worked in the field and made available the results of his work, and drew attention to a wealth of traditional material still part of the fabric of life in the Hebrides. For example, it was a careful and deliberate decision latterly to concentrate on the preparation of material for publication, rather than to attempt more recording until he was unable to continue this work effectively. Thus, in collaboration with the musicologist Francis Collinson, he published the three volumes of *Hebridean Folksongs* (1969, 1977, 1981). In the same spirit he had at an earlier stage published his remarkable and influential book of Gaelic stories from South Uist and Barra, transcribed and privately printed in 1939. His editorial preface to the *Sia Sgialachdan* includes the comments:

> In writing down these stories, whether from the speakers' own dictation or from Ediphone records, I have deliberately reproduced the dialects of the speakers. This is in accordance with the method used by contemporary Irish collectors of oral Gaelic literature, for example by most of the contributors to *Béaloideas* (The Journal of the Irish Folklore Society). In my opinion, any attempt to force oral Gaelic literature into artificial mould of the standardised literary spelling and grammatical forms is a mistake, as it not only actually produces a false impression of the real language of the stories, but also obscures many interesting grammatical points.

John Lorne Campbell was aware that what he was hearing of the spoken language in the field was not at the time otherwise recorded, and that he must work hard to preserve the record of the spoken dialects which differed from the literary language, in some respects consistently. Transcriptions and published versions of earlier recorded material had usually been 'tidied up' with a consequent loss of detail, richness and variety, and the linguistic record had neglected the Outer Hebrides. He has commented:

> The collection of Gaelic folktales has been greatly improved by the coming of mechanical recording. It is obvious that when stories were

taken down by the pen, storyteller editors often condensed and substituted *oratio obliqua* [i.e. indirect speech] for *oratio recta.* The genuine storyteller produces pages of dialogue, as Angus MacLellan did. (Personal communication, 24th October 1989.)

In their approach to the study of Gaelic, he contended, Gaelic scholars had clearly neglected demotic speech, dialects, and even the songs and ballads still to be heard as the natural and living language of Gaelic oral tradition. John Lorne Campbell and other scholars have stressed that the earlier grammarians of Scottish Gaelic had simplified their task by dealing with the artificial literary dialect used in the translation of the Bible, and in a modified form by such early writers of Gaelic prose as Rev. Norman MacLeod, *Caraid nan Gàidheal.* Recording and transcribing presented other challenges. The language, as for example in the Fingalian stories, was usually complicated, and the standard dictionaries (which drew largely on literary sources) had tended to ignore the Outer Hebrides. The flowing, vigorous, vivid style of the practised storyteller, for whom reciting from memory was a natural art, produced long, complex sentences and stylised archaic language. John Lorne Campbell, living and working in the Outer Hebrides, began to use dictionaries of Irish such as Dinneen's to explain meanings since the authentic Gaelic of the eighteenth-century poets might often use Old Irish forms. To complete the linguistic record for Scottish Gaelic, there was a need for regional dialect glossaries such as John Lorne Campbell himself produced from the papers of Fr Allan McDonald (1859–1905), *Gaelic Words and Expressions from South Uist and Eriskay* (1958).

These guiding principles of recording and dissemination are assumed and exemplified in this selection of articles, reviews and translations written and made during sixty or more years' residence in the Hebrides. The book is written, as John Lorne Campbell emphasized, from the point of view of a West Highlander who writes from the inside looking out, and not that of a metropolitan visitor, from the outside looking in. Anthologies of the descriptions and comments of travellers in the Hebrides too frequently reveal a half-contemptuous, half-patronising attitude, as of 'tourists' encountering 'natives'; of their real needs, as of their language, poetry, oral literature and traditions, those looking in from outside were woefully ignorant. This had been pointed out as early as 1773 by Dr Samuel Johnson in a memorable passage in his *Journey to the Western Islands of Scotland* where he wrote:

> To the southern inhabitants of Scotland, the state of the mountains and the islands is equally unknown with that of Borneo or Sumatra. Of both they have only heard a little, and guess the rest. They are strangers

to the language and the manners, to the advantages and wants of the people, whose life they would model, and whose evils they would remedy.

John Lorne Campbell argued that much the same blinkered attitude could be found in Scottish historians, especially those who think that any knowledge of Gaelic is unnecessary when writing about the Highlands and Islands; for such persons only the record written in English counted. With the Gaelic record outlawed, Highland history was simpler but poorer, since there was no challenge to an official record which was at times as tendentious and untruthful as official propaganda ever is. The following essays bear witness to the author's exultant exploration of that other linguistic and literary record, and to his careful and constructive quarrying of the rich sources still to hand for the student of Celtic Studies and the Gaelic language. The offering is a veritable *Brosnachadh Fear Chanaidh* or challenge from the Canna guidman.

The Editor
National Museums of Scotland
January 2000

Section 1

.

Hiorta or St Kilda

.

Early Visitors to Hiorta

.

On 29th May 1697, Martin Martin, whose curiosity about St Kilda had been aroused by various accounts he had been given about the island, after consulting Alexander MacLeod the Steward, took the chance of sailing over to St Kilda with the minister of Harris, the Rev. John Campbell, to whom MacLeod of Dunvegan had entrusted the care of the island. Departing from Ensay in the Sound of Harris and after a very rough crossing, during which they were out of sight of land for sixteen hours, they reached the shelter of the small island of Boreray, four miles north of St Kilda. There they had to face a violent storm which the crew believed had been raised by the witchcraft of *Ruairi Mór* the Imposter. Fortunately the sea fell calm and on the next day, 1st June, they reached the harbour, where the Steward, who was already on the island, and the people of St Kilda came down to welcome them.

The Rev. John Campbell himself was apparently the first Protestant clergyman ever to visit the island; and his arrival was opportune insofar as it was the means of freeing the St Kildans from the influence of the religious imposter called *Ruari Mór* (mentioned above) who was dominating and intimidating the islanders under the pretended or imagined inspiration of St John the Baptist.[1] The visit of the Steward, on the other hand, was an annual affair, alluded to by Dean Munro as far back as 1549, and the social and economic life of the island centred upon it, for it preserved an ancient medieval custom – the consumption of annual rent in kind on the spot. The system was as follows: St Kilda had belonged immemorially to MacLeod of MacLeod, who used to rent the Stewardship to some needy relation or clansman. The Steward then had to arrange for the annual expedition to the island at his own expense. On this expedition he took as many as sixty of his own relatives or dependents to consume the annual rent in kind – barley, mutton, seabirds and their eggs – and also such necessities as the St Kildans wanted for the next twelve months, probably mostly tobacco, for nearly everything the St Kildans had was home made. In return the

Steward took away with him the non-consumable rent of the St Kildans and their exportable produce, largely the feathers of fulmars and other seabirds. No cash changed hands on these occasions. In other words, the Steward had the monopoly of trade of the island as well as the right to the rent. Everything was regulated according to custom, and the interests of the St Kildans were represented by their Ground Officer who was formally elected by the community and who had the right of appealing to MacLeod in the event of disagreement with the Steward. The Steward's party used to remain for several weeks until the rent in kind had been consumed; Martin's party was allowed eighteen guillemot eggs and a barley cake per man per day; in three weeks, 16,000 eggs had been eaten.

This system of management may have been open to abuse: but it had the great advantage of regularly bringing life and interest into the community, and of mitigating the loneliness and introspection into which the islanders must (and eventually did) fall once the system broke down. From Martin's description it is clear that the people, although poorly housed, were well-fed and happy.

Comparatively few visitors before the Steward had come to the island during the preceding century or more and left any impression. In April 1615 after the fall of Dunyveg, the island received a visit from the famous Coll Ciotach MacDonald. This visitation is the subject of a contemporary letter from Rory Mór MacLeod of MacLeod to Lord Binning, dated 18th June 1615 (MacLeod, R.C. (1938–9), Vol. II, p. 53). In this letter MacLeod complains that during his absence on the mainland (where his children were being educated at Glasgow under the terms of the Statutes of Iona), Coll Ciotach, guided by some of the North Uist MacDonalds, had raided St Kilda and slain all the animals of the island, cattle, sheep and horses, removed the spoil and distributed it amongst their friends in North Uist.

This story has been swallowed by most writers on St Kilda, but it carries improbability on its face. The MacLeods and MacDonalds were not on good terms at this time, and the southern MacDonalds were also on bad terms with the Government. MacLeod's letter bears the appearance of a complaint that is pitched high with the hope of eliciting official compensation. In any case, it is not the only evidence on Coll Ciotach's expedition. A statement was made by one Robert Williamson to Sir Thomas Phillips in Ireland on 13th May 1615 on this matter (Smith, G. G. (1895), p. 263a). Williamson had been shanghaied by Coll to go along with his expedition. He was therefore an eye-witness; and according to him the party consisted of thirty men and boys armed with fourteen calivers, each having about twenty shot of powder, twenty-four swords, seventeen targes, and each a long *sgian dubh*. They had a boat of five or six tons, and had spent four days on Mull, a week in Canna, a week in North Uist and a month on St Kilda, where they had taken a 'giant store of barley and some thirty sheep for their provision'. In other words, they had done no more than requisition meal and sheep for their own consumption. MacLeod's story becomes impossible when it is remembered that there is 'No access to Hiorta but at one place, where the boat is heased (*sic*) up, loading and all, by the Inhabitants, there be some sixty families there.'[2] It would have been impossible to have loaded and removed all the livestock of St Kilda in a boat of five or six tons. In Martin's time this was two thousand sheep, ninety cows and eighteen horses, and many of the sheep were on the inaccessible islets of Soay and Boreray.

Williamson said there were only ten men and ten women on the island, but it is suggested that what he really meant was that there were ten families (ten married couples there). The statement hardly makes sense otherwise.

According to Alexander Buchan, of whom more later on, Coll paid another visit to St Kilda in 1641, when he found a priest living there, who was said not to have been very well educated. I have been entirely unable to find any confirmatory evidence to the effect that Coll Ciotach, then aged seventy-one, visited or took refuge in St Kilda in the year 1641. The historians of Clan Donald make no allusion to this visit. As for the priest, there were then so few priests working in the Highland mission that it would not have been possible to spare one to reside permanently on St Kilda; and the Irish Franciscans, who were then conducting this mission, were well-educated men. Buchan does not give the source of this story.

In 1686, the St Kildans were visited by some Spanish and French seamen wrecked at Rockall. Then, Martin and the Rev. John Campbell came in 1697; this was the first visit from a minister. Before the Reformation, as Munro says, a priest used usually to go with the Steward, and would baptise the children born during the preceding year. If he did not go, the people baptised their children themselves – a perfectly normal Catholic practice. Martin Martin described the St Kildans in 1697 as 'Christians, much of the Primitive Temper, neither inclined to Enthusiasm nor to Popery', but it is clear from what he goes on to say about their religious customs that some of these derived from the Old Religion; particularly the brass crucifix that was kept in one of their chapels (the roof of which had been maintained) and which was used, or handled, in marriages and in 'swearing decisive oaths'. Martin added that the St Kildans kept Christmas, Easter, Good Friday, St Columba's Day and All Saints (*recte* Michaelmas), when there was a cavalcade. These festivals were common to all the Hebridean islands, where the old customs had not been entirely rooted out.

The Rev. John Campbell, a tolerant man, did not interfere with any of these customs, marrying fifteen couples on 17th June 1697 in the traditional manner.

Fr Dermit Dugan's Projected Visit to St Kilda

·

On 5th May 1657, Fr Dermit Dugan the Lazarist missionary who had been working in Barra, South Uist and Benbecula since the spring of 1652, wrote to St Vincent de Paul in Paris to say that he was

> preparing to set out on the tenth of this month for Pabbay. I have not told you of this plan of mine, fearing that the trouble and danger might make you anxious, for it really is a strange and weird place. Still, the hope we have of bringing back many stray sheep to the Lord's fold, our trust in His goodness, and the grounds we have for hoping that the inhabitants of this island, not being infected with heresy, can, with God's grace, remain faithful to our religion if once instructed – these motives urge us to scorn the danger and even death and to set out with the help of God to Whose Will I submit myself.

Strange? Weird? Danger? Inhabitants not infected with heresy? The island referred to cannot have been the Pabbay south of Barra; the people of Barra had been reconciled to the Church by the Irish Franciscans. Nor can the Pabbay in the Sound of Harris be considered strange or weird. But as the late Rev. Dr Donald MacKinnon and Alick Morrison say

> the island of St Kilda was closely associated with Pabbay from the 17th century. The association was due to a remarkable MacLeod family – the Clann Alasdair Ruaidh. The leading members of this family possessed the tack of Kirktown (Baile na Cille) on Pabbay, where they resided: they were also the Stewards of St Kilda. The family is descended from Uilleam Cleireach (the Clerk) fifth chief of the Clan MacLeod of Harris and Dunvegan.
> *The MacLeods – the Genealogy of a Clan*, Section Three, Edinburgh, 1970, p. 199.

The only way that Fr Dermit could have got to St Kilda would have been to go with the Steward of St Kilda, on one of his annual visits, with his retinue going to consume the rents in kind on the spot. The visit took place in May. The danger to which Fr Dugan referred was the fifty mile crossing over the open Atlantic in a fairly small boat. Unfortunately, Fr Dugan fell ill and died in North Uist on 10th May of the same year, 1657, and never got to St Kilda.

The Religious Traditions of St Kilda, 1697

Before considering why the Society in Scotland for Propagating Christian Knowledge commissioned the Rev. Alexander Buchan to the remote island of St Kilda as SPCK schoolmaster in 1710, it is necessary to say something about the religion of the St Kildans that was practised before that time. We are fortunate in being extremely well-informed about this in Martin Martin's little book, *A Late Voyage to St Kilda*, published in London in 1698.

Martin Martin, c. 1660–1719, belonged to the well-known family of the Martins of Bealach in the Isle of Skye. He was a Gaelic-speaker, well-educated with degrees from Edinburgh and Leyden Universities, with a scientific approach to his subject; and he was one of the very few persons who have written about the Hebrides with these qualifications looking out from inside. He had visited St Kilda with the Rev. John Campbell, minister of Harris, whom MacLeod of Dunvegan had asked to look after St Kilda, in the summer of 1697, and had stayed there along with the Steward of St Kilda, who brought a party there annually to consume the rents in kind paid by the Laird of MacLeod's tenants there on the ground, for some time.

He describes the St Kildans as an egalitarian society ruled by an 'Officer', *Maor* in Gaelic, whom the heads of the St Kildan families had used to elect, but who was now appointed by MacLeod's Steward, and who acted in some ways as a church deacon there. Martin describes the religion of the St Kildans, who then numbered about 180 persons, as follows:

> The Inhabitants are *Christians*, much of the Primitive Temper, neither inclined to Enthusiasm[3] nor to Popery. They swear not the common Oaths that prevail in the World, instead their strong asseverations involved no profanity. They do not so much as name the Devil once in their lifetimes.[4]
>
> They believe in God the Father, the Son, and Holy Ghost, and a State of Future Happiness and Misery, and that all Events, whether Good or Bad, are determined by God. They use a set Form of Prayer at the Hoisting of their Sails: They lie down, rise, and begin their Labours in the Name of God.[5] They have a Notion, that Spirits are embodied; these they fancy to be locally in Rocks, Hills, and where-ever they list in an instant.[6]
>
> They leave off Working after Twelve of the Clock on *Saturday*, as being an ancient Custom delivered down to them from their Ancestors, and go no more to it till *Monday* morning. (Martin related how they had been scandalised by a Franco-Spanish and a Lowland crews which had worked on Sundays.)

8

Martin Martin tells how there were three chapels on St Kilda, at intervals of a quarter mile, Christ Chapel, St Columba's Chapel and St Brianan's or Brendan's Chapel. In Christ Chapel, a brazen crucifix not exceeding a foot in length, lay on the altar. He said that the St Kildans paid 'no kind of Adoration or Worship to it, nor do they handle or see it, except upon the Occasions of Marriage, and Swearing decisive Oaths, which puts an end to all strife, and both these ceremonies are Publickly performed'. The St Kildans took care to keep their graveyard scrupulously clean. They all came

to the Church-yard every Sunday morning, the Chappel not being Capacious enough to receive them; here they devoutly say the Lord's Prayer, Creed, and Ten Commandments.
They observe the Festivals of Christmas, Easter, Good Friday, St Columba's Day June 9th and that of All Saints November 1st.

On the last of these they had an 'Anniversary Cavalcade, the number of their Horses not exceeding Eighteen'. A similar event occurred in other islands on St Michael's Day in September.

They are very Charitable to their Poor, of whom there are not at present above three, and these carefully provided for by this little Commonwealth … at the time of their Festivals, they slay some Sheep on purpose to be distributed among their Poor, with Bread proportionable; they are charitable to Strangers in Distress.

This happened in the case of the Franco-Spanish crew wrecked on Rockall in 1686, who later met a priest on 'the next island', presumably Harris or Lewis, who spoke French – perhaps Fr Cahassie or Fr Devoyer.

Martin Martin also wrote that the St Kildans 'have very good Memories, and are resolute in their Undertakings, Chaste and Honest, and the men reputed Jealous of their Wives', also that there had not been 'one instance of Fornication or Adultery for many Ages', and that they are 'nice in observing the Degrees of Consanguinity before they Marry'; this shows the persistence of the discipline of the medieval Church.[7] This, with Martin's remark that 'the Inhabitants are Originally descended of those of the adjacent Isles, *Lewis, Harris, South* and *North Uist, Skiy*', gives the lie to the often repeated assertion that the St Kildans must have been an inbred society.

Readers of Martin Martin's careful and explicit account of the religious beliefs and practices of the St Kildans, which have all the appearance of a medieval survival preserved by people living in a different time-frame, can decide for themselves whether these merit the appellation of superstition, ignorance and immorality given to them by Alexander Buchan and repeated in the Minutes of the SPCK, statements which have all the appearance of sectarian propaganda aimed at raising money, but which too often have been accepted by Scottish historians as describing actual facts.[8]

Eventually, the domination of St Kilda by a succession of Calvinist ministers reduced its formerly happy egalitarian society to one of people preoccupied with the idea that they were predestined to eternal damnation, to avoid which harmless entertainments like secular Gaelic poetry and music and children's games must be prohibited, frequent church services where sermons lasting up to two hours must be attended, and anyone who fell asleep was roundly rebuked from the pulpit. It is no wonder that after the annual visit of MacLeod of Dunvegan's Steward and his party ceased, and this kind of religion was forced on them, the St Kildans became more and more introspective and inhibited.

Martin Martin concluded his book on St Kilda with the following passage:

> The Inhabitants of *St Kilda*, are very much happier than the generality of Mankind, as being almost the only People in the World who feel the sweetness of true Liberty … free from solicitous Cares, and anxious Covetousness; from Envy, Deceit, and Dissimulation; from Ambition and Pride, and the Consequences that attend them. They are altogether ignorant of the Vices of Foreigners, and are governed by the Dictates of Reason and Christianity.

What a pity they could not have been left to live in peace, perfectly adapted to their environment as they were, an environment in which most of the writers who have criticised or despised them would not have survived for more than a week, to be guided by more reasonable religious leaders than Buchan and many of his successors; and if only they could have been provided with such amenities in more modern times as a jetty, even infrequent scheduled calls from a proper shipping service, and the radio link with the outside world which a German submarine destroyed in World War I, restored, things which St Kilda would certainly have had from a more sympathetic government had it been a small island off the coast of Norway, like Röst in the Lofotens, or Mykines in the Faeroes. The society which most closely seems to resemble that of St Kilda in the old days, is that of Tristan da Cunha in the South Atlantic.

As regards Tristan da Cunha, the writer remarked that some of the critics of an article by Roland Svensson on that subject appear to be under the impression that a country like Great Britain has no responsibilities or obligations towards its outlying islands, and if people choose to live in such places, they deserve no encouragement, but should be left to put up with any discomforts they encounter. We who live in the Hebrides are not unacquainted with this attitude in our personal and political dealings with the mainland.

Happily, it is not universal; particularly in Scandinavia, to which Dr Svensson belongs, an entirely different attitude prevails; that is, that the men and women who are prepared to struggle with the difficulties that life presents in such situations, deserve official encouragement and help. It would surely not bankrupt the mighty British nation, of whose fast-vanishing Empire Tristan da Cunha may well be the last surviving colony before long, to help the Tristaners to repair their landing-place and their crayfish-canning factory.

Letter to the *Scotsman*, 13th April 1965

The same was true of St Kilda.

Alexander Buchan, SPCK Schoolmaster of St Kilda, 1710–29

The history of the sectarian persecution of the Gaelic language in Scotland was described by the writer in his *Gaelic in Scottish Education and Life* (1945, 1950). It included an Act passed by the Scottish Parliament in 1646 setting up (in theory) an English language school in every parish in the Highlands and Islands. Parliament was then under Presbyterian control. After the Restoration of the monarchy and Episcopalianism in 1662, this Act was repealed. After the Revolution of 1688–1689, King William granted the rents of the suppressed bishopric of Argyll and the Isles to the Synod of Argyll for the purpose of 'erecting of English schools for rooting out the Irish (i.e. Gaelic) language and other pious uses' (*sic*). The anti-Gaelic Education Act of 1646 was re-enacted in 1696, the year before Martin Martin visited St Kilda.

Dissatisfied with the progress of this policy, a number of wealthy Whigs in Edinburgh were incorporated under the title of 'The Society in Scotland for Propagating Christian Knowledge' in 1709. The writer has never seen it suggested by any historian that the inspiration for this must have come from the revelation made in Martin Martin's books on St Kilda in 1698 and on the Western Isles in 1703 that Catholic communities still existed in the Hebrides and that Catholic customs and festivals still survived in nominally Protestant ones. Martin Martin revealed that, from the point of view of the Edinburgh Presbyterians, the Hebrides were very 'imperfectly reformed'. It is significant that the SPCK's first appointment of a schoolteacher was that of Alexander Buchan in 1710. Buchan was already on the island, having been sent there by the Presbytery of Edinburgh, which had licensed him in 1705; he was ordained as a minister in 1710, and lived on the island until he died in 1729.

It is unlikely that any members of the Council or of the Committee of the SPCK had ever been to St Kilda, but there could have been apprehensions in some quarters that the island might be used as a back door for the entry of Jacobite agents or Catholic missionaries or arms and money into the Highlands and Islands, although in fact its exposed, remote position and unsatisfactory harbour made that extremely unlikely.

Nevertheless, Mr Alexander Buchan, a native of Aberdeenshire and a retired soldier,[9] who was licensed as catechist by the Presbytery of Edinburgh and sent to St Kilda by the Commission of Assembly in 1705. Most likely, Martin's book on St Kilda, published in 1698, had come to the notice of the Presbytery, for in 1708 it was recommended that 'a contribution be made for his (Buchan's) encouragement in propagating the knowledge of Christ and rooting out the pagan and popish superstitious customs so much yet in use among that people'. Buchan himself says that he 'having their idolatrous monuments to throw down, the razing whereof, and the getting them brought to a better temper of mind, cost him no small pains and trouble'. Buchan alleges that the Rev. John Campbell 'being no doubt assisted hereto by Mr Martin, the Steward, and his men' had 'thrown down several of their statues and altars' in 1697: the sneer at Martin is unmistakable – there is no allusion in Martin's book to such a happening. At any rate, the bronze crucifix disappeared; the old altars were thrown down; the ancient chapel fell into ruin; the festivals were forbidden. For this iconoclasm Buchan and the SPCK may safely be held responsible.

Buchan's 'book' on St Kilda, from which these remarks are quoted, was written in 1726 and first printed in 1727 and again in 1773 (or 1774) with a preface by his daughter Jean. It is an unashamed wholesale plagiarisation of Martin's book, with a few tart comments, mostly on religion, added by Buchan himself.

The Society in Scotland for Propagating Christian Knowledge was founded in Edinburgh in 1709, and there are many allusions to Buchan in the unpublished Minutes of its Committee. Hitherto Buchan himself, or his daughter Jean, have been the source of nearly everything that has been written about him. Now we can see him through other and more critical eyes, and in place of the flattering notices in *Fasti Ecclesiae Scoticanae* and Jean's preface to *A Description of St Kilda*, Buchan is revealed as a bigoted, narrow, ignorant, difficult person, married to a complaining wife; a person who caused the SPCK far more trouble than any of its other schoolmasters, in fact the kind of person sent to a remote place like St Kilda because he was not suitable for a more accessible situation, something from which the Hebrides have suffered a good deal off and on in their history.

Almost immediately after the SPCK was founded, Buchan applied for financial aid, early in 1710. At this date, of course, no interest had accrued on the Society's capital, and they were obliged to refuse. Buchan was then on the mainland, insisting that he could not return to St Kilda 'except some assurance be given that he will be taken care of'. In March 1710, the Society compromised by appealing to the tutors of the young MacLeod, Norman XXII of Dunvegan, born in July 1705, to support Buchan until their funds permitted their aiding him. In the same month he was ordained by the Presbytery of Edinburgh. This entitled him to the Stipend of St Kilda (such as it was).

In April 1710, Buchan was in Edinburgh and the Society moved that the Presbytery of Edinburgh 'may make tryall of Alexander Buchan's qualifications for being a schoolmaster'. The Committee gave him £10 8s. 6d. sterling. This trial was satisfactory and the SPCK appointed their first schoolmaster in the following terms:

13th April 1710

The Societie in Scotland for propagating Christian Knowledge erected by her Majesties Letters Patent being informed of the said condition of the Inhabitants of the Island of Hirta alias St Kilda which lyes at a great distance from any other land and not haveing formerly had any to instruct them on the principles of the Christian reformed protestant Religion nor any to teach them to read till of late that Alexander Buchan went thither but he being obliged to come hither for want of a subsistance there being no setled maintinance for one in his station in that place its informed yt Errour Superstition and Ignorance abound there, and seing the said Alexander has been tryed and examined by the Reverend Presbytery of Edinburgh at appointment of the Commission of the General Assembly and is found qualified and has produced ample Testificats thereof as also of his life and good conversation from other places where he hath resided from his infancie and he being willing to return to that place wee do by these presents authorise and impower him to erect and keep up a School in the said Island and to teach the Inhabitants thereof to read especially the holy Scriptures and other good and pious books as also to teach writting arithmetick and such lyke degrees of knowledge and to use such means for instructing the people in the Christian Reformed Protestant Religion as may be proper and he is appointed to observe the Instructions herewith given to him in all poynts.

Instructions by the Societie in Scotland for propagating Christian Knowledge given to Alexander Buchan.

1. Yow are to return to Hirta and according to your commission given by the said Societie Erect a School there and deall with the Inhabitants of that Island especially of the younger sort to come to yow to learn what yow are desired by the said Commission to teach.
2. When any comes to yow encourage them and shew them the advantage of Learning and take much pains on them that their profiting may encourage others.
3. Begin your meettings in your School in the morning and end it in the evening with prayer and be carefull to suppress lying curseing swearing and other immorality amongst the youth and have privy censures for that effect in the School.
4. When the day is short it will be fitt yow have but one meeting but when it is long yow may have two meetings if yow find the Children can be so long spared by their parents.

5. Be conscientiously carefull to instruct them in the principles of Religion according to the word of God the Confession of faith Larger and Shorter Catechisms of this Church these who can read cause them Learn the said Shorter Catechism by heart; but as to such who cannot read learn them some Questions concerning God and the Creation and the preciousness of Immortall Souls their sin and misery and redemption by Jesus Christ what he is and hath done and suffered for them and what they should do to be saved. Teach them the Ten Commands Beleif and Lords Prayer their Baptism and the nature of the Lords Supper what it signifies and the Covenant of Grace what was promised what they are bound to, and what God promiseth as also anent the Evil of Sin and the Sins that abound in the Countrey, the Evil of useing charming and other superstitious Customs and anent the Judgement to come and their state after this in heaven or hell.

6. When yow go from house to house to Instruct the Inhabitants commend what is good and vertuous and reprove vice and idleness and pray with and in the family and teach them to pray therein themselves and how to sanctify the Lords Day and how to carry in time of Divine Worship.

7. When yow converse with the Comon people shew them the evil and danger of Ignorance and vice and offer them your help and teach them as in the former directions and as yow shall be farther directed by the said Societie and presbytery or Synod of the bounds under whose Inspection yow are to be.

8. Be not morose or sullen nor too familiar or open but kind and courteous and of a wise and gaining conversation, that they may see yow are sent for their good and not your own profite nor any gain from them.

9. Walk circumspectly that your conversation may reprove and shame the vitious and commend our holy Religion to their Consciences Philipians second and fourteenth, fifteenth and sixteenth Titus second and tenth and use all means proper for suppressing of vice and immorality.

10. Be diligent not only to teach them to read English but also to write and lay it on such as profite by yow to do all they can for the edification of others and teach them their duty to their Superiors.

11. Study patience and be not soon angry but be meek and humble and be not given to unnecessary debates.

12. Be carefull of Instructing Murdo Campbell and ffinlay McDonald[10] and of their education in order to their being usefull in the said Island.

13. Be carefull of the books committed to your charge that they may be preserved for these who shall succeed yow in the forsaid Island and faill not when occasion offers to write to the said Societie or their Committee and give any account how matters go with yow.

Lastly Yow have need to be diligent and serious dayly in seeking God and his Councill and conduct in mannageing this design and mind proverbs third and sixth sixteenth and third of James and fifth verse, and study much the Holy Scriptures and make them your councellours psalms one hundred and ninteenth, twentie fourth ninty eight ninty nine.

Armed with the dual authority of a Minister and an SPCK Schoolmaster, Buchan returned to St Kilda and proceeded to get into a quarrel with the Ground Officer there, revenging himself by fining the Ground Officer's wife two merks[11] and forcing her to 'stand in sack-cloth for inducing two women to sell a dog on the Lord's Day' (Scott, H. (1915–61), Vol. VII, p. 193). We know nothing of the merits of this quarrel, but this looks like an abuse of clerical authority. (Nor do we know anything of the St Kildans' opinion of Buchan, for no attempt was ever made to collect their traditions.)

The next heard of Buchan in the SPCK Committee Minutes is on 25th February 1712 when:

> There was produced and read tuo Letters from Alexander Buchan Catechist in St Kilda, wherin he shows that he had been ill, but is some what recovered, and gives an account of his dilligence in his work and shews that he was resolved at his death to Leave the houses, and accommodations he had built, and all the plenishing therof and other moveables to Murdo Campbell, the best inclined, and most hopefull of his boys that he is educating, or to any other that shall succeed him as Catechist, & that if he could get the five pounds Sterling promised him he would sufficiently provide him and his successors in all necessaries, He desires to know if his litle book of the description of Hirta,[12] which he left with Mr Hart Minister be printed, and entreats that the third part of the money therof may be sent to him, to be given to Murdo Campbell to keep him at the Grammar Schooll and declares that he resolves to give him thirty merks of the Three hundred merks yearly that the Society has allowed him, with any more help he can give him, to train him up at Schools to fit him to succeed him, And that he must do this because the natives will let none of their children come to School that can work, unless he'l maintain them all the while, and he shews that he mantains eight or nine poor orphans in his family, and teaches them English, which they only can learn in his house.

The Committee approved this report and ordered 300 merks (£200 Scots) sent him as salary from Whitsuntide 1711 to Whitsuntide 1712. The trade of St Kilda being a monopoly of the Steward, Buchan's habit was to get goods on credit from the Steward against bills for all or part of his salary. This method of dealing led to trouble, as will be seen.

There was some talk at a later meeting about sending someone to St Kilda to inquire into Buchan's state of health, but this the

Committee decided that the Society could not, and need not, do 'because the Tutor of McLeod could get notice more easily, and as effectually, as by ane express, and should take care that enquiry should be made about him'.

At a meeting held on 2nd April 1713, a letter from Buchan was produced reporting progress, and saying he owed MacLeod 'these three years' 760 merks. The Committee ordered that three years' salary owing to Buchan (900 merks) should be remitted to MacLeod and his Tutors on Buchan's behalf. MacLeod's Factor was, of course, the sole source of supply for the St Kildans.

In October 1713 the Committee had another letter from Buchan, and agreed to allow him another year's salary until 15th April 1714, asking at the same time for an account of the necessaries supplied by the Tutor of MacLeod, and a receipt from Mr Buchan as soon as possible. At the same meeting he was allowed £10 Scots worth of books for the use of his pupils. The receipt was sent, and the books acknowledged by a letter received in December or January.

Here follows a gap in the SPCK Minutes, partly due to the troubles of the 1715, until on 15th May 1717, 'The Committee Reports that for these tuo years bygone or therby they have had no accompts what Mr Buchan is doing at Hirta.' The Committee of the SPCK asked the Commission of the General Assembly to take the matter up with the Presbytery of Skye, and at a meeting held on 5th September 1717,

> there was produced a Letter from Mr Archbald Mcqueen Minister, in name of the presbytery of Sky, shewing that Alexander Buchan at Hirta has been very successfull in his work in that place and that he had administrat the Sacrament of the Lords Supper in that island, and the people are desireous to have it again. And Therefor Craveing that the Elements may be sent there. The Committee transmitts this Letter to the Society, And are of opinion that some wine & flour should be next Spring sent to Hirta, and an encourageing Letter.

A more explicit, and very interesting, report on St Kilda was read at the following meeting on 4th November 1717:

> There was read a Letter from Mr Daniel Campbell, Minister of Glassrie dated the third day of October in favours of Alexander Buchan at Hirta, Representing his circumstances and entreating that an hundred merks yearly may be added to his salarie, and that his wife and daughter who are on their way to Edinburgh may be subsisted untill Summer next, that they return home, There was also produced a Catologue of books that Mr Buchan desires may be sent him & another of books that he has, which are not now usefull to him, Also an order to his children to

17

give of their substance to encourage teachers in St Kilda. He gives an account that he has only four Schollars beside his oun children, the poverty of the place & people hindering them to send their children to School except in stormy weather, when they cannot be otherwayes imployed, he gives an account of six children that he has, and that the eldest being a girle, teaches the catechisme to all the girles in the Island upon Saturdays and Sundays afternoon, being the only time they can spare, and that he himself is always present to help her, There was also produced & read a Supplication by Katharine Campbell spouse to Alexander Buchan, giveing an account of her husbands circumstances viz. That notwithstanding that he diligently attends his duty both as Minister and School Master, yet he labours under many discourage-ments both as to spiritualls and temporalls, haveing no Minister or experienced Christian to converse with, and give him advice in his many difficulties, That through want of a Magistrat to assist him in discipline, his hands are very much weakened that way, That his family is encresced to the number of ten, viz. themselves tuo, six children, a maid servant and a nurse whom she is obliged to keep, her oun milk having gone from her by the change of her diet, That they are obliged to hire the natives to grind their meall in quirns, cast & lead their peats, herd their few cattle thatch their oun house and do other services, where through the Three hundered merks allowed by the Society to her husband, is every year exhausted long before the Stewart come to the Island, and they are put to the borrowing which exposes them to disdain & reproach, That they are forced to wear shirts of plaiding & other such things which exposes them to contempt, That they have no bread but what's made of old barley, and the Country affords no Liquors but water, their few cows not being sufficient to affoord them milk & whey, and they have only six weathers allowed them in the year by the Chamberland in part of their Three hundered merks, And Therefor she Craves that the Society would add another hundered merks to their former allowance, and in part thereof to allow them tuo bolls oat meall, and a boll of peese to be put up in barrells at Neill McCallums house in Glasgow, to be sent to them yearly with the boats of Harreis, also tuenty ells of Course Linnen at eight pence the yard, and eight ells at sixteen pence the yard, She also entreats that the books mentioned in her husbands Catalogue may be sent, And that a Letter may be sent to the Tutor of McLeod, and Roderick his son the Baillie of Harreis to give her husband all suteable encouragement for strengthening his hands in discipline, and obligeing the natives to pay him the ordinary dues for marriages and baptisms, which he once possesst but is now deprived of And also that they would oblige the natives to help to cast & lead her husbands peats as is usuall in other places, And that the Society would send some competent number of Irish Psalm books, and Bibles both English and Irish for the use of the children, and such as can read, And she entreats that a copie may be sent to her husband of whatever is written in his favours to the Tutor & Baillie that he may be able to let them see what the Society orders about him, She also begs that some way may be fallen upon to subsist her and her daughter untill May next that they return.

The Committee's comment was:

That Mr Buchans success both as Minister and School Master should be particularly enquired into and what's the reason that he has so few Schollars, and they think the Society should give him all encouragement, and should grant the desire of the above Petition.

Mrs Buchan spent the winter on the mainland and on 17th March the Committee ordered that the balance of Buchan's salary should be paid to her so she could buy what she needed and take it home. However, when the accounts were looked into it was found that very little balance remained owing on Mr Buchan's salary, 'effects to the value therof being got from the Laird of Mcleod's Chamberlanes' and the Committee had to pay Mrs Buchan an additional 100 merks of salary to buy meal etc to take home. They also arranged for her to leave her oldest daughter, then aged about ten, for a year, to be educated through charity. They also directed '... that a Letter be writen to the Tutor of McLeod and others concerned in that Island to take more care in obligeing people to send their children to Mr Buchan to be taught, and also to see that all due encouragement [be given him] and be not extortioned as to the pryce of necessaries furnished to him, otherwayes he will be removed and sent else where', although attendance at SPCK schools was not supposed to be compulsory. On 3rd April it was reported that Mrs Buchan had gone to Glasgow to return home, taking the school books, and was leaving her daughter there to be boarded at £15 Scots a quarter, to be educated free in the 'trades hospital'.

From this time onwards the financial troubles of the Buchans take up a good deal of the SPCK Committee Minutes relating to St Kilda. Obviously the system whereby bills drawn on the Treasurer of the SPCK for Buchan's salary were lodged with MacLeod's steward against goods supplied on the visits made by that official to St Kilda once or twice a year was open to difficulties. On 13th January 1719,

There was also produced a Letter from Alexander Buchan Minister in Saint Kilda shewing that at last compting with Mr Mcleods Baillie, there is only sixteen merks resting him, he gives a long account of the rate of things, he buyes in that place he sayes he has seven children and a servant lade [lass] that he is teaching to read, and that there are five of the natives, and three of his own children that can read the Bible, and that there are other two young ones whom their parents have promised to send to School, he sayes he has given the Sacrament a second time, and that he had many more Communicants then he had the first time.

On 23rd June 1720, a letter was received by the Committee

shewing that Mr Alexander Buchan at Hirta has two daughters at Glasgow and that some years agoe one hundred merks was added to Mr Buchans yearly Sallary upon account of Education of his Children and his self denyal in condescending to continue in that Remote Island, and that yet nothing of that money had been given to the two daughters at Glasgow, and the Charitable people there, had hitherto taken care of them, But its not to be expected they will continue to do so, and if the Society will not do something for them she cannot keep them Longer.

At the next meeting the Treasurer was asked to pay the last quarter's board for one of the daughters. This was done again in October 1720. On 8th December 1720, it was reported that Buchan had authorised the payment of 100 merks for the education of his two children in Glasgow, and, enough remaining to meet that sum, payment was ordered. Next March, Mrs Buchan appeared before the Committee with another recital of woe.

Katharine Campbell spouse to Alexander Buchan at Hirta having come to this place compeared before the Committee and represented her husbands Circumstances in that place and their bad accomodation and how needfull it is, that she have some money to furnish meal and other necessaries to carry home with her, having no food there but barley meal and meal of black oats, Sea fowels and fish, and as for cloaths and other things furnished them by those who serve under the Laird of McLeod they are obliged to pay very dear for the same; The Committee considering that the said Mr Buchans Salary of three hundered merks Commenced only from the fifteen of April one thousand seven hundred and eleven as payable by the Society, his Service preceeding that time being paid by Collection, and partly out of the members of the Society their pockets as appears by their Minutes April tenth Jmviic and ten which Salaries the fifteen of April Last amounts to two thousand pounds Scots, which is all paid except fifty merks. The Committee appoints their Treasurer to pay the said sume of fifty merks to Mrs Buchan as also one hundered pounds more per advance which clears that part of his Salary of three hundered merks to himself till the fifteen of October nixt and appoints the Treasurer to pay the sume of one hundered merks allowed Mr Buchan the seventeen of Novr Jmviic and Seventeen of additional Salarie to Alexander ffinlayson to be paid to those who keep two of the said Mr Buchans daughters at Glasgow which clears what is due of that additional Salary till November Last there being one hundered merks paid Mrs Buchan twenty seven March Jmviic and eighteen and another

hundered merks to Baillie Murdo thirteen December Jmviic and
twenty; as to the Second additional Salary allowed Mr Buchan by the
General meeting thirteen August Jmviic and nineteen it is only to
continue one year or two, and all that is due is already paid in to Mrs
Mckewan for boarding Jean Buchan and appoints a Letter to be written
to Mr Alexander Buchan.

The next summer Mr Buchan wrote to the Committee in a depressed
strain.

The Clerk presented a Letter from Alexander Buchan at Hirta the twenty
second of July last Shewing that he had formerly last year Sent a Letter
giving an account of the great mortality that had been there but the Letter
was Lost and that the sad case of the people in that Island had occasioned
the Scattering of the School but that there is twenty yet alive that can read
the Bible and other four that was Learning in the proverbs besides some
who began to Learn and went back he shews that there is a great aversion
among the Children to Learning and the parents and friends are not
encouraging thereto So that he is not to blame for the paucity of Schollars
That there is a Poor boy both fatherless and motherless that came of his
own accord to the School whom the said Mr Buchan had maintained in
food and Rayment for two years and this is the third and proposeing
twenty or thirty merks to help to maintain him ffor he assists in teaching
the School and reads the Bible well and the Catechism every Sabbath
afternoon to the Children and he and an other of the natives can read
the Irish psalm book[13] That all the young men that marries there must
have the Catechism by heart and the young women the Like That the
Generality of the people answer as well as he had Seen Illiterate people
do, whereof they will give prooff when Ministers come to visite the place
He shews that he is failing much this year and he thinks drawing near his
end, He seeks some Catechisms. The Committee having heard this Letter
are of opinion that the poor boy recommended by Mr Buchan have twenty
merks yearly from this time during the Societies pleasure and that Mr
Alexander Buchan be written to to take care of the Instruction of that
Boy, in order to qualifie him to be usefull in that place.

The year 1722 and part of 1723 is taken up with bills drawn on
Mr Buchan's salary in favour of MacLeod's tutors. On 27th June
1723 a letter from Buchan was produced in which he complained
that most of the people would not send their children to school
and those who did attend forgot what they had learned – in English
– after leaving. He called for the balance of his salary, which he
believed to be 130 merks, but the Committee, having to check this
claim against MacLeod's steward's accounts, had to postpone
settlement. On 6th March 1724, the Committee recorded they had
no other report from St Kilda for 1723 but this. By this year the
number of Buchan's daughters being educated in Glasgow had

increased to three, and these asked that 100 merks of the salary of 300 merks be given them to buy necessaries which could be got cheaper and better in Glasgow than from MacLeod's steward. This the Committee could not do, but they wrote to Buchan suggesting he make the arrangement himself. The 7th May the same year a letter from Buchan was read complaining that the natives only sent their children to school during summer and when compelled to by MacLeod's steward. The Committee replied asking him to send in the names of his scholars, and forbidding him to teach any of them to read the Bible in their native language, Gaelic.

In March 1725 another of Buchan's reports, self-commendatory in tone, came in:

> The Clerk produced and read a Letter from Mr James Campbell at Kirkmichael of Glassary dated the twenty second of ffebruary Last, Shewing that he had that day received a Letter from Mr Buchan in Hirta with one inclosed to the Clerk of the Societie which he had transcribed for the more easie reading and it bears that Notwithstanding of the people of that place's great Ignorance Superstition and Immoralitie yet now they are come to know Not only the principles of Christianitie But to make wonderfull advances in the ways of Godliness from the Least even to the greatest that they all have the shorter Catechism by heart and that he had taught more than three score to read of which many are dead, and he blessed God who by the Bounty of the Societie had enabled him to be an Instrument of any good tho in the remottest and most incivilized Corner of this vineyeard and have moved them and other Charitable people to shew so great kindness to him and his poor Children and prays that God may reward that Labour of Love, hoping the Societie will continue to make his Circumstances in that Solitary place Comfortable and therefore the said Mr Campbell concludes that endeavours may be used to get his Children here the management of sending him necessaries from Glasgow, which may be had at an easier rate than what the Baillie or Stewart of Hirta does. The Committee remitted to the Treasurer and Clerk to consider the state of the said Alexander Buchans Accompts and what Children he has here and how maintained and report.

Trouble, however, was to follow. At the next meeting, on 1st April 1725:

> The Treasurer gave in a State of Alexander Buchan in Hirta's accompt whereby it appears that upon the fifteen day of this moneth there will be resting him of Salaries two hundered pounds Scots, and yet he has drawn for one hundred and thirty three pounds six shilling eight pennies more and by a Bill dated the twenty of July last he draws for more payable to his daughters.

Buchan was overdrawn, besides which his daughter Jean was present asking for 100 merks 'to buy necessars with at Glasgow to be sent to Hirta'. The Committee recommended that Mr Finlayson Town Clerk of Glasgow be written to to find out if anything else had been advanced to Buchan's daughters against repayment by the SPCK. If not, the money could be spent in that way, and school books were to be sent to Buchan as requested with a warning not to overdraw on his salary again. MacLeod's steward was also to be advised not to give him further credit.

Trouble about Mr Buchan's overdrawing continued, however. At a meeting of 9th September 1726 the Treasurer reported that his salary had been paid up to Withsuntide 1726, and that his additional salary of 100 merks per annum had ceased at Whitsuntide 1725, his daughters by then being considered capable of looking after themselves, the other 100 merks allowed him being quarterly paid for boarding his son George Buchan. Alexander Buchan himself was only due less than five months' pay on a yearly salary of 300 merks by September 1726, yet he had already drawn bills for 250 merks payable out of this salary. The Committee warned Mr Buchan again about overdrawing and refused to grant any further money to his daughters.

The Committee, still clearly dissatisfied, recorded on 20th October 1726 that they had never had any 'account of the diligence Carriage and Success of Mr Alexander Buchan in Hirta, but from himself' and recommended that one of the ministers of the presbytery of the Long Island or of Skye should go to St Kilda next summer with the Steward and 'not only enquire into the said Alexander Buchans Carriage But Catechise the people and report to the presbytery who are to send hither a Copie thereof'. The Minister chosen was the Rev. Daniel MacAulay of Bracadale, Skye, and the Committee sent him a copy of their original instructions to Mr Buchan in order that he could see how they were being kept. This is recorded in a Minute dated 19th January 1727; but Mr MacAulay's report was not received until the summer of 1728. Meanwhile another letter from Mr Buchan was received (Minute of 7th December 1727) dated 28th August 1727 in which he reported his intention of holding a Communion Service, and announced that he had sent his youngest daughter Christian to be boarded with her sisters in Glasgow, allowing for her board fifty merks out of the 'first of his three hundred merks of salary'. Worse news was to follow. On 10th June 1728

> The Clerk produced a Memoriall from James Dewar Schoolmaster in Edinburgh Representing that George and Dougal Buchans sons to Alexander Buchan Schoolmaster in Hirta had been for some time past

boarded with him and that they are altogether destitut of Cloathing and their shirts past all mending and that their time with him is now expired and Craving payment of their Board wages and a Crown a year for each of them for washing and dressing their Linnens. The Committee having considered the premisses and heard the Reverend Mr William Miller represent to them That he had seen Christian Buchan Daughter of the said Alexander who was sent to Mrs McIlwrath in very good cloathing and that she had profited as much with her as she could have done in any School of this City, and that she was extremely kind to her and finding That it was formerly recommended to the Treasurer to enter the said Dougal Buchan an Apprentice in this place They laid it on the Treasurer and Secretary who is also Cashier to His Majestie's Royal Bounty to look their Books and report to the next meeting what is resting the said Mr Buchan as Minister and Schoolmaster That orders may be given for providing the foresaid tuo Boys in Cloaths and Linnens and paying their Board and laid it upon Mr Miller to speak to Doctor Dundas and acquaint him of their necessitous condition as also Recommended to the said Mr Miller and Baillie Osburn to use their endeavours to settle the said Dougal Buchan apprentice to a Wright in this Place as easy as possible and report.

Next came the Rev. Daniel MacAulay's report, produced at the meeting on 26th July 1728.

Produced a Letter from the Reverend Mr Daniel McAulay Minister at Braccadale dated the twenty ninth of June last Shewing That he being appointed to go and visit the Island of St Kilda, had obey'd the Appointment and when he came there, was surprised with the lamentable account of the Depopulation of that Place by the small pox For of the twenty one Families that were there, only four remain'd Which bore the Burden of twenty six orphans left by the other Seventeen their Parents being cutt off by the foresaid Disease, and that the Escape of the Few remaining is owing to a remarkable act of Divine Providence For about the Fifteenth of August last, Three men and Eight boys were left in a Rock in order to catch a loading of young Solan Geese which is the Chief Product of that Island, and while they were there, the Inhabitants who were left to bring them out of that Rock were cutt off by the Small Pox, so that the foresaid Persons continued in the Rock untill the thirteenth of May, At which time they were relieved by the Baillie of Hirta's Brother, and that the said Mr McAulay had hear'd Mr Buchan Minister of the Island Preach, and finds him pretty well read in the Scriptures But otherways of low qualifications and his Stock of Prudence is not very large and that he is fitter for that Place than any other he knows; And that after Sermon, He asked at Mr Buchan and the People Several Questions, and got satisfying answers thereto as mention'd in the said Letter and found thereby That there were only tuo living that he had taught to read. The Committee having hear'd the said Letter read and considered the same were very much concern'd at the Depopulation of that Island and were of Opinion, That it would be a great hardship upon the Poor People now in their dismal circumstances to take Mr Buchan from them, and seeing The Committee for Reformation of the Highlands have continued his Salary as a Minister there for one year, agreed that his salary as Schoolmaster be likewise continued and considering That the said Mr Buchan is become very old, and that every one will not go there to succeed him, are of opinion that Dougald Buchan his son now here, be bred to be a Schoolmaster in that Island.

The SPCK had certainly got the worst of the bargain, for after having supported Mr Buchan on St Kilda for eighteen years it found there were only two persons living there, apart from Buchan's own family, who had learned to read, while the Society had the responsibility for several of his own children on their hands.

George and Dougal Buchan appeared before the Committee on 5th September 1728 when a 'Watts Grammar, an Arithmetick book, a Copie book, and a Music Book' were ordered for Dougal. George was considered unfit for a clerical career. A month later the question of clothes for George and Dougal came up again, Rev. Mr William Miller having spent 25s. sterling on shirts for them. The Committee decided that this kind of expense should be a charge on Mr Buchan's salary from the Royal Bounty, and recommended that George should be apprenticed to a trade.

At a meeting of 6th February 1729 a letter from Buchan to the Rev. James Campbell Minister of Kilbrandon was produced, in which Buchan asked, as usual, for a larger salary and for the care and education of his children to be looked after. The Committee could not agree to pay Buchan any more 'seeing he has learned so few in the Island to read' and suggested that as a Minister he should be referred to the Royal Bounty. A bursary was to be sought for George, and Dougal was to go back to St Kilda to keep school under his father as soon as he was capable of doing this. Three daughters are recorded as being of age and able to support themselves, the fourth, Christian, was still being looked after by Mrs McIlwraith. Mr Buchan was informed of these decisions. In April the Committee recommended that Dougal should go to St Kilda as a schoolmaster for the Society with a salary of 100 merks a year, and that Mr Buchan himself as Minister should be transferred to the payroll of the Royal Bounty. Dougal's salary was conditional on the people's learning to read. On 23rd April the Committee allowed Dougal 'a big coat'. The Committee seemed to be on their way to solve the financial problems in which the Buchan family had involved them; but the trouble was not yet over. On 3rd July 1729 a memorial of James

Dewar Schoolmaster was read in which he said flatly he could not keep George and Dougal longer than 20th August 1729. Dougal meanwhile decided he did not want to be a schoolmaster in St Kilda, for on 30th December 1729,

> The Clerk produced a Letter from Margaret Buchan one of Mr Alexander Buchan's Daughters dated the nineteenth current, Shewing That one Mr Niel Buchannan Merchant in Glasgow is willing to take her Brother Dougal as his apprentice to serve on board a ship for five years without any fee But he demands a Cautioner. The Committee finding That the Boy inclines most to a seafaring Business and is averse from what was formerly proposed about his teaching a School in Hirta and besides that by reason of the late Mortality there there are few to be taught They approved of his engaging with the said Mr Buchannan and agreed that fourty shillings sterling be allowed him for buying of seacloaths and other necessars and that out of any Salarys that may be due to his deceased father and in case it be found that none is due, They recommend to the Committee for the Royal Bounty to give the same out of what may be due to his said father as one of their Missionarys, But refused to meddle in the Matter of the Cautionry.

Alexander Buchan had died during 1729, not in 1730 as has been said. For the next two years his widow Katherine Campbell and his eldest daughter Jean Buchan importuned the Society for financial help. Mrs Buchan asked (the Meeting of 27th February 1730) for the Society to interpose with the Barons of the Exchequer for a yearly allowance out of His Majesty's Charity. On 12th June 1730 George Buchan asked for new clothes; this was refused. On 9th March 1731 the Committee decided to spend the small balance of Buchan's salary on the education of George

> he being presently at the college in this city with a view to his being fitted to succeed his father in Hirta, and his Mother and the other Children should be told that there is nothing due of the foresaid Salaries save the above Ballance destinat for George's Education, and that the Society cannot dispose of any of their Money for other uses than is allow'd by the Letters Patent.

On 1st April 1731 a letter from Jean asking for £5 sterling

> for providing her Younger Brother Dougal in Sea Cloaths and for his Portarrage and Teaching him Navigation during his apprenticeship of which she & her sisters were not able to bear the charge and that the same might be depositate in the hands of Provost Murdoch in Glasgow one of the ouners of the ship in which her said brother is.

This was refused, in terms of the previous decision to use the money educating George for the Society purposes. In May 1731,

Jean asked for money to buy clothes for George. This was remitted for consideration and, on 15th August 1731, the Kirk Session of Findo-Gask in Perthshire gave Mrs Buchan 18s. (Seton, G. (1878), p. 20).

In all the annals of the SPCK it is very doubtful if any of their schoolmasters gave so much trouble and expense to the Society in return for such little practical success, as the Rev. Alexander Buchan did. Nearly a hundred years later (1822), the Rev. Dr. John MacDonald visited St Kilda and found the people still unable to read, still given to using asseverations (the expressions which he records are by no means so horrifying as his comments suggest), and still retaining notions of free will, which he did his best to eradicate. Buchan himself was obviously far too long on the island for his own good, or for the good of the inhabitants; apart from which the regulation of the SPCK regarding the total prohibition of the use or teaching of Gaelic in their schools would have been enough of a handicap for any schoolmaster in such a situation.

Notes and References to Section 1

[1]Very much in the style of the leaders of various weird modern American sects whose leaders derive personal advantages from their ascendency over their followers.

[2]A late seventeenth century account, *Macfarlane's Geographical Collections*, Vol. III, p. 94. The number of families cannot have been sixty.

[3]Enthusiasm in the sense of 'a conceit of divine favour or communication' or 'ill-regulated religious emotion or speculation' is meant.

[4]Fr Allan McDonald recorded that in South Uist and Eriskay 'it would be considered dreadful and as grating on all their traditional feelings if a priest in preaching were to say *diabhol*, devil'. The word is avoided by the use of many kennings in Gaelic.

[5]Examples of these prayers can be found in Alexander Carmichael's *Carmina Gadelica*. See also the first paragraph of Section 26 in James Kirkwood's *A Collection of Highland Rites and Customes* (ed. J. L. Campbell) and John Carswell's addition to his translation of the *Book of Common Order*, p. 110 of Scottish Gaelic Texts Society edition. The first section of Alexander MacDonald's long poem in praise of Clanranald's galley is devoted to this subject.

[6]This is an allusion to the Highland belief in the Fairy people. See the complete text of Robert Kirk's *Secret Commonwealth* as published by Mario M. Rossi in his *Il Cappellano delle Fate*, Naples, 1964. Kirk refers to fairy mounds as 'hills' or 'hillocks' and to persons hearing noises in these mounds by putting their ears to crevices in adjacent rocks.

[7]An interesting survival was the use of the mild asseverations 'by my soul', 'by Mary' and 'by the Book' which so horrified the Rev. Dr. John MacDonald of Ferintosh in 1822 (in Gaelic '*air m'anam fhéin*', '*Mhuire, Mhuire*', '*a*

Leabhara, tha'); the 'Book' was probably the Missal. These asseverations are still used on the Catholic islands today.

[8]Lachlan MacLean, after a visit to St Kilda in 1838, quoted by F. Thompson, p. 44, asserted that Martin Martin 'was to them another Knox, in throwing down their altars and scourging their will-worship (*sic*)'. I can find nothing in Martin's sympathetic account of St Kilda to justify this remark.

[9]He is described as 'an old soldier of the Marlborough wars' in Alick Morrison's preface to the Harris Estate Papers, 1724–1754, *Transactions of the Gaelic Society of Inverness* XLV, p. 61. The Duke of Marlborough's wars took place between 1689 and 1711; his most famous victory was at the battle of Blenheim in 1704.

[10]This may very well be the Finlay Macdonald who later attended to Lady Grange during her exile in the island, 1734–1742.

[11]1 merk = 13s. 4d. Scots. 1s. Scots = 1d. sterling.

[12]Buchan's book as published was written when he had been 21 years on the island, i.e. in 1726.

[13]The edition of 1694, or one of the reprints of it.

Section 2

·

Uist Tradition

·

Mór Bean Nill

.

Mrs Neil Campbell (Mór Bean Nill or Mór Aonghuis 'ic Eachainn), Marion daughter of Angus the son of Hector, sister of Aonghas Beag (Angus MacLellan MBE) the well-known Gaelic storyteller, whose recorded life history was published in English under the title of 'The Furrow behind Me', was born in 1868 and died in 1970. She is said to have been the last monoglot Gaelic speaker on South Uist. The family belonged to the Loch Eynort district of the island, but lived latterly along with Angus at Frobost. On visits to South Uist the writer spent many a happy evening listening to the wonderful store of traditional songs and ballads and stories told by Aonghas Beag and Mór Bean Nill. He was also present at the ceilidh held at Frobost to celebrate her hundredth birthday in 1967. She had a great store of interesting old waulking songs; twenty-seven such songs recorded from her are published in the three volumes of *Hebridean Folksongs* by Francis Collinson and the writer, and she was the sole source of the airs of eight of them.

She had a great command of vivid, witty Gaelic, of which the two stories here about the time when, at the age of about fourteen, she went to a job on a farm on the mainland of Scotland, without knowing a word of English. The stories of her experiences then were first printed in Vols 8 and 9 of *Gairm*, and are translated here. The outcome of them was that her parish priest in South Uist advised her to stay there for her future wellbeing.

She also recorded some anecdotes connected with Uist, and some interesting versions of old Ossianic ballads, including the airs to which she sung them. There is a long article about her in the *Times Educational Supplement* of 6th June 1964 by B. R. S. Megaw, then the Director of the School of Scottish Studies, and another by Donald Archie MacDonald of the School in *The People's Journal* of 24th February 1968. She and her brother Angus lived latterly with her married daughter Mary and Mary's husband Peter MacPhee at Frobost.

The First Time I Left Uist
.
Mór Bean Nill

Translated from Gaelic, recorded on tape. Text printed in *Gairm* 8: 314.

I was only young the first time I left Uist. I was engaged at harvesting work at Ormaclait at the wage of a shilling a day. I did harvest work there; I saved a pound from my wages. I had a lot of things to get with the pound. I needed a dress, and a lot of other things. No doubt I had seen other people proud when I myself was without the means to buy anything; and I had saved up the pound.

Sunday came, and I went to church. When the congregation was dispersing, a girl called Rachel MacDonald came out and said:

'Is there anyone here who'll go to a good place to earn good wages?'

No one said a word. I said, rashly, as I was a bit forward, 'I'll go there'.

'Oh, darling, come here' she said, 'come with me, I'm leaving tomorrow, and I'll see you on the floor of your master's house, and I'll go any day to see you there.'

Oh, that was what suited me. I went along with her to her home at Stoneybridge, and I told that I had a pound, thinking myself rich, that it would never run out on me! Well, the fare on the steamer from Uist to Oban was then five shillings (i.e. 25 pence). I left on Monday morning, taking with me my few possessions in a small bundle; I was wearing everything I had anyway. Well, when we reached Oban, though Rachel had plenty of Gaelic, only English was to be heard, and I didn't have any English, I had no schooling; I was to be pitied.

'Oh' she said, 'you'll get anything you need here (on credit) to be paid at term time,[1] but give me a few shillings so I can go in and pay for an umbrella which I had broken and set to be mended here when I was going home.'

Oh, I gave her that, I was well off! She went into the shop with me then, and said 'Will a farm-servant here be able to get something to be paid for at the term?' 'She will' said the shopkeeper 'if she has a letter from her master.'

That was something I didn't have; I wasn't looking for a master myself, Rachel was going to leave me with one. I wasn't for appearing myself.

That was all right; then we went to the train. I didn't know where I was going; I was following Rachel. When we reached Loch Awe, Rachel opened the window, and started looking out. A boat was going to come across Loch Awe to fetch her; she was all right, she was going back to where she had been before. She turned to me and said: 'Well, you get out at the next station; if you don't, only great God will know where you'll get to.' I began to cry then; I didn't know what to say or do.

'I'm getting out here' she said 'and if you don't get out then, only God knows where you'll be.'

One of the women who were in the carriage turned to me and said 'Have you been to school, my girl?'

'No' I said.

'Have you got English?'

'No.'

'Well, I pity you without schooling or English.'

I was only crying. They all got out of the carriage then. But a working-man got in, and sat down opposite to me. He would say now and again 'Come over close to me, I'm sure you'd make a wife for me.' I was only crying.

'Have you any money?' he said.

'No' I said.

'And where are you going?'

'Indeed, I don't know where I'm going, but I have to get out at the next station.'

'Well, I'm getting out there too' he said. 'And are you going to a job?'

'I am' I said.

'Well' he said, 'you only have to speak to the policeman when you get out of the train.'

'I don't know how to talk to policemen, I'm no good at it.'

'Oh' he said 'he used to speak Gaelic.'

Well, when we reached Dalmally, I came out of the train, and the working-man came out. He went to get the policeman and the policeman came. He spoke to me, and asked where I was going, and I said that I was going to a man called MacKillop. The policeman looked at me for a moment, shaking his head. 'Oh' he said 'there's only one person of that name here, and he isn't keeping a maidservant at all. He never has a maidservant.' I was only crouching there.

Then the working-man who had been with me came back with a packet of biscuits for me, and a flask in his pocket, from which he gave me a drop of whisky. The policeman went away, and left me there; and came back again after a short time.

'Oh' he said, 'now, lass, I understand where you're going. See that piece of a wood over there.' It was five miles away, that wood, but indeed it was large, and a bit apart from the rest. 'That's where you're going' said the policeman, 'that's where the house you're going to is, where that piece of woodland is.' But I wasn't willing to move from the spot where I was for that, I didn't know where I was going to go.

Then two well-grown lads came, and one of them said to me: 'Are you from Uist?'

'I am.'

'Was it Rachel MacDonald who got you to come?'

'It was.'

'Oh, well' he said, 'you'll be coming with us.' I went along with them then, and when I arrived at the place I had only a piece of written paper and two or three stamps and a shilling or two, that was all that was left of my pound. I was only there for six months, and indeed I wasn't very happy there. That's what happened to me the first time I went away!

The Next Place I Went To

Mór Bean Nill

Translated from Gaelic, recorded on tape. Gaelic text printed in
Gairm 9: 51.

The wife was nice and kind to me, I was getting extra pay from her
for staying there, because I was standing up to the old fellow. No
doubt he was not unkind, but he was given to drink; he was terribly
bad for drinking, especially at lambing time (April) and when the
rams were let out (November), he had special times for it. He was
just bringing home five gallon jars (of whisky), he was living far
from a hotel or anything, and he would have the jars here; when he
began drinking, he would keep at it without stopping.

One morning, they were going to gather the sheep and dip them,
but – I heard an uproar in the room downstairs, and fearful smashing
and crashing; I didn't go down [the house] or any thing, I heard
people climbing the stairs, and I was afraid to go down. Then he
came up and caught me by the shoulder and sang a verse of a song.

'Do you know that?' he said.

'No.'

'If you don't, you can get in the dog-house!'

'I don't need to' I said, 'I'm there already.'

He used to grind his teeth, he would scare anyone with the noise
he would make grinding his teeth. Here he returned downstairs.
'We'd better go and dip the rams' he said.

'Oh, I don't know' I said.

He went; he prepared himself. He didn't put anything over his face
at all. We began dipping the rams; he was catching a ram and turning
it over on its back, and getting hold of its head, and I would be at its
feet; when I had caught hold of its two back feet, he would be putting
it on its back in the trough. And he had one ram there, a prize ram, for
which he had paid nine pounds (at the Sale) at Killin. I myself saw the
ram as it went from the dipper, going past like this, like that.

'Oh' I said, 'the big ram must be ill.'

He looked. 'Oh, isn't it devilish.'

There was a river a good bit away from us; he and I went with the
ram between us, and it was no small burden! We went with the ram
and washed it in the river, and let it back from the river.

'Off with you' he said 'home and tell the mistress to give you a glass of whisky.'

I went over (to the house). 'What have you done wrong now?' she said, 'you poor creature.'

'Nothing' I said, 'but the so-and-so was complaining I had not put an apron on him. The old fellow called an apron a *cearb*, a 'rag'. He'd say always 'why didn't you put a rag on me, girl?''

Then she gave me a glass of whisky, and I took a drop which I drank. 'Try to be brave' she said.

'Oh, the devil' I said, 'I won't make an impression of him!'

Anyway, that was over. The sheep came (into the fank) and the rams went out. The big ram was falling back and forth like this, as if he were being tripped; before it was nine in the evening, the big ram died.

But dear me, the next day they were going back to gather. But my God! If there was uproar the day before, there was uproar today in the room below. He broke the grate. There was a fearful noise there. One of the lads, the one called Colin, came and went out past me in the kitchen without saying a word. I went out to the well, and I heard a window being lifted high above me.

'Oh, lassie!' said his wife, putting her head out of the window, 'don't be slack for him, or you'll be getting just what I'm getting. Curse, and the priest will give you forgiveness!'

'Son of the devil' I said, 'why am I going to curse him?'

'Oh' she said, 'if you're slack for him, you'll get just what I did.'

I came in. He was downstairs, talking to himself. He came up to me.

'Are you there, girl?' he said.

'I am' I said.

'Come here' he said, 'come here.'

Well, I had to make some kind of answer, and do what he told me. He had made a hole in the door, one of the panel doors, he had put his foot through it, and there was a hole in it. He caught me by the shoulder.

'Put your head in there' he said.

'I won't' I said.

'Put your head in there!'

'I won't' I said, growing bolder.

'If you won't, go to hell!' he said.

'Well, I'm very near it already' I said.

I went back upstairs. He was downstairs, letting off steam! It was then (midday) dinner-time, and I began to make the dinner for the men who were out on the moor. I peeled the potatoes. The lads came in to the fank with the sheep. When he saw them, he said:

'Go and tell Colin that I want him.' That was the one he had tried to choke, his own son. 'Tell Colin that I want him.'

I went and called to Colin that his father was wanting him. It wasn't the best of answers I got. He was cursing his father. Anyway, when I came back, I found the lads' dinner had been put on the floor in an ashette, and five terriers were at work eating it, the potatoes which I had peeled. He put his head in at the door, and said 'I did that, my girl, on you as a trick'. 'You did that, you hellhound' I said, taking hold of the poker 'out of spite, but come along there, and the devil take me if I don't take your nose off. You devil.' I didn't hold back then from damning him!

Anyway, he went away then; they were there. Things settled down a little. They collected together for tea in the evening; he came along. I think he just didn't care what he did to score off me. I had just given notice of leaving. He was always saying 'I'll not say that you're bad, girl.'

'Oh' I said, 'I'm only asking what I've earned.'

'I won't say you're bad' he'd say.

'Go, girl, and bring back the cattle which are down there in the Dail Bhan.'

I went off; I left them at their tea. When I came back, I went in by the door of the kitchen, and he was standing, just, on the middle of the floor, and his wife was opposite him. The tea dishes had been put done until I took them to the scullery. He got hold of three cups and three dishes on top of each other, and lifted them like that; he let go of them. They fell and broke into fragments as if they were made of ice.

'Pick that up, girl' he said.

'Pick it up!' I said, 'It was more picked up as it was before. You only need to pick it up yourself!'

'Ah, aren't you devilish!' he said.

Then he took a box of matches out. 'Come here' he said 'so I can put you in there. Come here!'

I didn't say a word. He then came over close to me, and his wife turned to him. 'Is it going to strike the girl you are?'

'Let him strike me, the hell's son' I said 'and he won't do it again. It will be the worst turn he ever did since he was born if he puts a finger on me!'

'A-a-a-h' he said, 'you're only a devil. You're a b——.'

'Well' I said 'I'm working for a b—— as long as I'm working for you!'

After that the old fellow and I were on good enough terms, as good as any two people, but we were often enough at loggerheads on account of the drink. O, I spent a year working for him, bad as he was; but his wife was kind; she was to be pitied.

Angus MacLellan MBE (Aonghus Beag), 1869–1966

Published in *Scottish Studies* Vol. 10, 1966, 193–197

With the death of Angus MacLellan in March 1966 at Frobost in South Uist in the ninety-seventh year of his age, we lost one of the last of the great Gaelic storytellers of the Hebrides recorded by the School of Scottish Studies. Aonghus Beag was one of the comparatively small number of Gaelic storytellers who survived, fortunately, into the days of the tape recorder. I shall not attempt to compare him with others whom I have known, such as Duncan MacDonald, Seonaidh Caimbeul (Seonaidh mac Dhombnaill 'ic Iain Bhàin), James MacKinnon in Barra (Seumas Iain Ghunnairigh) or Neil Gillies (Niall Mhìcheil Nill) all of whom, alas, have also passed away. It is enough to say here that all of them were strong and interesting personalities, the like of whom can hardly long survive the disappearance of monoglot Gaelic speakers; but Angus MacLellan was particularly interesting, and particularly valuable to the School of Scottish Studies, owing to the enormous amount of material which he preserved with a memory which was unclouded up to the time of his death at a very advanced age, and to the very vivid and lively way in which his stories were told. He is a person to whom the folklorist and the social historians of the future are going to be greatly indebted.

My personal acquaintance with Aonghus Beag went back to the winter of 1948–49, when he was living in the house of his nephew, the well-known piper Mr Angus Campbell, and I was taken there by the late Rev. Fr Alec MacKellaig, parish priest of Bornish, to meet Angus MacLellan and hear some of his stories. At that time, no recording machine was available. In November of 1949 I returned to South Uist with an American machine, the Webster wire recorder, on an expense grant given by the Leverhulme Foundation.[2] The late Dr Calum MacLean was then working in Benbecula with Angus

39

MacMillan (Aonghus Barrach) and other reciters; as he had not time to reach Angus MacLellan himself, he suggested that I should undertake the recording of some of his stories, although at the time the principal purpose of my visits to Uist was to record songs, particularly waulking songs.

In those days there was no electricity in South Uist apart from the Lochboisdale Hotel, Daliburgh Hospital and one or two private houses. To the Lochboisdale Hotel Angus MacLellan very kindly came on 23rd November 1949 for a first session, and recorded three ballads and two stories, the Ballads of the Sea-Hag (*Muilgheartach*), of the Smithy, and of Kismul,[3] and the stories of the Widow's Revenge on Clanranald and the Reason why the Sea is Salt. During the next two years (when I was also working with many other reciters), he recorded a further thirteen stories for me on wire. All this material was copied on to tape for the School of Scottish Studies, and probably all of it was recorded from him directly on to tape again after 1957.

So vigorous was Angus MacLellan both physically and mentally that in 1949 I had the impression that he must be a man of about 65 years of age at the most. I was astonished to learn years later that, by November 1949, he had passed his eightieth birthday. Even then, and for some years later, it was his habit to spend several weeks alone every summer in the thatched house beside Loch Eynort in which he had been born on the 4th July 1869, in order to look after his sheep; he had the reputation in Uist of being a first-class handler of sheep.

By late 1951 it was apparent that even such a good wire recorder as the Webster was going to be superseded by tape, and it was also clear that when the proposed installation of electricity by the Hydro Board in South Uist took place, recording was going to be very much easier to do there. It was resumed in the winter of 1957–58 with a Grundig, my machine being at times used by the Rev. Fr John MacLean, parish priest of Bornish, and from the spring of 1958 many more visits were made to Uist with the main object of recording Angus MacLellan and his sister Mrs Campbell, in view of their age, the vividness of their memories, the immense amount of traditional material which they knew, and their eagerness to record it. Between this time and his death in March 1966, Angus was also recorded for the School of Scottish Studies by the late Dr Calum Maclean (from 1958 to 1960, 111 items), then by Mr D. A. MacDonald (1963 to 1965, eighty items) and by Dr Alan Bruford in November 1965 (six items). Fr MacLean recorded eighteen items in 1957–58, and the writer over 200 items (of which about ninety were auto-biographical) between April 1958 and August 1965.

As a precise catalogue of all this material would take up a considerable amount of space, and would also necessitate the checking of recordings both in the School of Scottish Studies and the Canna archives, it is not attempted here. It is sufficient to say that Angus MacLellan's stock of tales included all kinds of things, Fingalian stories and ballads, international folk-tales, ghost stories (not that he himself believed in ghosts), fairy stories, local history, and many personal reminiscences. Also, every now and again he would break into song, singing with a remarkably strong and true voice such things as songs made by the Bard of Laisgeir which I have certainly never heard sung by anyone else. He had a most interesting version of the air of *Oran na Comhachaig*, 'The Owl of Strone', which has been transcribed and printed by Mr Francis Collinson in his *Traditional and National Music of Scotland* (London, 1966, p. 60); this kind of air may have been used for the chanting of bardic verse. Evenings spent at Frobost in recording songs and stories from Angus MacLellan and his sister (now – 1966 – in her hundredth year) passed very quickly and often lasted into the small hours of the morning. All folklorists who have visited them have been much indebted to the help, kindness and hospitality of Angus MacLellan's niece and her husband, Mr and Mrs Patrick MacPhee.

Some of the stories and ballads Angus MacLellan used to recite are among the classics of traditional oral Gaelic literature, and it is exceptionally fortunate that most of these were recorded more than once from him by different persons. Such stories were the Youthful Exploits of Fionn MacCumhail,[4] How the Fingalians Lost their Hunting, the Rowan Mansion, the Death of Diarmaid, the story of Conall Gulbann,[5] the story of the Donn Ghualainn,[6] *An Gadaiche Greugach* ('The Old Robber relates three adventures to free the sons of the King of Ireland'), Bobban the Carpenter, and others. In many cases too, Angus MacLellan could remember the names of the persons from whom he had originally learnt the stories, a matter of some interest in connection with the transmission of such traditional material.

All these and many other songs and stories, and Angus MacLellan's many personal reminiscences — he was reliving the first thirty years of his life, including the years he spent working on mainland farms, with great vividness while I was working with him in 1960 and 1961 — were told with great verve and vigour and with particularly effective dialogue, the more so since Angus MacLellan possessed to a remarkable degree the capacity for acting the different characters in his stories, and could imitate their Gaelic dialects when doing so, as listeners who heard some of his shorter tales broadcast by the BBC will remember.

In the 1965 New Year's Honours list, Angus MacLellan received the award of the MBE for his extensive contribution to the preservation of Gaelic oral literature, an award which gave the greatest pleasure to his many friends, not only for personal reasons, but because of the honour that it reflected on Gaelic storytellers as a class and the recognition of the value of the oral Gaelic tradition that it implied. This honour was celebrated by a very well attended céilidh held in Bornish parish hall on 13th May 1965, where Angus MacLellan himself recited a ballad, and not a word of English was used throughout the proceedings. His sister was unable to come to this céilidh, but a tape recording of most of it was played to her afterwards.

In the same year Angus MacLellan was elected a chieftain of the Gaelic Society of Inverness. It was then the fervent hope of his friends that he would live to reach his hundred years, and record still more traditional songs and stories while doing so. This, however, was not to be. In the severe winter of 1965–66 there were signs that his vitality was beginning to lessen, and on 16th March 1966 he passed away after a brief spell of illness. He had lived a long life and had faced the hardships of poverty in South Uist and ill-paid hard work on mainland farms with good humour, courage and integrity sustained by his religion, circumstances common in the old Gaelic world; in old age he had achieved well-deserved honour and comfort. He leaves behind him recordings of Gaelic folk-tales and folklore on which scholars may work for many years to come,[7] and an account of Scottish rural life in the 1890s from the ploughman's point of view which should be of permanent interest to social historians.[8] He must have been one of the greatest contributors to the archives of the School of Scottish Studies. These things are his memorial.

The Last Catholic on Tiree

•

Recorded and transcribed by the late John MacLean MA, Barra.
Translated from Gaelic by John Lorne Campbell

•

At the time of the persecution of the Catholic religion in Scotland, a priest was being pursued in South Uist, and was finally caught behind the Beinn Mhor near the mouth of Loch Eynort. Now the persons who caught him did not want to have his blood on their hands, though they were very willing to get him out of the place by some means or other.

They thought that as the wind was in the south-west, they would let him go in a boat without a sail, without any oars, without a bailer, and without food or drink. In this way they thought he would be dead before he could reach land. The boat went until it struck land on the west side of Tiree. When the Tiree men saw the boat coming, they went down and took the poor man to the nearest house, and made him welcome with food, drink and warmth, in ignorance of who the stranger was or from where he had come.

After a little time, the stranger heard a fit of coughing from the other end of the house; when the coughing stopped, he heard the words 'May God not let me die without a priest'.[9] The priest asked the householder if he might see the man who was coughing there. 'You may' said his host, 'but he's only an old fellow who's been bedridden for many years'. The priest went along and bent over the old man, and said 'I'm a priest'. The old man put his hand to the side of the bed and lifted a big wooden stick, to strike the stranger. The priest realised that people had been mocking and playing jokes on the old man, and told him that he need not be threatening to strike him with the stick, for he really was a priest. 'If you really are a priest' said the old man, 'you will not leave this house until you have said Mass; and I'll serve it.'

'Very well' said the priest, 'but I can't say Mass today, as I've taken food,[10] but early tomorrow morning when the cock crows, I'll be here.' So it fell out; early next morning the priest said Mass, and the old man served it. He then made confession and penance and was anointed, and died after two days. Before he died, he called for his son, the man of the house, and said to him 'Will you fulfil my last request?' 'I will' said his son, 'if it's at all within my power.' 'Well then' said his old father, 'you will not tell anyone that the stranger is a priest, and when I die, you'll go with him and leave him on the mainland unharmed.' When the old man died – he was the last Catholic on Tiree – the old man's son went with the priest, and left him safe and well on the Mainland.

Note

The story related here could easily be true; it could have happened in the seventeenth century at the time of the Irish Franciscan mission to the Hebrides, which began in 1619. There is no reference to such an incident in their reports which, however, are not completely preserved. Their success in reconciling the Gaelic-speaking population of the islands which they visited, was so striking that it was hardly believed by the authorities in Rome.

Martin Martin writing in 1695 described the inhabitants of Tiree and Coll as Protestants, still observing the traditional religious festivals of Christmas, Good Friday, Easter, and St Michael's Day. Thomas Pennant in his *Tour* (1766) wrote that 'the Protestant natives of many of the isles observe Yule and Pasch, or Christmas and Easter, which among rigid presbyterians is esteemed so horrid a super-stition, that I have heard of a minister who underwent a censure for having a goose for dinner on Christmas Day; as if any one day was more holy than another, or to be distinguished by any external marks of festivity.'

I think it is unquestionable that the revelation of this situation, that Catholicism survived in a number of the islands like Barra, South Uist, Benbecula, Eigg and Canna, and that elsewhere nominal Protestants still observed Catholic festivals, must have aroused the rigid presbyterians of Edinburgh to the fact that from their point of view, there were large areas in the Highlands and Islands which were only very imperfectly reformed. Awareness of this stimulated them to form, in 1709, the Society for the Propagation of Christian Knowledge with its avowed purpose of abolishing Catholicism and the Gaelic language from that part of Scotland, a purpose for which they were granted in 1725 a yearly subsidy of £1,000 by King George I. St Kilda, which must have been feared as a possible backdoor to the entry of Jacobite agents into the Highlands, was the first position to which a SPCK schoolmaster was sent.[11]

The Rev. John Fraser, born in Mull, and Episcopalian (later non-jurant) minister of Coll and Tiree from 1678 to 1704, is said to have converted Catholic families of Coll not long after his appointment.

The idea of leaving it to Providence to decide if an inconvenient person should live or die by putting him in small boat without oars.

sail, or food and water, and pushing the boat out in an offshore wind, was known in the islands; according to the Skye version of the story of the massacre of the people in the Eigg cave as related by Canon R. C. MacLeod, it was the provocation for the attack made by the MacLeods on Eigg, after the small boat came ashore and the transportees told their story (see pp. 127–130).

Seonaidh Caimbeul

'Shony' Campbell whose name will be familiar to readers of *Folksongs and Folklore of South Uist* and *From the Alleghenies to the Hebrides* by Margaret Fay Shaw, was born at South Lochboisdale on 18th September 1859. Gaelic readers will know him from his songs, some of which were collected by the late John MacInnes (Iain Pheadair) MBE and published in 1936, and his stories which were published in *Sia Sgialachdan* in 1939. Neither book contains everything that was taken down from him by Iain Pheadair and the writer. Tape recorders were not available in his time – he died in 1944 – but his splendidly clear, slow diction made it comparatively easy to follow him and take down in abbreviated script what he had to say.

Shony could well remember the bad old days before 1886 and the Crofters' Act, before crofters had the right to security of tenure and compensation for improvements, and the hard times old people in the islands often had before the introduction of the Old Age Pension in 1908, and its increase in 1928–1929, when it was increased from five shillings a week to ten, and the elderly qualified for it at the age of sixty-five instead of seventy.

The Law of the Lairds

Shony Campbell

(Taken down in Gaelic, 1935.)

As I first remember (before 1886) the only law there was, was the law of the lairds; when a landowner wanted any law that he considered suitable to make on his own estate, the law would be made; and many a law was made by the factors of the lairds on the estates, and not only were laws made by the factors, they were made by the ground officers too, who were under the hand of the factors.

Many a time perhaps the factor did not know what the ground officers were doing; at that time, if the ground officer took a dislike to you, you could be certain that if it could be done, you would lose your holding. It often happened. And you could not do anything whatever against the laws of the factor, for if the factor did not hear anything about it, the ground officer would, and you would not be any the less blamed for it for that.

I remember hearing how men began – about the Crofters' Act, and the law which the (Crofters') Commissioners were going to bring out, that neither ground officer nor factor nor even the Laird could put you out of your holding as long as you paid your rent. That greatly pleased the crofters who heard of it, though it was not proclaimed yet.

Many a man who had the chance to do good work on his croft by dyking and draining, and there were many who would do so, was saying to himself 'what use is it for me to do such work if it's likely I'll lose my croft next year?' And many things were neglected on account of that, which would have been done if people had had the security that they have today. But now since the Crofting Law has come out with the Commissioners, everyone is trying to make his croft as good as possible, and with that a great change has come over the country altogether, since the Law came out.

A Song on the Pension
·
Shony Campbell

(Published in Caimbeul, I.L., *Orain Ghaidhlig le Seonaidh Caimbeul*
1936, pp. 75–79.)

1. Many a man will be saying how poor he is, how employment
    has failed, there is nothing to do on kelp or on seaweed. They'll
    go along where Ruairi MacMillan (the district clerk) is, and get
    work in the quarry or on the road – miserable work, I wouldn't
    stand it for a day, I'd flee from it.

2. I'd prefer to be at the fishing, though we'd suffer from hard
    weather at times, wet by night and by day, on the skerry or on
    shore or in caves; when morning came, whether we'd caught
    anything or not, when we'd been at the inn for a time, our
    hope would be just as good.

3. A great chance has come compared to when I was at the fishing,
    there was no rest there but to be seeking them everywhere,
    setting lines and searching for whelks and at each so exposed,
    compared going to get the Pension every Friday morning, as
    long as I was well.

4. It's great the fair-play and the freedom old people have
    everywhere, now that they've got the Pension, and it's bound
    to them for ever, when they grow old and none of them are
    very strong – it benefits the young folk too, if they're living with
    relations who have grown old.

5. There's no old man or woman between Arran and Knoydart,
    between Barra Head and Harris Sound and Lewis, who isn't
    often on their knees, willingly praying for the first man (Lloyd
    George) who arose to arrange it and give it out.

6. It gained respect for the old men and comfort for old women,
    who'd been a bit surly sitting at the corner of the fireside, no
    less than they grow haughty, striving to keep up conversation,
    saying 'I've got the Pension, I'll have you as my servant', that's
    what they think.

7. When you go to the shop, you'll have an eye for what you see
    there, you'll forget the shyness that kept you down for so long;
    the merchant will always be willing to talk with you, when he
    sees what you have of two-shilling coins, he'll be sure you'll take
    something with you.

8. Things have changed greatly compared with how I saw them sixty years ago, I'm telling nothing but the truth; there was no Dole then or Pension that would get anything that you needed, until the day of the (cattle) sale came, but how would it be, if you didn't sell the stirk?

9. Many a thing was dogging you, keeping you from rising; even if stirks were fetching a good price, you'd only have one of them; though he were as big as a bull, perhaps after you'd gone to the sale with him, when you got there you'd have to find a way to take him home.

10. The Factor and the stonemason, the ill-tempered blacksmith, the creel-maker, will come, and you can't do without them, the shoemaker, or the tailor; you can't keep warm without clothing; when the Poor Relief man comes, you'll scarcely dare to show your face, you needn't trouble to.

11. When they all go away, and there's no more word of them, your mind will be at rest, though you've been sighing and thinking, sitting outside regarding the sight of the world, the merchant would come up behind you, and say in a low voice 'my good man, did you sell the stirk?'

12. You'll tell him in a small voice, 'I've not sold it so far, they say there's no price for stirks; if a fellow-countryman would come who'd keep it in a field for me, along with others like it, so it would be a little bit better, see if it can't stand out'.

13. Many young people think that the song is partly made up of lies; they are very willing to draw a veil over my words; when the Dole and the Transitional are respected as the rule, and the Old Age Pension, which will not change for ever, that is good.

The Old Age Pension was introduced in 1908; it was then five shillings a week, payable only to persons over seventy years of age whose support did not exceed thirty guineas (i.e. £31.50) a year. Shony was not eligible then, of course; he reached the age of seventy in 1929, around the time when the pension was increased to ten shillings a week, and eligibility for it was reduced to sixty-five.

The 'ill-tempered blacksmith' mentioned in verse 10 suggests that Shony is reminded of the surly smith whom Fionn Mac Cumhail and his friends met in *Duan na Ceardaich*, 'The Lay of the Smithy', see *Folksongs and Folklore of South Uist*, p. 31. See also 'Songs of the Fair', pp. 122–127 in the same book.

Peigi MacRae

The name of Peigi MacRae will be well known to readers of Margaret Fay Shaw's *Folksongs and Folklore of South Uist* (1955, 1977, 1999) and her *From the Alleghenies to the Hebrides* (1993, 1999). Born in North Uist in 1874, Peigi's account of the hard days her family spent there are given in translation here. The family later moved to South Uist and occupied a croft on marginal land at North Glendale, as is described by Margaret Fay Shaw.

Always cheerful, witty in repartee, and full of Gaelic songs, which she never stopped singing, especially when doing anything, Peigi recorded 270 songs in all, some on visits to Canna House, where electricity was available. Fifty-two songs sung by Peigi and her sister Mary can be found in 'Folksongs and Folklore of South Uist', taken down by Miss Shaw in the days before tape recorders were available. Peigi MacRae died in May 1969 much regretted by her many friends.

Childhood in North Uist

Peigi MacRae

We were all born at the foot of Beinn Li, near Lochmaddy, except two of us; the two were born here, Mairi and Donald. Our home was at a place called Loch Hunder. Our home was at Na h-Ostrach. My father was from a different district, from Kintail. When the tacksman at Lochmaddy heard the name of the district to which my father belonged he was set against him. He put him out of his house. He was against any stranger coming into the place.

It was then that my father came down here to South Uist. John Ferguson sent for him as a shepherd. Though we were living near Lochmaddy my mother had hard work. She had no one to help her; my father was in the militia. She had everything to do both indoors and out. We had one cow and whenever anything happened to the cow she had to go to get milk from the house of her sister three miles away. When she came home perhaps there was a child in the cradle and another child running around the milk pail. She had to go and get milk like that all the time. There was no one else in the house except the little children.

There was a bit of a girl about the size of Seumas Iain's daughter, smaller than Seumas Iain's daughter. She was left in the house with the children while she went to the west side of North Uist to get the milk. She used to carry the bottles wrapped up in a shawl on her back.

On one of these journeys she came back with the milk, the child in the cot was crying and crying and wouldn't stop crying. She didn't know what was the matter with her. She said to the girl, 'When I go away don't you take the child out of the cradle! Don't you lift it out of the cradle at all until I come back.' However, with the way the baby kept crying out loud the girl had to lift it to try to stop it crying. When she lifted it up with her two arms, I don't know how big she was, she let it fall. It fell against the front of the cradle and broke its back. They didn't know what to do about it; they got the doctor, and they sent for the doctor and the doctor said, 'There's no cure for it'. Any way it wasn't long before the child died.

Things were like that; there was no end to the hard times we had in the house and after having all that hard time at home, she often had to go to the other side of the island to the shop to get something for them to eat, or to Lochmaddy; she had to go round like that;

she had a miserable time. She had to go to the shore sometimes to get shellfish, she would get a pailful of shellfish and bring the shellfish home and prepare them for the family to eat. She would go to the west side with a basket to get fish and when the basket was full of little saithe, flounders and little fish to take home, she would make bundles of the little fish, and perhaps she would go to the minister's house when she was out of flour or sugar, or she would take them to the shop. She would have to go to the shop with the fish.

There was an old fellow at the shop, his son was running the shop; she couldn't get anything from the shop until she'd seen the old fellow who was bed-ridden. Every time he heard that Bean Anndra, Anndra's wife had come, he would shout for her to be sent up to see him. She would sit beside the bed and he would write down everything she was ordering from the shop and she would take the paper down to his son, Hugh. 'Hugh will give you everything you want,' he said. This was the way she was managing all the time she was at Lochmaddy.

My father came home from the militia and about that time she had another baby. She had a baby at this very time. She was working at planting potatoes in lazy-beds outside the house and it's likely she was planting potatoes at the time, until she finished planting all the seed potatoes from a bag that was hung from her neck. She said to herself, I'll finish this before I go home. She finished it and then she came home. She made a fire then and made food for herself. James was there then and Angus was there and I was there and there wasn't much use in any of us for making a fire or doing any kind of work.

Anyway, my mother had to do everything else. When the time came, she had to go and get the man who lived next door to go for the nurse. But before the nurse came at all, the baby was about to come into the world. And she had it at the fireside, at the chimney – the fire was between two stones there, that's the way the fire was in the chimney. She cut two sheaves of oats outside, and laid them out beside the fire, and put blankets on top of them. She lay down there and the baby was born there, without anyone in the house but herself.

The nurse came then, and everything was all right. It was on his back that he carried the nurse half the way, she was weak; she was old. Anyway, that was over.

It was like that, you know. Eleven of us were born in North Uist; two others after we came here to South Uist.

This was the way she was busy, she was keeping very busy. There wasn't a house in the place except our house and one other; there were only two houses. The other house was as far away as Angus Ruadh's house here; further than that. The neighbours' family was about the same age as ourselves. They were rather wild lumps like ourselves.

Every day when my mother used to go to the west side to get milk, James and I used to go and get a board, a board of a chest, and we'd tie string to it, and we'd go to a ruin, called the Shepherd's ruined house, we'd go over there, we'd take butter and pieces of bread, and a linen cloth with us, we would spread the cloth on the ground. Before you could say 'Jack Robinson' the cloth would be full of starlings eating the bread. When the cloth on the ground was full of starlings, we'd let out the rope, we would slacken the rope, and the board would fall on top of the starlings, and we'd have a potful of starlings. That was some pot!

They were good – anyway at the time we thought them good! They were so fat then. There was really gravy on them, so fat they were!

The Fever

•

Peigi MacRae

Recorded in Gaelic, on tape, 30th November 1958.

There were two kinds of fever, there was a fever in the house of Iain MacSheumais, the father of Peter, when the family was young. It arose from the spring at the door, an old spring that was at the door, and they began to draw water, and it was from that well – the fever that was in Peter's house. It was only in Peter's house itself. No one else caught it, nor did anyone die from it.

The fever of which Fr George Rigg died was in the house of the father of Hector's wife, Eachann Beag's house. A cousin of theirs, over one day from Eriskay, had gone to see them during the night, and she looked in on us – she was with us for a night on her way home. She had failed to get over to Eriskay, and she was in our house all night, having come from the fever house. She had heard it was there, but she thought she wouldn't bring it with her. She went home when she heard the fever was there, she was in our house all night, but she didn't leave the fever with us. Wasn't it strange she didn't leave the fever with us? She died of it herself after she had gone home to Eriskay, she only lived about a week before she died of this fever.

No one would go into that house except Fr George. Not a living soul would go near it, and the people inside, Hector and his wife, and their three children, were in bed, and not a soul would go inside along of them to give them anything. But as long as they themselves could move, until they got so ill they couldn't move, they used to get up and get themselves something that they needed inside. An old woman then began coming there with milk and it was on the end of a fishing-rod that they were putting in the milk through the window. The fishing rod reached as far as one of the beds, and they used to catch the pail at the end of the rod. That is what she was doing; but she wouldn't go in nearer than that.

They were so wretched that at last Fr George began coming there, and he used to take off his clothes, put them in the byre, and he used to leave the clothes he had on outside and to put on other old clothes, and he used to go in and look after the people there all day, until he himself caught the fever from them, and died of it. His

54

name is now given to one of Peter's sons, Seòras. He was the only one of them who died. He died, poor man, and it was a loss.

The only other person who died of the fever was this girl; the fever was only in the one house (in Uist) but it was in Eriskay, but plenty of people in Eriskay died of it. It emptied houses there.

Catriana, Daughter of Hector
.
Peigi MacRae

Recorded in April 1951. Published in *The Scots Magazine* 1955 and in Gaelic in *Gairm* 3: 58-68.

When the late Fr Allan McDonald had settled down as parish priest of Daliburgh in South Uist in 1884, he started to keep a notebook in which he entered anecdotes, folktales and old songs from time to time, often when he was waiting for a boat to take him from Uist to Eriskay, or vice versa.

The Uist port for his crossings was Glendale on the south coast of Uist opposite to Eriskay. At Glendale there lived an old woman called Catriana Nighean Eachainn, or Catriana daughter of Hector, a Campbell.

Catriana was a very remarkable person. She possessed the art of divination, and people used to have resort to her in order to learn the condition of an absent friend, or whether a sick person would recover, or how to find something that was lost, and so on (a practice explicitly forbidden in the Gaelic Catechism).

These divinations were performed by the seeress's getting up at dawn, going around her house sunwise while reciting a prayer, and then looking out over the landscape through the circle made by putting thumb and forefinger together. According to the position of men, animals or natural objects, the future was foretold.

There was a regular system of signs for this, and in 1887 or 1888 Fr Allan persuaded Catriana to let him write them down. Through the use of his material by other writers, Catriana has become an important source of information about the way such divinations were performed in the Hebrides.

The following anecdotes about her were recorded in Gaelic by Miss Peigi MacRae of North Glendale, South Uist, whose family were then her only neighbours, about two miles away by a very rough track over which Fr Allan used to walk on his way to Eriskay.

Shepherds used to stay at South Glendale, near Catriana, for a night or two at shearing time, but that was all the human company she eventually had, for reasons that these reminiscences make very clear. The Gaelic text of this story appeared in *Gairm*, in 1954; my English version is shortened and rearranged so as to be in chronological order.

Here is a translation of Miss Peigi MacRae's account:

Catriana was extraordinarily good at foretelling things and at making divinations, and at advising people what to do, though she was only a poor old woman herself. Once upon a time, my father, who was a shepherd, was looking for a ram he had lost, and he could not find it, though he was searching for it for several days. My mother at last said to him, 'Why don't you go to see Catriana?' 'I don't want to at all' said my father, 'I don't believe in that kind of thing.' 'Very well' said my mother, 'go and look for the ram, maybe you'll never find him.'

However, the next day as he was going to the hill, it occurred to my father to go down the road and see Catriana. When he called she said, 'Did you find the ram, Andrew?' 'I didn't find the ram yet.' 'Where are you looking for him?' 'I am looking for it here and there through the hill, and there isn't a part of the hill that I didn't walk looking for him, by now.' 'Did you go out in the Gàradh Beag yet?' said she. 'No,' he said, 'I don't believe I did go out there.' 'You go out to the Gàradh Beag today,' said she, 'if you are going out, and see what meets you, or what you find; maybe you'll find this ram, dead or alive.'

He went out that day, and climbed up until he reached the Gàradh Beag and he kept along the Gàradh Beag all the way, and the ram met him coming, standing there on the road chewing his cud happily, coming home by himself. My father found the ram this way through Catriana, and he believed in Catriana ever afterwards, and in whatever she said or did.

Everyone used to go to see her like this about things they had lost or wanted, and people who were thinking of getting married went to ask whom they would get as a wife or husband, or people who wanted to know how they would get on in the world, would go to her and she would tell them everything. She told one man, a neighbour of ours, whom he was going to marry, and how his parents would be annoyed at his marrying, and how he was going to take a farm in a place he had never seen, where there would be his hornless sheep on the hill about his house. All this came true.

One night a woman called Harriet came to Glendale to buy wool and only Catriana was at home. The shepherd had gone to Eriskay to see the girl he was courting, and was to be away until the next day. Only Catriana was at home, and night fell, and she would not let Harriet go. 'Stay tonight,' said Catriana, 'and you'll have wool to take away tomorrow, and you'll be all right then.' Harriet stayed.

Around six in the evening, the two women were sitting, one on each side of the fireplace in silence. Suddenly Harriet heard the chain of the door being rattled and shaken roughly.

'Someone is at the door Catriana,' said Harriet.

'Oh well,' said Catriana, 'whatever you hear, or whoever comes to the door or anything that you think is coming around, don't let on that you hear it; don't say a word, keep quiet, deaf and dumb where you are, nothing is going to happen to you.' Harriet kept quiet and said nothing.

The chain rattled again, and the third time it rattled Catriana got up and went to the door with a stick in her hand. Harriet remained deaf and dumb beside the fire, her feet shaking with fear. When Catriana reached the entrance, she left the door of the room open and went to the front door, and opened it. Harriet could hear a murmured conversation outside, but she couldn't understand a word of it. Catriana was outside for half an hour, and when she came in again she looked very, very wretched. She came in and shut the front door, and when she was coming through the kitchen door Harriet saw the top half of the ghost coming in after her. He had a long white beard down his chest. Harriet did not let on she had seen him and when she looked again after taking her eye off him for a moment he had vanished. Catriana came into the kitchen then, sat down beside the fire again, moaning and groaning as if she were dying. Harriet did not say a word, or let on she had noticed anything.

The next day Harriet could hardly wait until the dawn to take her feet out of the house, and as soon as it lightened she was off. Harriet herself told my mother this story, and my mother would not have believed it if she had not heard it from Harriet's own mouth. 'Though I live for years,' Harriet said, 'I wouldn't spend a night at Glendale again.'

One night my aunt was at work looking after the shepherds at Glendale, and she spent the night in Catriana's house. She went to sleep, and after a while she woke up and saw a man (a ghost) entering the house. She watched the man's shadow go past her own bed to where Catriana was. She had never been frightened before, but she was frightened that night. He went over to Catriana and they were talking and talking there, but my aunt couldn't make out what they were saying. She saw the man make his way out of the house again, and after two or three minutes Catriana got up and went out after him, taking the tongs. About five in the morning she came back. She didn't bring the tongs back with her, and her face was all scratched and bleeding.

When my aunt got up to make the shepherds' breakfast, she started to look for the tongs, and the tongs couldn't be found. She asked Catriana, 'where are the tongs? Have you seen the tongs?' 'No,' said Catriana, 'I haven't seen them at all.' She did not admit having taken them at all, at first. 'But,' said my aunt, 'she did admit it at last when I grew cross about the tongs and told her how I had seen her get up the night before and go out with them. She told me then the tongs were down at the big sheep fank. 'And if you like,' said she, 'go and look for them down there.'

'I will not go and look for them just now,' said my aunt, 'I'll try to make the fire with two sticks rather than look for the tongs down there.' She asked one of the shepherds, after they had got up that morning, to go down and look for the tongs at the fank. One of them went and returned with the tongs, which he had found where she had told him, and the tongs were covered with blood as if they had been used in a fight. My aunt never spent a night in Glendale again, she went straight home and left the shepherds to look after themselves. After that, Catriana was alone: no one would stay with her any more.

Eventually she became ill and there was no one there to look after her. My mother was going over to attend to her every day she could (we lived two miles away) but there were days she could not go over to see her at all. Catriana's son said that she ought to go over to Eriskay and stay with him, and not go on living by herself. 'I shall never go to Eriskay,' said Catriana, 'until I know I shall only be with you for a week, and then I'll go. Don't come to get me until I send for you.' Her son didn't come to get her until word came from her. 'Now,' she said, 'I will go over to Eriskay with you today. Go to the shop and buy what will do us until the end of the week, and no more. I'll go over with you when you come back from the shop. Is your boat here?' 'Yes.' 'Well, I'll go over with you.'

When he came back from the shop, she went over with him. She gave her hens and everything else she had to my mother. She had a big chest in the house. She made her son open the big chest, and there were seven smaller chests inside the big one, all locked. She gave the keys to my mother. 'Now,' she said, 'take all the chests, and take everything out of them. If there is food in them, use it, if it can be used.' When my mother opened the chests everything in them had got mixed up and gone bad – all the tea, sugar, flour, butter and cheese, and every sort of food that Catriana had been getting from the women who used to come to see her to ask her to foretell the future for them.

She went to Eriskay, as I said, and at the end of the week news came of her death, which she had foretold.

Note

Very fortunately the signs by which Catriana's divinations were made, and the ritual that preceded the divination itself, were taken down from Catriana, daughter of Hector herself by Fr Allan McDonald in 1887 or 1888. They were published by William MacKenzie the Gaelic-speaking secretary of the Crofters' Commission of 1883 with full acknowledgement to Fr Allan, in MacKenzie's paper on 'Gaelic Incantations, Charms, and Blessings of the Hebrides' read to the Gaelic Society of Inverness on 23rd March 1892, and published in Volume XVIII of the Society's *Transactions*, pp. 97–182, where Catriana's divinations are given on pp. 104–108 (later published in book form). They were printed again ten years later in the *Journal of the Folklore Society*, XIII, pp. 47–49, in a paper read to the Society entitled 'More Folklore from the Hebrides' read to the Society on 6th November 1901 by Ada Goodrich Freer, who made no reference to their earlier printing in the Gaelic Society of Inverness's *Transactions*, though she had herself read a paper on 'Highland Second Sight' to this Society on 30th April 1896.

This paper appears to consist almost entirely of material from Fr Allan McDonald's notebooks. In an opening paragraph, Miss Freer writes that his opportunity for collecting folklore had been unique 'and without him – his knowledge, sympathy, and erudition – the folklore, songs, hymns, customs and tales of these islands could never have been collected'. She avoids mentioning Alexander Carmichael, except to say that Fr Allan had been a fount for him as well as for her. She writes the article in the first person plural 'we', implying that she had accompanied Fr Allan on his folklore collecting expeditions, and that she herself understood Gaelic, whereas all the Gaelic quotations made in the article had been translated into English for her by him. Had she known Gaelic, she would not have allowed such misspellings as *deachanch* for *deachamh*, *sluath* for *sluagh*, *fuoitrag* for *faoiteag*, or *raum* for *rann*, to pass into print.

See the next article, in the Eriskay section of this book, and also J. L. Campbell and Trevor Hall, *Strange Things*, 1969. Could these divinations and what they indicated be sometimes considered as cases of what C. G. Jung called 'a-causal synchronicity'?

Notes and References to Section 2

[1]i.e. at the end of the term of six months for which Scottish farm workers usually engaged in those days.

[2]Apart from this, official encouragement took the form of the impounding of this wire recorder by the British Customs for six months after arrival from America. Wire recorders are usually denigrated, but the Webster was a good machine and must have been the best of them.

[3]See Donald MacLeod, *Orain Nuadh Ghaeleach* (Inverness 1811). The ballad is not in praise of Kismul Castle as is sometimes supposed, but in praise of a house built by a Ruairi MacNeil at Steinn in Skye which is likened to Kismul Castle. There is a wood-cut of the house at the end of the poem, p. 176.

[4]Compare the version taken down by Fr Allan McDonald from Alasdair Johnston on Eriskay in 1892–93 and printed by the Rev. Dr George Henderson in the *Celtic Review* Vols II and III.

[5]See Alan Bruford's important article on *Eachtra Chonaill Gulban* in *Béaloideas* Vol. XXXI (1963), pp. 1–50. A transcription of the recording of *Conall Gulbann* made by Angus MacLellan was printed in the *Transactions of the Gaelic Society of Inverness* Vol. XLIV (1964–66), pp. 153–92.

[6]A version of the Tain Bó Cuailgne story. This was printed by Dr Calum Maclean (1959) *Arv* 15:160–80.

[7]See *Stories from South Uist Told by Angus MacLellan*. Translated by John Lorne Campbell (1997), Birlinn.

[8]See *The Furrow Behind Me Told by Angus MacLellan*. Translated by John Lorne Campbell (1997), Birlinn.

[9]Consider the Gaelic imprecation *Bàs gun sagart dhuit* spoken as a curse, 'May you die without a priest'.

[10]Formerly it was necessary to fast from midnight before taking communion at Mass, now only for an hour before Mass.

[11]See Section 1, *Hiorta* or St Kilda.

Section 3

·

Eriskay Tradition

·

Eriskay

To the Eist of this Ile of Fuday[1] be three myle of sea lyes ane Ile callit Eriskeray, twa myle lang, inhabit and manurit.[2] In this Ile ther is daylie gott in aboundance of verey grate pintill fische sandeels at Ebb seas and als verey guid for uther fishing. pertaining to Mackneill of Barray.

(Dean Monro said of the Western Isles, as quoted in *Macfarlane's Geographical Collections*, iii 289)

Pintill fish must be sandeels; there are two species in British waters, the Greater and the Lesser. They are called *Siolag* in Gaelic. They are excellent eating, but now either left to the puffins, or fished professionally for cat food. When pursued, they take instant refuge in the sand, from which they used to be caught by the use of a toothed sickle called *corran siolaig* drawn through the sand at low spring tides at full moon in the autumn. The writer remembers very well a considerable stranding of Greater Sandeels on a pebble beach on Canna, when baskets could be collected when wading ankle deep in the water. They made excellent eating when fried.

Eriskay and the south end of South Uist belonged to the MacNeils of Barra for a time, but later were acquired or recovered by the MacDonalds of Clanranald. Small though the island is, some important persons have been associated with it. The best known of these was Prince Charles Edward Stewart, who landed on it with his small party on 23rd July 1745, the first time he set foot in Scotland. Alexander MacDonald of Boisdale (Alasdair Mór nam Mart), a successful cattle-dealer, came to see the Prince and told him that as MacLeod of Dunvegan and MacDonald of Sleat did not mean to rise for him, he had better go home, to which the Prince replied 'I am come home'.

Apart from Prince Charles Edward, Eriskay is associated with three important persons, all MacDonalds. These were Domhnall mac Iain 'ic Sheumais, a redoutable warrior related to the MacDonalds of Sleat; see the poem in his praise printed as No. CIV in *Hebridean*

65

Folksongs Vol. III, and the notes thereon. He won a notable victory over a superior force of MacLeods who had raided North Uist in 1601, at the battle of Carinish. The second was John of Moidart (Iain Muideartach) who was Chief of Clanranald, born about 1590 and died on Eriskay in 1670, and was buried at Howmore in South Uist; he had held out for the Royalist cause even after the death of the Marquess of Montrose. Iain Muideartach, his son Donald (Domhnall Dubh), Domhnall mac Iain 'ic Sheumais and MacDonald of Glengarry, were all summoned to appear before the Synod of Argyll in May 1656, on pain of excommunication (which then meant social, political, and religious ostracism, as far as the Covenanters were concerned). None appeared; actually Clanranald and Glengarry had been excommunicated already. Iain Muideartach's marriage to Marion, daughter of Sir Rory Mor MacLeod of Dunvegan, had marked an end to the disgraceful feud between the MacDonalds and the MacLeods which had lasted through the sixteenth century.

The third of these persons was the Rev. Allan McDonald, who belonged to the Keppoch branch of the clan; he was born in Fort William in 1859, and educated at Blairs College in Aberdeenshire and the Real Colegio de los Escoces in Valladolid in Spain, ordained in 1882 by the Archbishop of Glasgow, and appointed to the mission of Daliburgh in South Uist by the Rt Rev. Angus MacDonald, a member of the Glenaladale family, in 1884; the parish then included the island of Eriskay. He did not spare himself in the course of his parochial duties, and from 1887 on he also made a collection of folklore and local history from the rich Gaelic oral tradition of South Uist; the collection became famous. In late 1894 Eriskay was disjoined from Daliburgh and put in Fr Allan's sole charge. Something of Fr Allan's folklore collection is told in the first article here, which was published in *Scottish Studies* in 1958 and is brought up to date here.

The Late Fr Allan McDonald, Miss Goodrich Freer and Hebridean Folklore[3]

.

Published in *Scottish Studies*, Vol. 2, 1958, pp. 175–188

At the time of the death of the late Fr Allan McDonald of Eriskay in October 1905, it was well known that he had compiled a large collection of South Uist folklore during the twenty-one years he was a parish priest at Daliburgh and Eriskay, and that this collection had been acquired by the late Walter B. Blaikie for publication in the *Celtic Review*, as is stated on page 192 of Volume 5 (1908–9) of that Journal. But apart from a few folk-anecdotes which appeared in the *Celtic Review*[4] shortly after his death, the collection vanished.

The reason why no attempt was made to publish it by Fr Allan McDonald's contemporaries is explained in the following pages. Writing his obituary for the *Catholic Directory*, Mgr Canon A. Mackintosh remarked of Fr Allan that 'he gave (all too freely it may be said) of his gleanings and valuable assistance to other workers in the Celtic field'. The chief beneficiary of Fr Allan's generosity in this report was Miss Goodrich Freer. The rediscovery of Fr Allan McDonald's MSS, for which I began a search before the Second World War, which was greatly aided by various friends such as Mgr Canon MacMaster, the Rev J. McBride, Professor Angus McIntosh and Professor Angus Matheson, has made it at long last possible for an assessment to be made of Miss Freer's methods, and of her indebtedness (almost total) to the collecting work of Fr Allan McDonald. But for the fact that part of the material he collected was collected with her encouragement, and was put by him at her disposal for arrangement and publication one would be justified in saying that she made an unabashed use of his folklore collections in the interest of her literary career, but I doubt very much indeed if he intended that it should be published in a way which implied that she was the collector, for to have done so would have been becoming accessory to a deception of the public, a thing which it was entirely contrary to Fr Allan's nature to do.

At any rate, the harm was done, and done before Fr Allan's death. In a letter written on 6th January 1902 to Fr Allan, Alexander Carmichael remarked that:

> Mr Henderson (i.e. Dr George Henderson) says that Miss Freer has made such free use of your MSS in her various publications that she has

not left much of much value. This is very vexing, for both Mr Henderson and Mr Blaikie were very desirous that all your MSS should be published in full and under your own name.

Carmichael's statement that Miss Freer had not left much of much value is fortunately not correct: she had been entirely unable to make use of material recorded only in Gaelic, and in consequence had left untouched many folk-tales, folk-songs, traditional prayers, proverbs and all lexicographical material. But as far as Fr Allan's collection contained material that appealed to the popular interest in general folklore, it had been gutted.

Miss Freer took a good deal of trouble to arrange and classify this material. But her method involved very serious defects. She was not acquainted with the language of the people with whose folklore she was dealing, still less with their oral tradition as a whole. And, while we need not reproach her for not having instituted comparisons with Irish or Scandinavian folklore, because a straightforward presentation of Hebridean folklore would have been valuable enough, the limitation of her method involved the neglect of anything that could not have been understood by her or presented as sensational (in the same way Mrs Kennedy Fraser was only interested in Hebridean folksong insofar as it was suitable for adaptation to the concert platform). Eventually, as will be seen, Miss Freer got herself into the position where the greater her status as an expert on Hebridean folklore appeared to be, the more difficult it was to sustain.

Certainly it would have been far better if Fr Allan McDonald had published his collection himself. There is a refreshing charm about his style which is lost in Miss Freer's condensation, and as a man on the spot, fully acquainted with the background of the tradition and the language of the people, he would have avoided the misleading generalisations and the errors of translation introduced by Miss Freer. It was unfortunate that Blaikie and Carmichael only became interested in his collection after the harm had been done, but now that *The Outer Isles* and the earlier volumes of *Folklore* are out of print, the opportunity to publish Fr Allan McDonald's own words may yet occur.

In July 1884, Fr Allan McDonald, a native of Fort William who had been educated for the priesthood at Blairs and Valladolid, was appointed by the Bishop of Argyll and the Isles, the Rt Rev. Angus MacDonald, as parish priest of Daliburgh, a parish which comprised the southernmost third of South Uist and the Island of Eriskay, with a congregation of 2300 souls, all Gaelic speakers except two or three, and many, especially of the older generation, knowing little or no English.

Fr Allan, as he is always known locally, applied himself to his parochial duties zealously. He soon mastered the local Gaelic dialect, in which all his own verse and prose compositions were later to be written. Having a sensitive and intelligent mind, he could not fail to see that he was living in the midst of a local oral tradition of great interest and antiquity; and, probably with the encouragement of the Rev. Alexander Campbell, an old priest born in Uist in 1819 or 1820 and living there in retirement, he began to note down local traditions, songs, proverbs, sayings and customs in 1887, often giving the actual Gaelic words of the reciters. By December 1892 he had filled two large quarto notebooks with such material, the first containing 480 items, the second 105. These dates are important, for they prove that Fr Allan had already collected a large quantity of folklore before any outside influence was brought to bear on, or outside interest taken in, him. A large part of his second notebook is taken up with Fingalian stories taken down in Eriskay, and later printed in the *Celtic Review* by the late Rev. Dr George Henderson (1905–9). In the winter of 1892–3 Fr Allan's health broke down from overwork, and Bishop Angus MacDonald made Eriskay a separate parish, and transferred him there so that his burden of work would be less heavy.

Five more quarto notebooks were filled by Fr Allan while living in Eriskay. The first two of these, Nos. III and IV, have unfortunately disappeared, but we can safely assign them to the period 1893–5, and, as will be seen, some of the material they contained survives, though in condensed form. Nos. V and VI are extant, the first covering the period January 1896 to January 1897, and the latter February 1897 to March 1898. A seventh notebook contains various material collected between 1895 and 1899 besides a number of his own compositions, including his famous Gaelic poem on Eriskay. Three more notebooks contain hymns, waulking songs, and lexicographical material respectively. The total amount of material collected cannot be very much less than 350,000 words and it amounts to one of the most important local collections of folklore ever made anywhere.

It was not long before Fr Allan's interest in these matters became known. Letters to him from Alexander Carmichael, the well-known editor of *Carmina Gadelica*, are extant from April 1893, and he also corresponded with, and enjoyed the friendship of, the late Rev. Dr George Henderson, at one time lecturer in Celtic at Glasgow

University, whose extant letters to Fr Allan date from June of the same year; and in both cases it appears that the correspondence had already been going on for some time. These, and other, scholars were in the habit of frequently consulting Fr Allan, who had easy access to some of the best reciters, on questions of folklore and lexicography.

Towards the end of 1893 the Society for Psychical Research, which was participating in a 'Census of Hallucinations in every part of the World', sent out 2000 copies of a circular, at the expense of the then Marquess of Bute, to clergymen and schoolmasters, etc., living in the Highlands and Islands, for the purpose of discovering to what extent belief in second sight still survived. Only sixty recipients troubled to reply, of whom half answered in the affirmative. Six months later another circular, written by the Marquess of Bute himself, elicited 210 answers of which sixty-four were in the affirmative.

Associated with this inquiry was a Miss Goodrich Freer, a lady who in the Hebrides is usually referred to as an American, though she described herself to the Gaelic Society of Inverness in 1896 as 'born south of the Tweed'. Miss Freer had access to the replies to the Marquess of Bute's circular; in the autumn of 1894 she visited the 'districts specially indicated' at the request of the Society for Psychical Research, to which she read papers on the rather meagre results of the inquiry, on 7th December 1894 and 6th December 1895, under the pseudonym of 'Miss X'. On 30th April 1896 she delivered a lecture to the Gaelic Society of Inverness on the subject of 'Second Sight in the Highlands'. The audience, many of whom could hardly have been totally ignorant of the subject, must have felt somewhat disappointed, when, instead of producing any interesting anecdotes about second sight, Miss Freer subjected them to a long and rather naive address about the Society for Psychical Research's circular issued through the Marquess of Bute's liberality, with a few clichés about psychic Gaels and materialistic Saxons thrown in, and an exhortation to further the inquiry itself. They might well have asked what qualifications she possessed to direct and organise research of this kind.

If the answers to these circulars have been preserved, they are not now accessible to students. But it is probable enough that Fr Allan was one of the few who replied, and replied in the affirmative, for he had already noted a number of anecdotes about second sight. It is certain that the Rev. Peter Dewar, the first secretary of the Society for Psychical Research's Second Sight Enquiry, had visited Fr Allan

McDonald in August 1894, at the suggestion of William MacKenzie, secretary of the Crofters' Commission; Ada Goodrich Freer, who took over the Enquiry from Dewar, went to see Fr Allan in the autumn of 1895, discovering his extensive folklore collection, which she advised Lord Bute to attempt to purchase. However, the Second Sight Enquiry foundered in the row that broke out in the summer of 1897, when the Ballechin House ghost hunt financed by Lord Bute came to grief after a volley of attacks on the Society in the correspondence columns of the London *Times*, resulting in a permanent breach between Miss Freer and F. W. Myers, the secretary of the Society for Psychical Research, in which Lord Bute took Miss Freer's side.

However, the visit to Eriskay had provided Miss Freer with a mine of important literary and folklore material. Within a few years article after article was to come from her pen: 'Christian Legends of the Hebrides' (*Contemporary Review* 74: 390–412, September 1898); 'The Powers of Evil in the Outer Hebrides' read to the Folklore Society on 15th February 1899 and printed in *Folklore* 10: 259–82, in September 1899; 'Eriskay and Prince Charles' (*Blackwood's Edinburgh Magazine* 169: 232–41, February 1901); 'More Folklore from the Hebrides' read to the Folklore Society on 6th November 1901 and printed in *Folklore* 13: 29–62, 25th March 1902; and finally her book *The Outer Isles* published in London later the same year. All were substantial articles, implying authoritative knowledge and profound research. They were vitiated by one thing, that is, that all the folklore material in them relating to Eriskay and South Uist (and also other material relating to Barra and Lochaber) was taken practically verbatim from the notebooks of Fr Allan McDonald.

This was not done without a measure of consent on the part of the original collector; nor without a measure of acknowledgment on the part of Miss Freer. Nor can it be denied that part at least of Fr Allan's collecting was inspired by her interest and encouragement. But the free use of his material under her own name coupled with acknowledgments that leave the reader with the impression that he was simply her collaborator in work which she initiated, goes beyond the bounds of what is permissible and eventually left Fr Allan with his collection sucked dry of some of its most interesting contents and without the public recognition which he merited and which would have been his, had it been published under his own name.

In order to demonstrate Miss Freer's methods I must again remind readers that a considerable part of his collection, including some very interesting items, had been made before he had met Miss Freer in 1894. It is therefore obvious that the folklore these volumes contain cannot have been collected by Miss Freer herself, nor could she have accompanied Fr Allan while he was collecting it. It is also demonstrable that Miss Freer was not in Eriskay between September 1897 and June 1898 and that material taken down between those dates must have been given to Fr Allan alone.[5] In any case Fr Allan's informants imparted their material to him in Gaelic, which Miss Freer did not understand.

Miss Freer's methods in publishing this material were as follows: (1) Admitting indebtedness to Fr Allan in apparently generous acknowledgement, but concealing the fact that what she was printing was actually his material or a précis of it; (2) referring to Fr Allan as 'a priest', 'my informant' and as 'Fr Allan', this giving the impression that there were three different people involved; (3) quoting verbatim remarks of reciters entered in Fr Allan's notebooks in a way that implies these remarks were made to her; (4) constantly using the first person plural, implying that she and Fr Allan had gone folklore-collecting together; (5) using Fr Allan's comments on customs, etc., as if they were her own.

The following examples, taken for the most part from folklore collected by Fr Allan before he met Miss Freer, show what I mean:

Fr Allan, Notebook I No. 67:

A man Campbell was going to mass early one Sunday morning to Kildonan. On the strand he found a woman and her daughter actively '*a deilbh buidseachd*', framing witchcrafts, by crossing threads of varied colours in various manners, just as is done when threads are arranged for the loom. He tore up the whole apparatus and chid them with their breach of the Sunday and their malice. The witches entreated him not to mention what he had seen them doing, and they promised him immunity from injury. After mass he told all the people about the matter, and shortly afterwards, when about to sail to the mainland a crow stood on the mast, and after they started from shore a storm arose in which he perished. This occurrence did not take place within the memory of the present generation.

Miss Freer, Folklore *10 (1899), 282:*

I will conclude with a warning against lightly meddling with matters so serious as these. A man named C. was going to Mass early on Sunday morning to Kiloanan. (*sic:* this is what the word looks like in Fr Allan's writing, but anyone who knew Uist would have known 'Kildonan' was meant.) As he crossed the strand, he found a woman and her daughter actively engaged in framing witchcrafts by means of pieces of thread of various colours. He tore up the whole apparatus and rebuked them for malice and for breach of the Sunday. They entreated him not to reveal what he had seen, and promised their protection in return for his silence. Nevertheless after Mass he told the story. Shortly after, when he was about to sail for the mainland, a black crow settled on the mast of the boat and a storm arose in which he perished. The story is not only true, but of recent occurrence.

The whole story suffers through Miss Freer's condensation, and her last remark is the entire contrary of what Fr Allan himself wrote, and produces a misleading impression as to the contemporaneity of witchcraft in South Uist.

Fr Allan, Notebook I No. 170:

On Hallowe'en six plates were placed on the floor each with separate contents and the girls of the house were blindfolded and led to the spot where the plates were laid down, and the first she touched foretold her fate

Uisge glan	A husband against whom nothing could be said
Salann	A sailor
Min	A farmer
Uir	Death
Uisge salach	A disreputable husband
Eanghlas bhainne	Foretold adultery.
	Cf. page 97 (on which page Fr Allan noted the story of the Adultery of Cú-Chulainn and Bláthmat as recounted by Rhys).

Following the first five Gaelic entries are the English equivalents in Miss Freer's handwriting, 'Pure water, salt, meal, earth, dirty water'. A question mark in her hand follows *Eanghlas bhainne,* and after it Fr Allan has added the explanation 'milk and water mixed'.

In Folklore *13 (1902), 53, this divination is given by Miss Freer as follows:*

On Hallowe'en six plates were placed on the floor each with separate contents, and the girl (*sic*) of the house came blindfolded. The first she touched foretold her fate. 1. Pure water portended an unexceptionable husband. 2. Salt, a sailor. 3. Meal, a farmer. 4. Earth, a death. 5. Dirty water, a disreputable husband. 6. An empty plate, no husband.

The sixth divination given by Miss Freer here is quite in keeping with the others; but it is certainly not what Fr Allan McDonald, from whom she copied this item, noted down. The impression given is one of bowdlerisation.

Fr Allan, Notebook I No. 37 (taken down on Eriskay in 1887):

The sea is considered much more blessed than the land. A man will stay all night alone in a boat a few yards from the shore without fear, yet he would not stay an hour in the darkness alone on the shore so near him. The boats of course are always blessed and holy water is kept in each boat as a rule. On one occasion going to Eriskay after nightfall I was made aware of this idea of the sea's blessedness. I asked the man who came for me what place on shore would his companion be in, who was awaiting us. 'He won't be on the shore at all, by the book. He will be in the boat itself. The sea is holier to live on than the shore.'

Miss Freer, Folklore 10 (1899), 260–1:

The sea is much more blessed than the land. A man will not be afraid to stay all night in a boat a few yards from shore, but he would not stay an hour alone in the dark on land.

A priest told me that one day he was crossing the dangerous Minch, which lies between Uist and Eriskay, on a dark night to visit some sick person. He asked the man who had fetched him where his companion, who was awaiting them, would shelter on the shore. 'He won't be on the shore at all, by the Book! It is in the boat itself he will be. The sea is holier to live on than the shore.'

Fr Allan, Notebook I No. 83 (taken down in 1887 or 1888):

It is customary on New Year's Eve for the children to go and ask their Hogmanay. From the fourth line of the subjoined rhyme it seems that the custom was kept formerly on the Eve of Xmas, as the Spaniards keep their 'Noche Buena'.

> *'S mise nochd dol a Chullaig*
> *Dh'ùrachadh eubh na Calluig*
> *A dh'innse 'mhnathan a bhaile*
> *Gur e màireach latha Nollaig.'* etc.

Miss Freer, Folklore 13 (1902), 45 (the translation of the Gaelic is of course by Fr Allan, and unacknowledged):

Hogmany (*sic*) Night has naturally its especial customs. The children go round to the houses on New Year's Eve to ask their Hogmany. It appears from the fourth line of their rhyme as if the custom obtained formerly on *Christmas* Eve, as among the Spaniards,[6] who keep then their *Noche Buena.*

> 'I tonight am going a Hogmanying,
> Going to renew the shout of the Kalends,
> To tell the women of the township
> That tomorrow is the Day of Christmas.'

Fr Allan, Notebook V No. 162:

> Yew, *iubhair beinne,* is kept in a house as preservative against fire. Was it ever used for 'Palms' on Palm Sunday? If so, the custom is the same as the Spanish one of placing palm branches on balconies against lightning. (Noted from Dougal MacMillan, Eriskay, on 11th November 1896.)

Miss Freer, Folklore *13 (1902), 32:*

> Branches of yew are kept in the house as a preservative against fire – it may be a survival of keeping the Palm Sunday boughs. (In Spain they are placed in balconies against lightning.)

The way that this item of folklore is presented by Miss Freer illustrates several of the shortcomings of her method.

(1) A botanical error made by Fr Allan is copied. *Iubhair beinne* is not yew, but the creeping juniper that grows in some inaccessible places in the isles. No doubt by now this item has been incorporated into the general folklore of the yew-tree by copyists!

(2) 'Kept in *the* house' is substituted for 'kept in *a* house', and thereby a custom, learnt from only one informant and probably by no means universal, is generalised and presented as part of a system of Hebridean folk-belief.

(3) Fr Allan's speculation upon the origin of the custom, and his allusion to a foreign parallel, are included as if they were Miss Freer's own comments.

Fr Allan, Notebook VI No. 106:

> When a person is asked to go late at night for water and is unwilling to go the following proverb is quoted: *Is iasgaidh òm na mhaduinn.* I don't know what *òm* is. VI 247 (36): *Is iasgaidh om* ((pronounced) like *com*) '*na maduinn,* better do it at once.

Miss Freer, Folklore *10 (1899), 72:*

> Another mysterious entity who appears only in a proverb is '*Om*', of whom it is said: 'Om is most active in his morning.' The phrase is used to anyone who wishes at night to put off doing something till next day.

Though Fr Allan was puzzled by this expression himself, the difficulty could have been solved by consulting Nicolson's *Collection of Gaelic Proverbs. Is èasgaidhe nòin na madainn,* 'noon is more lively than morning', p. 234. The same expression is found in Irish, see Dinneen's *Dictionary* under *éascaidh.* In Scotland it appears to have been corrupted in transmission, for Mackintosh recorded it as *is ea-*

sgith nò madain, 'people are readier to act at night than in the morning' (the same sense is that given by Dinneen). No such 'entity' as 'Om' exists in Scottish Gaelic folklore; his name may be safely deleted from the list of Highland hobgoblins.

Fr Allan, Notebook VI No. 258 (from Miss Christina MacInnes, Coilleag, Eriskay):

> The raven is not liked because he did not come back to the ark but remained eating the carcases he found floating and lying about, and he acquired such experience then in finding out carcases, that ever since he always knows where a carcase is and has meat (flesh) always. This knowledge of his is proverbially known as '*fios fithich*' the raven's knowledge.

Fr Allan, Notebook I No. 480:

> When Cuchulainn was dying it is said that the host of his enemies despatched a crow *feannag* to see if he were dead. His dying attitude was so lifelike being propped up by spears, (as related, so Fr Allan tells us, in a narrative in the *Transactions of the Gaelic Society of Inverness* [Carmichael 1873: 25–39]) that
>
> > The *feannag* returned and said
> > *Chaog an t'sùil,*
> > *'S cham am bial.*
>
> And thereby intimated that his life was extinct.

Miss Freer fused these two items together, suppressed the reference to Alexander Carmichael, and produced the following:

Miss Freer, Folklore 13 (1902), 35:

> Knowledge of the whereabouts of the lost, if dead, is called raven's knowledge. When Cuchullin was dying the host of his enemies despatched a crow (*fiannag*) (*sic:* this is what Fr Allan's handwriting would suggest to a person ignorant of Gaelic) to see if he were dead. His dying attitude was so life-like, propped up with spears, that the raven (*sic*) returning, could only say:
>
> > The eye looks askance
> > And the mouth is awry.

On p. 33 of this article in *Folklore* 13, Miss Freer states that 'the sort of story which, in *Aesop's Fables*, is attributed to the fox, is in the Outer Hebrides where foxes are unknown, related to the cat.' But as anyone with first-hand knowledge of Hebridean folklore is aware, the islanders know perfectly well what a fox is, and it figures in folk-anecdotes in the oral tradition; and in fact, Fr Allan took down the story of the fox, the wolf and the butter in Notebook VI, No. 45.

One of the most striking proofs of Miss Freer's ignorance of Gaelic and her unreliability as a 'folklorist' is her treatment of the word *toradh*. The original passage occurs in Fr Allan Notebook I, item No. 86:

> A plant called *caoibhreachan* was considered lucky and a sufficient protection against witchcraft. They say it is impossible that any milk or *toradh* can be witched out of a house, where the *caoibhrichean* is kept under an upturned vessel.

Miss Freer, Folklore *10 (1899), 275:*

> The marsh-ragwort (*caoibhreachan*) is valuable against the *torradh* (*sic*) and the Evil Eye generally.
> Of all forms of evil influence none is more dreaded than this *torradh*, or the charming away of milk from cattle.

And in the glossary to *The Outer Isles:* '*toradh*, a form of evil influence, the charming away of milk from cattle'. Thus is Gaelic folklore given to the world! *Toradh* means nothing more than 'produce'! Milk is the produce of cows; *toradh* is what the witches tried to charm away, not the charming away itself.

In a long passage on 'Divination' (*Folklore* 13 (1902), 47) that is copied from Fr Allan (Vol. I, items 146 and 350, Vol. V, item 103), Miss Freer (to whom the innocent reader would think the whole passage had been told) betrays herself completely by not realising that 'Catriana MacEachan' who is referred to in Vol. V, item 103, was the same person as the 'very old woman' referred to as a Campbell in Vol. I, item 146! Two informants are given when only one existed (Campbell 1955).

These instances could be multiplied wholesale. Each of the four of Fr Allan's folklore notebooks which I have seen (I, II, V, VI) have ticks against the material which Miss Freer copied, along with marginal and indexing comments in her writing. Volume VII, fortunately, never came into her hands and remains unmarked.

Miss Freer concluded her last talk to the Folklore Society, given on 6th November 1901, with the following words:

> The above miscellaneous gatherings are, so to speak, the flotsam and jetsam of the wild seas of the Outer Hebrides. They present, I believe, considerable material for the commentator and the comparative folklorist, but the task of discussion is one for which the present writer lacks – among other things – at this moment, leisure, though she looks forward to the attempt on some future occasion.

The 'above miscellaneous gatherings' in fact represented much of the contents of Fr Allan McDonald's notebooks; and the disinclination of the lecturer for the 'task of discussion' may very well have arisen from the fact that she had utilised his material to a point where the illusion that it actually represented the proceeds of her own inquiries would be more than a little difficult to sustain, and could hardly have been sustained if there had been a Gaelic-speaking questioner, familiar with the Hebrides, in her audience that evening.

When it is added that in her preface to this paper in Vol. 13 (1902) of *Folklore* Miss Freer claimed copyright in the material printed and asserted that Fr Allan had been a common source for both Alexander Carmichael's *Carmina Gadelica* and for herself, it is not surprising that Fr Allan's friends rebelled.

As early as 13th August 1901, Alexander Carmichael had written Fr Allan complaining of the way Miss Freer had received his wife when she (Mrs Carmichael) called on her in London. 'Ella' (his daughter) 'was told when in London that Miss Freer is not what she seems, and draws upon her imagination a good deal for her facts'. On 7th October of the same year he wrote: 'We hear from various sources that Miss Freer is not genuine and some call her a clever imposter. I never got my wife to believe in her.'

The assertion that Fr Allan was a source for *Carmina Gadelica* angered Carmichael greatly. He had explicitly denied this in the preface to *Carmina Gadelica* which appeared in 1900. In March 1902 he wrote: 'I thought much, very much, of Miss Freer. I think less, much less, of her now.' On 1st June 1902 Dr George Henderson wrote: 'Has Miss Freer republished your articles?' (i.e. the articles from *Folklore* in her book *The Outer Isles*; 'Your articles' means the articles she prepared from Fr Allan's notebooks) 'I think she is rather bold in writing her name over them with such meagre acknowledgement to you. Of course I know you well, but I don't admire that sort of thing.'

Fr Allan, to whose kindly and generous nature Dr Henderson alludes, had in fact been taken advantage of. It must have been a painful moment for him. The person who he had believed to be a friend and an encourager of his work had in fact made use of him to advance her reputation as a folklorist and her career as a writer.

Fr Allan wrote a disclaimer, as regards his material being used by Carmichael in *Carmina Gadelica*, which was printed in *Folklore* 14 (1903), 87. Carmichael had not used it (in his first two volumes anyway) though he had often consulted Fr Allan about meanings of words and about variant readings. He did not need it. There the matter ended for the time being. Miss Freer had married and gone to live in Jerusalem, where she interested herself in the folklore of the Arabs. Fr Allan died in 1905. He did not collect any folklore after the end of 1899; his manuscripts disappeared for nearly forty-five years until traced by the writer of this article with the help of friends. Amy Murray, who visited Eriskay in the summer of 1905, wrote in her book *Father Allan's Island* (p. 203) that he 'had been little pleased with the working up one pair of hands, at least, had given them' (i.e. his folklore collections). There can be no doubt of what he meant by this, for the only hands besides Miss Freer's through which his notebook had passed were those of his friends Alexander Carmichael and Dr George Henderson.

Miss Freer died in America in 1931. She did not preserve Fr Allan McDonald's letters to her, or the copies she made of the material she chose from his notes to use in her lectures and articles: and most of her letters to him are now lost. She received a very favourable obituary in *Folklore* 41 (1930), 299, as, amongst other things, an important contributor to Hebridean folklore. The death of Fr Allan McDonald, the real collector, in 1905, passed unnoticed by that journal.

SOME ERRATA TO MISS FREER'S ARTICLES IN *FOLKLORE*

(*a*) Vol. 10 (1899) 'The Powers of Evil in the Outer Hebrides'.

p. 265 for *diathol*	read *diabhol*
p. 268 for *dessil*	read *deiseil* (and elsewhere)
p. 273 for Seacoch	read Leacach
p. 273 for Stuolaval	read Staolaval
p. 275 for *Lus Columcille*	read *Lus Chalum-chille*
(*lus* does not mean 'armpit', as she implies)	
p. 281 for *eolas*	read *eòlas*
p. 282 for Kiloanan	read Kildonan

(*b*) Vol. 13 (1902) 'More Folklore from the Hebrides'.

p. 31n for *sluath*	read *sluagh*
p. 35 for *deachanch*	read *deachamh*
p. 35 for *fiannag*	read *feannag*
p. 36 line 2, for 'raven'	read 'crow'
p. 36 for *Mhurchadh bheg*	read *Mhurchaidh bhig*
p. 36 for *nid*	read *niod*

p. 36 for *uisiag*	read *uiseag*
p. 36 for *glaissean*	read *glaisean* (and elsewhere)
p. 37 for *fuoitreag*	read *faoiteag*
p. 38 line 1, for 'aphis'	read 'harvestman' (*Phalangium*)

p. 41 It is implied, in the remarks about the Beltane bannock, that Fr Allan McDonald's grandmother came from South Uist. This is not the case: in the original, he says she was from Strathspey.

p. 43 for *galium verum* Fr Allan has 'rue'.

p. 44 for 'Son of the fall of the Rocks', read 'Son of the hall of the Rocks'.

p. 44 for *mìn*	read *min*
p. 49 for *raum*	read *rann*
p. 50 for *Mohr*	read *Mór*
p. 56 for *Dioja*	read *Dioga*
p. 56 for *chelusgan*	read *cheeusgan*
p. 56 for *M'hor*	read *Mhór*
p. 57 for *barrin*	read *barran*
p. 57 for *Greinn Gulmain*	read *Greim Gulmain*
p. 62 for Tochar	read Iochar

Note

This article, which some critics considered contentious and unchivalrous when it was published in 1958, was amply justified by the further researches of the writer in collaboration with the late Trevor H. Hall, published under the title of *Strange Things. The Enquiry by the Society for Psychical Research into Second Sight in the Scottish Highlands* (Routledge & Kegan Paul, London) ten years later.

Fr Allan McDonald's Diary for March 1898

.

The diary was kept in Gaelic during this month. This is a
translation by J. L. Campbell and was published in Gaelic in
Gairm (1952–3) 1–2.

March 1st (Tuesday) When I got up in the morning the ground was
white with snow. It is likely that spring will end well since it has
begun so badly. If the proverb is true ... of March will be very fine,
this year. But why ... complain of the bad weather this time of
year, when ... long since the sage said, 'Autumn until Christmas
and winter until St Patrick's Day?' Anyway, I have no reason to
complain when I need not move from the fireside. It is the poor
fishermen who are out on the bare back of the sea, wet and frozen,
in this windy weather, with incessant sleet squalls and hail stone
about their ears, who are to be pitied. If only they had a fair chance,
but they are ill-met and ill-clothed in every way. After all it is little
profit they make though the fish are plentiful around the coast.
May God send them a sufficiency of it and may He preserve their
lives to them.

(218)   It is often said that the Gael lacks diligence. I would like to
see the people who most frequently make this charge confined for a
while to a sea island without any sustenance except what they could
win by their own diligence from the sea in the kind of weather we have
at present. I am very much afraid none of them would be alive to tell
the tale within a week. Whatever is wrong with the Eriskay man, not
even the person who dislikes him most can truthfully say that he lacks
diligence. There he is, wet every day, exposed to rain, snow and storm,
without a dry stitch to his back from dawn to dusk, living on dry bread
and on a drop of black tea so strong it could tan his long-lines, without
a drop of milk in it, without a fair chance, without justice or joy or any
worldly pleasures, but what he gets from the smell of the smoke of the
pipe beneath his nose to disperse hunger and weariness – and there is
not amongst high or low in Scotland (219) a man who is so happy and
contented in his worldly lot as he is. Worldly cares burden him but
little, and his mind is as light as the white seagull which flies above his
boat. I earnestly pray that God may prosper the poor fisherman and
keep him safely from the greedy maw of the ocean wherever the poor
man must voyage, through the far-away seas of the Atlantic, through
the swelling waves of the Irish Sea through the many waters south and

north, without and within on the East Coast, through the hidden lochs and the broad fjords of the mainland and the islands.

It became very wild about three o'clock in the afternoon. A little boat was coming into the Sound at the time and she had a bad time of it before she made the land. It was all right as they were so near the land. If this wind had caught her in the open sea there would have been danger enough of their being lost, but the Sound was not so rough and though the wind was just as strong as it was outside the danger was not so great.

(220) I don't know when I felt the time so long as I have felt it during these days. I don't believe I ever did. I would like to turn to doing something, but I don't know what to turn to. Not knowing this is what has put me to this idle pastime [i.e. keeping a diary]. Sometimes it occurs to me to put my hand to making a poem. At others I feel like writing a story, but between the two ideas, like the man who was sitting on two benches together, I am on the floor, and nothing gets accomplished. It would be something – in order to pass the time – if I might stretch my legs and take a walk through the Island, but the weather is so unpleasant, that it is much wiser for me to stay indoors, than to be splashing and plashing outside – coming home a wretched object covered with mud and slime or blinded with spindrift – and none the better. Since I have no (221) better employment may I not as well be sharpening my blunt Gaelic? It would be none the worse for having some of its rustiness removed, and if I continue to pare it with the tool which I have in my hand at present I hope that I will get some grain of the rust rubbed off, if rust is in grains. I read Gaelic every day. To tell the truth reading it on these gloomy days has been a third of my life – but I must admit that I have written only a little of it for some time – at any rate out of my own head. I daresay I was not diligent enough at carefully collecting and writing down every fragment of verse and poetry, anecdote or story I heard, in the books in which I kept everything of that kind, but it is a year, or two, or three, or four perhaps since I tried to compose even a single verse of a hymn in Gaelic. No wonder it is (222) pretty rusty for that. But how I envy the people who can speak fluent well-pronounced Gaelic, as fluently and as sweetly as the lark[7] singing, and as sweet as the honey which the buzzing bee sucks from the flower blossoms[8] in autumn! It can't be helped. In spite of diligence, practice in youth is better. That is where I lost – brought up in a village half Lowland and half Highland[9] without as much as even the Paternoster, let alone any schooling in Gaelic, but shut up from dawn till dusk in an English-language school – in

a Latin and Greek school if you like – while the language which was most expressive and most natural to us was forbidden. The effect of that is there – the twist English put in my mouth then is still there and will remain. In consequence of it I will never have been completely at ease in Gaelic, and though I hate it with heart and with spleen, my Gaelic will always have the harsh stammering unpleasant accent of the English speaker which a tongue-tied, stiff-worded English education has left in my head.

The Old Life in the Islands

As told by Fr Allan McDonald to Walter Blaikie in the summer of 1898. Blaikie was visiting Eriskay and South Uist in the footsteps of Prince Charles Edward, whose itinerary of 1745–46 he was studying.

Fr Allan (Eriskay) tells me that the people ate the root of silverweed[10] before the days of potatoes, and that the root of sneezewort was used as tobacco. On the failure of the potatoes (from blight) they ate gooseweed.[11] They ate also dulse (*duileasg*), the leaf of a tangle (*liaghag*), sloke (boiled with butter, tastes well), *cruaigean* or carrageen, a seaweed; curly kale (*càl greannach*) (*càl* – cabbage). Nettles were also used, black oats, bere, barley and rye.

Crockery was unknown. Wooden vessels with sheepskin bottoms were used. Porridge (from black oats) was made like gruel – handed round. Each crofter killed a sheep at Christmas – a hogg.

Potatoes are planted in the Western Isles in the 'lazybed' system. Hard peat soil or land long out of cultivation sandwich the seaweed. It takes thirteen carts of decayed seaweed to raise one barrel of potatoes, and four carts of fresh seaweed to make one cart of decayed.[12] All cultivation spade labour done by women, not men. Men do the lazybeds.

They use the root of tormentil for tanning. They ate shellfish, cockles, wild fowls. There are shoals of limpet shells in ancient signs of habitation.

At weddings they kill (about) forty hens; when a guest leaves kills poultry (*sic*).

They set weirs in tidal runs to catch saithe and cuddies.

In most of the islands there is a rock (*carraig* or fishing rock) with a hole, in which bait is mixed up for use with a bagnet.[13]

Notes and References to Section 3

[1] In Barra Sound.

[2] Cultivated.

[3] The author of this article had traced most of the literary remains of the late Fr Allan McDonald with the help of various friends, and had been engaged in preparing them for publication.

[4] 'An Sithean Ruadh', *Celtic Review* 3 (1906–7), 77–83; 'Calum-Cille Agus Dobhran a Bhrathair', 5 (1908–9); 'Tarbh Mór na h-Iorbhaig', 5 (1908–9), 259–66; 'Piobairean Smearcleit', 5 (1908–9), 345–7; 'Cluich na Cloinne – Children's Games', 7 (1911–12), 371–6; 'Children's Rimes', 8 (1912–13), 166–8.

[5]In making comparisons between Fr Allan's work and that of Miss Freer, I am much indebted to Miss Sheila J. Lockett's assistance in cataloguing Fr Allan's MSS.

[6]Fr Allan had studied for the priesthood at Valladolid, hence the references to Spanish customs.

[7]*druideag.*

[8]*dithein,* yellow flower.

[9]Fort William.

[10]*Brisgein.* Elsewhere Fr Allan wrote that '*brisgein* was in great request for food in the islands. Roderick MacPark from Harris, who was in Boisdale, told Neil Johnston, Eriskay, that he saw a large chest full in his grandfather's house in Harris for winter use, and Roderick's grandfather said that the land in Harris used to be divided amongst the peasantry at ploughing time or tillage time so that each might have their proper share of the *brisgein* which are more easily found when the land is being tilled. The land was then worked communally, being all in common, no people having separate crofts.'

[11]*Bloinigean.* Elsewhere Fr Allan wrote 'About fifty years ago (i.e. about 1848) in the times of the (potato) blight and evictions, food was so scarce in Eriskay that separate spots in the Island were marked off for separate families for collecting *bloinigean,* and each family as confined to that spot in their collection of it. No person eats it now. It grows where seaweed heaps have been lying long on land.'

[12]There follows here the sentence '360 ... to make ... 3 feet wide'. The two words are illegible.

[13]Cp. 'Verses Made to Eriskay', verse 14 (ref. John Lorne Campbell, *Bàrdachd Mhgr. Ailein. The Gaelic Poems of Fr Allan McDonald of Eriskay* Edinburgh 1965, 84).

Section 4

·

Barra, Mingulay and Bernera

·

The MacNeils of Barra and the Irish Franciscans

Published in *The Innes Review* Vol. 5 (1954), pp. 33–8

On 12th November 1625 the Irish Franciscan friar Cornelius Ward (Conchobhair Mac an Bháird) who had gone that autumn to South Uist with the approval of Clanranald, was invited to go to Barra by a gentleman to perform a baptism '*ad quendam valde nominatum nobilem gratia baptizandae suae prolis invitatus, appuli in insulam Barram*'.[1]

Father Ward was apparently the first Catholic priest to visit Barra since the Reformation. He found the church dedicated to St Barr (which is situated at the north end of the Island) roofless but still possessing the statue of the saint, who was greatly venerated by the inhabitants. 'For the sea, as often as it is sprinkled with the dust of the grave of this saint is accustomed, as the inhabitants affirm, to cease from all storm.'

Fr Ward remained in Barra until 21st November 1625, celebrated Mass three times and preached four times, reconciling 101 persons including the sister of the principal laird (*soror domini principalis*) with some of the gentry (*cum aliquot nobilibus*). He also baptised two sons of the principal laird (*duos filos domini principalis*) and forty-two other persons, nearly all adults, among them a woman of sixty and a man of seventy. On the small island called Fuday (Ude) in Barra Sound Fr Ward reconciled a 'noble' with his wife, that is to say, the tacksman of the island – and baptised four others. Fr Ward relates that when he gave the Sacrament on Barra, a young man who had not been to confession previously, mingled with the communicants and after receiving the Host was unable to swallow it, an incident which occurred again when the Lazarist Fr Dugan visited Barra in 1654 (Campbell, J. L. (1936), p. 10).

Fr Ward then returned to Uist. After the new year he intended to return to Ireland by Kintyre with some Catholics who were making the journey, but bad weather prevented them from leaving the island, and instead he paid a second visit to Barra in February 1626, on which occasion he reconciled a further 117 persons. 'One of these a man of noble birth and the lawful heir of the island I joined in marriage. His younger brother, however, having seized the castle by force and having apprehended his father and this elder brother, did not release the father until his death, nor his brother until he had made by oath renunciation of his inheritance. Since he was usurping the castle and his brother's estates, he refused the faith, as is believed, in order that he might not be compelled to restore them.'[2]

Fr Ward's account is of importance concerning (a) the continuity of the Catholic tradition on Barra; (b) the succession of the MacNeils of Barra, which is disputed for this generation (MacLean Sinclair, A. (1904), 216–23; MacNeil, R. L. (1923)). As regards the first, the continuity of the Catholic tradition on Barra is now finally proved. As late as 1593 it was reported that the Barramen were in the habit of making pilgrimages to Cruach Phàdruig in Mayo (Mackenzie, W. C. (1949), p. 184). They cannot have been Protestant then, and if they had been evangelised between 1593 and 1625, Fr Ward would not have found St Barr's image still standing in Kilbar Chapel nor would he have been invited to go from Uist to Barra to perform baptisms. Twenty-four years later than the event, it was alleged by Lord Lorne that Ranald MacDonald of Benbecula, brother-in-law of the then MacNeil of Barra, had murdered John MacNeil parson and minister of Barra in 1609 (MacPhail, J. R. N. (1934), p. 227). This allegation was never put to the proof, but if such an incident did occur it is difficult to understand why the authorities did not act immediately. If it did occur, it probably bore some relation to the struggle then going on in Barra between Campbell (or MacLean) and MacDonald influences in the form of a contention for the heirship to Ruairi an Tartair between his illegitimate and legitimate families, of which more later. Protestantism can never have taken root in Barra, judging from Fr Ward's invitation and reception and what he found there.

Apart from illustrating the continuity of the Catholic tradition on Barra, Fr Ward's narrative throws some light upon a difficulty in the MacNeil of Barra genealogy, that is, the succession to Ruairi an Tartair, the chief who died around 1620, imprisoned, as Fr Ward tells, by a son who was not the rightful heir. Here it is necessary to consider the version of MacNeil of Barra pedigree printed in *Burke's Landed Gentry* in 1850 during the lifetime of General Roderick MacNeil of Barra, the last MacNeil of Barra in the direct line, who died in 1863. This pedigree must be taken to represent the tradition existing in General MacNeil's family, though as printed in *Burke* it is disappointingly bald and gives the impression of having been written up from memory or at any rate without access to some important sources of information.

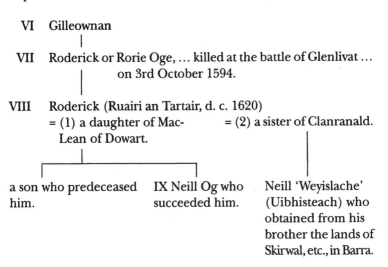

VI   Gilleownan

VII   Roderick or Rorie Oge, ... killed at the battle of Glenlivat ... on 3rd October 1594.

VIII Roderick (Ruairi an Tartair, d. c. 1620)
      = (1) a daughter of Mac-   = (2) a sister of Clanranald.
      Lean of Dowart.

a son who predeceased   IX Neill Og who   Neill 'Weyislache'
him.   succeeded him.   (Uibhisteach) who
                                            obtained from his
                                            brother the lands of
                                            Skirwal, etc., in Barra.

This pedigree was amplified by the late Rev. A. MacLean Sinclair in the *Celtic Review* III, pp. 216–223. MacLean Sinclair inserted two Rodericks into the succession, making Ruairi an Tartair[3] out to be the tenth chief. He also asserted that Ruairi an Tartair was probably succeeded by Neill Uibhisteach,[4] as Neill Og was not legitimate. R. L. MacNeil of Barra in his book *The Clan MacNeil* (New York, 1923) further elaborated the pedigree, quoting freely from contemporary records, and asserted that the successor to Ruairi an Tartair was not Neill Uibhisteach but Neill Og. He assumed that Ruari was married to Neill Og's mother and handfasted with Neill Uibhisteach's mother, but this contradicts the evidence of the complaint to the Privy Council made by Rory MacNeil of Barra (Ruairi an Tartair) in 1613 which is quoted below.

According to both these authors, Rory Og, whom MacLean Sinclair calls the ninth and R. L. MacNeil calls the thirty-fourth MacNeil of Barra, was married to Mary, daughter and only child of William MacLeod of Dunvegan, grand-daughter of Lord Lovat and widow of Duncan Campbell of Auchinbreck, their heir and successor being Ruairi an Tartair. Nothing whatever is said about this marriage in General MacNeil of Barra's account of his genealogy, quoted above, but in the MacLeod of MacLeod pedigree printed in the same edition of *Burke's Landed Gentry,* Mary, only daughter of William MacLeod, is said to have been married first to Duncan Campbell of Castle Sween and secondly to MacNeil of Barra (no Christian name given), as stated above.

Chronologically it is impossible for Mary MacLeod to have been the mother of Ruairi an Tartair. Her parents were married between 12th April and 31st July 1540 (MacLeod, R. C. (1938–9), Vol. I, p. 51). The exact date of her birth is not known, but it was probably between 1541 and 1545. As heiress of the MacLeods, she was an important person, and her wardship was eagerly sought for by various nobles, and was eventually secured by the Earl of Argyll, who married her off to Duncan Campbell of Castle Sween, second son and ultimate successor of Archibald Campbell of Auchinbreck. This marriage took place in 1573 according to *Collectanea de Rebus Albanicis* where a number of documents relating to Mary MacLeod are printed (pp. 136–51), but a receipt for part of her dowry printed in the *Book of Dunvegan* (Vol. I, p. 212) seems to imply that she was already married to Duncan Campbell in February 1569–70. She was certainly still married to him in 1577 (MacLeod, R. C. (1938–9), Vol. I, p. 51) – if the date is correctly transcribed. According to *The Clan Campbell* she had three children by Duncan Campbell, who died before 19 August 1581.[5] It was therefore quite impossible for Mary MacLeod to have married Rory Og MacNeil of Barra in her widowhood and to have been the mother of Ruairi an Tartair by him, for Ruairi an Tartair had two families of full-grown sons by 1610[6] and is described as a very old man around 1620 (Mitchell, A. and Clark, J. J. (1906–8), Vol. II, p. 180).

Dr I. F. Grant tells me that there is a tradition at Dunvegan that Mary MacLeod was already in love with MacNeil of Barra when she was married off to Duncan Campbell against her will, and that as soon as Duncan Campbell died she went to Barra. That is quite probably correct; the only alternative (for which there is no evidence) is that she eloped to Barra in her youth, and was brought back by Kenneth MacKenzie of Kintail who produced her in Edinburgh on 21st May 1562 and whose position with regard to her is a little difficult to understand.

The authority for Mary MacLeod's marriage with MacNeil of Barra (which MacNeil is not stated) seems to be Rev. James Fraser, minister of Wardlaw, in his account of the Bissets and the Frasers of Lovat, written around 1670 (Clark, J. T. (1900), Vol. I, p. 93). But in an entry of the *Register of the Privy Council* (Vol. VI, p. 725) dated 23rd April 1602, John Stewart of Ardmoleis, Sheriff of Bute, and a number of other persons, are ordered 'not to harm Marie McCloyd relict of Duncane Campbell captain of Castle Sune', and two other persons. She is not described as the wife or widow of MacNeil of Barra. Apparently some kind of feud was on at the time between her son, Dugald Campbell of Auchinbreck, and the men of Bute. This allusion implies she was not then living in Barra.

On 11th March 1613 the *Register of the Privy Council* (Vol. X, p. 6–7) recorded a complaint by

> Rorie McNeill of Barray, and Gillevuan Oig McNeill, his lauchfull sone lauchfullie procreat betwix him and Moir Nine Allan (Mór nighean Ailein), his lauchfull spous, and sister to Donald McAllan of Yllantyrum (Eilean Tioram) Capitane of the Clanrannald ... upon the – day of October last bypast, thay being within thair awne house and Castle of Kismule in the Yle of Barray, thair doing thair lauchfull effaris in sober and quiet manner, lippyning for (expecting) no violence, injurie, nor oppressioun to have bene done to thame be ony person, it is of treuth that Neill Oig McNeill and Gillevuan McNeill, sones naturall to the said Rorie, unlauchfullie procreat betwixt him and – , mother to Sir Dougall Campbell of Auchinbreck

accompanied by various persons bearing arms

> come to said castle of Kismule, enterit violentlie thairintill and pat violent handis on the saidis complenaris, took and apprehendit thame, layed thame fast in yrnis, mannit the said house, maid thame selffis maisteris and commanderis thairof

and had fortified the castle and detained Rorie MacNeil and his legitimate son Gillevuan Og (Gill' Eóghanain) prisoners in it. This was the beginning of the story of which Fr Ward relates the end. Neill Og and 'Gillevuan' were declared rebels and Clanranald was given a commission to apprehend and produce them, which he had every reason to do in his own nephew's interest; but there is no record of this having been done; Clanranald was getting old by 1613 (he died in 1618) and was probably involved in other affairs.

There is no doubt whatever that Mary MacLeod was the person meant by the 'mother to Sir Dougall Campbell of Auchinbreck'; this is borne out by the entries in *Inquisitiones Generales* Nos. 1580 and 8582 – 'Dominus Dougallus Campbell de Auchinbreck miles baronettus *haeres* Mariae McCloyde, matris' – dates 1st March 1630 and 31st March 1630. There can be little doubt that her association was with Ruairi an Tartair himself, not with Rory Og[7] (if indeed Rory Og and Ruairi an Tartair were not one and the same person), that it was not a lawful marriage, and that Neill Og and 'Gillevuan' were her sons by Ruairi an Tartair; even though James Primrose refers to the strife in Barra at this time as having been between the sons of a MacLean mother and those of a MacDonald mother, the complaint to the Privy Council quoted above seems to be authoritative on this point.

There is circumstantial evidence for Mary MacLeod's interest in Barra in the fact that the lease of the teinds of the Bishop's Isles (the small islands south of Barra) were at one time held by Sir Dugald Campbell of Aucinbreck, her son. In 1617 the Bishop of the Isles complained to the Privy Council that the tack duty had not been paid by Sir Dugald since 1611 (*Register of the Privy Council*, Vol. XI, p. 244). In 1623 Ruairi Mór MacLeod of Dunvegan gave a lease of these teinds to Neil Og McNeil; they had been assigned to Ruairi Mór by Sir Duncan (? Dugald) Campbell of Auchinbreck.[8] This is strong evidence in favour of the supposition that Neil Og had succeeded Ruairi an Tartair as *de facto* laird of Barra, and was the same person as the usurper mentioned by Fr Ward. One is reminded of the remark made about Castle Kismul and the MacNeils of Barra by Fr Alexander Leslie in his report on his visitation of 1679 – 'Whatever member of the (MacNeil) family is in possession of it (i.e. Kismul) even though not the eldest, is regarded as chief of the whole island' (Campbell, J. L. (1936), p. 17). It is probable that Neil Og remained in possession, nothing more being done to oust him. A clue to what may have happened is given in the account of Barra printed in Vol. II of *Macfarlane's Geographical Collections* (Mitchell, A. and Clark, J. T. (1906–8)) already referred to, where we read that

> This McNeill (i.e. Ruairi an Tartair) had several Noblemen daughters and had sundrie bairnes, and at last everie one of them thinking and esteeming himself to be worthie of the Countrie (i.e. Barra) after the fathers deceass being on lyff as yet, the said sons having sundrie mothers, at last everie one of them did kill others except one that is alyff and another drowned in the sea.
>
> Campbell, J. L. (ed.) *Book of Barra* (1936), p. 17

This account is said to have been written around 1630, and it clearly implies that by that time all Ruairi an Tartair's sons had been eliminated except one. At this time the superiority of Barra belonged to the MacKenzies of Tarbat, so there is no record of MacNeil successions in *Inquisitionum ad Capellam Domini Regis*. Fr Cathaldus Giblin O.F.M. tells me he has found no further references to this question in the Franciscan documents he has seen.

One may conclude this article by some further allusions to the religion of the MacNeils of Barra during the seventeenth and eighteenth centuries. Mr R. L. MacNeil states that the religion of Gilleonan 'XXXVII' c. 1625–90 'cannot be stated definitely' and that Roderick 'XXXVIII' c. 1655–1718 and Roderick 'XXXIX' 1693–1763 were 'nominally Protestants' (MacNeil, R. L. (1923), p. 149). As regards Neil Og, Mr R. L. MacNeil appears to be under the impression that because he received a commission in 1629 to apprehend priests and Jesuits, he must have been a Protestant himself. That, of course, is not necessarily the case; the commission was given on account of his hereditary position and not on account of his religious convictions, whatever they were at the time; such commissions indeed might well be given to embarrass a Highland chief of Catholic sympathies. Though the 'usurper' refused the faith in 1626, Fr Ward makes it clear that he did so on account of his usurpation and not for any heretical convictions. On 25th May 1643 this same MacNeil of Barra was denounced by Mr Martin MacPherson, minister of South Uist, to the Synod of Argyle for having a statue of Our Lady and her Child in his private chapel (Mactavish, D. C. (1943), Vol. I. p. 68).

For Gilleonan 'XXXVII' we have the evidence of Fr Dugan in 1652 and 1654 and of Fr Francis MacDonnell in 1671 (Campbell, J. L. (1936), pp. 9, 10, 15). For Roderick 'XXXVIII' there is the important list of Highland Catholics drawn up in 1703, where MacNeil of Barra (Roderick 'XXXVIII') and his five children and two brothers are described as Catholics. The report goes on to say that

> the Captain of Clanranald, Kinlochmudart, Benbecula, Morar, all McDonalds and McNeil of Bara are the principal patrons and promoters of popery in their bounds giving shelter and encouragement to their priests and Jesuits.
>
> *Maitland Club Miscellany*, Vol. III, pp. 389–95

In 1714 (MacPhail, J. R. N. (1920), p. 59), 1724 (General Wade's Report, In: Allardyce, J. (1895), p. 145) and 1746 (Macbean, A. Rev. (1916), p. 79) there are equally explicit references to the Catholicism of the chiefs of the MacNeils of Barra; they were certainly not considered by the authorities to be Protestants at any time during the first half of the eighteenth century, and might reasonably have been commended by the chronicler of their clan for their constancy to the 'Old Religion' under penal laws.

The MacNeils of Barra in the Forty-five

Published in The Innes Review Vol. 17 (1966), pp. 82–90

The fact that the MacNeils of Barra were Catholics until the middle of the eighteenth century is well known, and Barra itself is still predominantly Catholic[9]; the part played by the chief of the MacNeils in the Rising of 1745 has been hitherto rather obscure, but the investigation of a number of unpublished documents has made it possible to elucidate this obscurity considerably.

In 1703 a 'list of children under popish parents, tutors or curators' in South Uist and Barra, drawn up by the Synod of Argyll, included the 'Lairde of Barra' who had 'five children of which tuo only ar come to the years of instruction', his brothers Murdo and John MacNeil with two and three children respectively, and 'Donald McNeile and tuo young Girles children to the deceast Hector McNeile of Vattersay' (the island immediately south of Barra) who were under the Laird of Barra's curatorship.[10]

It is rather surprising to find this Donald MacNeil of Vatersay later named as a correspondent of the very anti-Catholic Society in Scotland for Propagating Christian Knowledge in January 1725, and writing to the Society towards the end of 1727 that 'if a school were setled at Bara a Large popish Island he would encourage it, and that no place in Scotland stands more in need of one'.[11] Possibly a second marriage to a daughter of Norman MacLeod of Greshornish[12] may account for Donald MacNeil of Vatersay's conversion. Since Barra was a Catholic island with a Catholic proprietor, Roderick MacNeil (1693–1763), claimed as 39th chief, one may suspect that Vatersay, who was a cousin of MacNeil, one of whose sisters had been his first wife, was intriguing with the SPCK in the hope of compromising MacNeil and securing the estate of Barra for himself as nearest Protestant heir under the Penal Laws.[13] As subsequent events were to prove, Vatersay (like a number of other persons thought well-affected by the SPCK) had a foot in each camp.

At any rate, his zeal on behalf of the SPCK between 1727 and 1732 is amply attested from the Minutes of the Committee of the Society. We find him writing again (Minute dated 24th October 1728), when

> The Clerk presented a letter from Donald McNeil of Vattersay dated the twenty sixth of August last shewing that a Popish Bishop with five

more priests were lately in Bara and Southuist visiting and confirming their people,[14] and yet it is hoped that in process of time they will be losing ground by the diligence of the protestant ministers ... The Committee delayed the consideration of a school for Bara till another diet, and in the mean time referred to the Clerk to look over the list of Schools, and see if any of them may be removed to that place.

At a meeting held on 6th February 1729, the Committee decided to send one Peter King, schoolmaster at Brig of Turk, to Barra. On 20th March 1729

The Clerk produced a letter from Donald McNiel of Vatersay Putting the Society in mind of a school for the Isle of Bara, and reported that the Committee for the Royal Bounty[15] had allowed Peter King ten pounds as a Catechist in that Isle, according to this Committee's Recommendation the sixth of February last, The Committee ordered the Clerk to return Vatersay an answer shewing that the said Peter King is appointed to repair to Bara once in May next, and desiring that accommodations be prepared for him, and as to poor scholars there, especially such Papists as are willing to allow their children to be taught at the Society's School and to observe the Society's Rule, appointed that the Formula thereanent be sent to Vatersay that Certificates may be returned according thereunto.

Peter King actually reached Barra early in June, and at a meeting of the Committee dated 17 July 1729 his report on his reception there is recorded:

The Clerk presented and read a Memorial given in by Peter King now on the place, Bearing, That he came to Bara the sixth of June last, and being a stranger and the country in hard Circumstances for want of meal, he could get no Victuals for money; That he was informed by one Donald MacNeil in Vatersay a Protestant, That it was impossible to get any Scholars conveened there, or accommodation in Boarding till the country were better supplyed with the necessaries of Life, and having waited of Mcneil of Bara was told by him that there was little, if any Prospect of Success for him in that Island, and therefore seeing there was no Schoolhouse, no Scholars or Books, and there being no way of living there by Reason of the Scarcity of Victuals, he was oblidged to return hither in order to lay the case before the Society, and receive their Directions; Produced likewise a letter from the said Donald McNiel dated the tenth of June last, Shewing that the people in the said Island being all gone to the Hills,[16] and Victuals so scarce there, they could not send their children to school sooner than August next, and that the said Peter King could not be certified as Catechist till November next, when Murdo Mcniels commission as such is to expire. The Committee having considered the premises, Did agree to delay sending any Schoolmaster to the said Isle of Bara for some time and ordered a

Commission to be given to the said Peter King in the parish of Kilmalie with the Salary of one hundred merks allowed to Bara.

This set-back did not discourage Vatersay. On 11th October 1729, he wrote the Committee that

Peter King was expected back to Bara in August last, and he had bought a House for the School, and craving that if he is not to come, the Presbytery be impowered to get a Schoolmaster, and settle him in that place, for the need of a school there still continues.

The Committee decided to refer the matter to the Presbytery. On 12th February 1730, Vatersay wrote again, saying

that the People in Bara are very desirous of a School, and that he had bought a House for one which is vacant, and he suggests, That if Peter King is not to come thither, There is one Thomson who keeps a school in Gia near Kintyre who is willing to come as Catechist and Schoolmaster which would prevent the People's setting up an old doted Papist whom they design as Schoolmaster

The Committee remitted this, and another letter written by Vatersay on 24th February 1731, to the Joint Committee for settling schoolmasters and catechists, a definite decision being reached on 23rd May 1732, when

As to the School allowed for Bara, The Committee agrees that how soon a school house is built and a fit person certified by the Presbytery to whom it is hereby recommended to look out for one to serve therein, the person so certified shall have his Commission furthwith sent him in order that he may enter to his work, after he receives the Commission, and its recommended to the Presbytery to return the Society's thanks to Donald McNiel of Vatersay for his Zeal for the Protestant's Interest in that Countrey and intreating him to contribute his assistance for having a schoolhouse built therein without delay.

The same year Alexander Gunn, whose qualifications were certified by the Presbytery of Dornoch, was appointed SPCK schoolmaster in Barra with a salary of £4 10s. 0d. as Schoolmaster from the Society and as much again as Catechist from the Royal Bounty.

Vatersay got his way, but it cannot be said that the school was a success. For in 1746, according to John Cameron, Presbyterian chaplain at Fort William, 'tho' in the Islands belonging to (MacNeil of) Barra there will be about 4 or 500 souls there is but one gentleman (presumably Vatersay himself) and seven or eight common people that are Protestants', one of whom had been hanged by Captain Caroline Scott on the charge of having been out in arms for the Prince, though there were plenty of witnesses to prove him innocent (Paton, H. (1895–6), Vol. I, p. 94).

Barra and its adjacent islands were the first land of Scotland sighted by the Prince and his friends on board the *Du Teillay*, 22nd July 1745.[17] They anchored in Barra Sound, off Eriskay, piloted by MacNeil's piper whom Duncan Cameron had met while ashore. A messenger was sent to MacNeil (who no longer lived in Kismul Castle at this date), but he was away from home, whether by accident or on purpose is uncertain.

From Barra Sound the *Du Teillay* sailed for Loch nan Uamh on the mainland, and what followed is common knowledge. Knowing the political predilections of the Barramen, who had fought under Claverhouse at Killiecrankie and had been 'out' in the Fifteen, one might have expected MacNeil and his clan to have joined the Prince in 1745. Their doing so was prevented by an easily understandable combination of circumstances.

When the *Du Teillay* left for the mainland, the islanders could of course only have formed the vaguest surmise of what was likely to follow. They might have hopes, but they would have heard of MacDonald of Boisdale's refusal to help, and they would have seen that the *Du Teillay* was alone, without the French aid so many considered necessary for the success of such a venture. In addition, they were faced with the immediate necessity of securing their harvest in the second of two wet summers. When at last news did arrive, and the crops were secure, the Prince and his army were too far away for it to seem likely that a contingent from the Outer Isles could catch up with them in time, it might have been thought, for the coronation. So the Islesmen stayed at home.

At the same time, Barra owing to its geographical position and the political sympathies of its inhabitants, was an ideal place for the landing of money and supplies from France and Spain for reshipment to the mainland for the insurgents. In October or November 1745, a Spanish ship commanded by Don Ultan Kindelan of the Ultonia Regiment of Spanish Infantry, and piloted by John MacLean from Iona, landed £4,000 and 2,500 stands of arms in Barra. Kindelan went on to Perth to join Lord John Drummond, leaving his junior, Don Mauricio McMahon, of the same regiment, to distribute the arms and money. McMahon was captured by Captain Duff of the *Terror* after Culloden and his papers fell into the hands of the Hanoverians, implicating many of the Island proprietors.[18]

After Kindelan had crossed from Barra to the mainland, he wrote o McMahon as follows:

Kinloghilard, Decemr. ye 1st, 1745.

Dr McMahon

I received an Anser from the Prince to the letter I wrote to His Royal Highness from Colansay with orders to Deliver all the Cash, Arms etc to Mr Sandey Mac Lochlen who has Directions to Supply all those that raises their Men for RH service with Arms etc. And that you should make the greater haste Mr Angus MacDonald goes there with the large boat that you may carry the whole at once with you, see that if the two boats be not sufficient and that the La(i)rd Barra does not come with you with all his Men, hire as many boats as you may want that you may leave nothing behind, there are 3,000 Men waiting for us at Perth and thereabouts, most of them according to H R H orders to be supply'd with them Arms etc so that your delaying any time may be of very bad consequence.

There is no doubt but that the Prince's younger brother is arrived in England at the head of a French Army of 6,000 men. His Royal Highness writes to me in his Letter dated a day before he left Edenborough, that he expected to meet them in a short time with the Scotch Highlanders. I fear we shall arrive too late to have our share of the Glory, in crowning our lawfull King. You will supply Lt Angus McDonald with what money he may want in case the cost of all the Men that may follow him and bring with you as many as you can but lett nothing delay you in coming to the Mainland with the Arms, Cash etc. Give my service to Mr McNoal of Watersaw [*MacNeil of Vatersay*] and apply to him for his assistance for your quick despatch. My respects to his Lady & three daughters & belive me to be dear Mac Mahon

> Your most Humble
> Obedient Servant
> Ultan Kindelan

My service to the young
Minister & his Brother.

After I finish'd my letter Mr. Alexr Cameron came here to acquaint us of a French Army being arrived in England of 6,000 Men headed by the Prince's younger Brother and that the Scotch Army was within a few days March of the [*blank in the original*] Carlile being taken by the Latter, he has sintt here to hasten us up to Perth, where we shall meet a strong Body of our people waiting for us that we may march together to England, so that I beg you may make all the haste possible, acquaint Barra & Clan of this.[19]

At the time this letter was written, the Prince's Army was at Macclesfield; five days later the retreat from Derby was to begin. Whether, as is perfectly possible, the Barra contingent was prevented by gales from crossing at all, or whether they heard of the retreat before they were ready and then decided not to go, is unknown; but at all events they never came to the mainland.

After Culloden, as has been said, McMahon was arrested; according to a letter from Mr Tolme to Norman MacLeod of MacLeod, dated from Dunvegan, 30th June, 1746:

> The Generall (General Campbell) and his Party went upon Fryday last from Bernera to North Uist by land, and from thence They go to Southuist and Barra, in both places I believe they will ffeel their Weight, Buysdale, Hector McNeil, Vatersay's son,[20] and Archibald McNeill are prisoners on Board of Capt Hay's Ship ... The General himself told me, That he had seized upon a Servant of one of the Mac Ma'ans, who had been of a long time in Southuist and Barra dispersing money and arms and with Whom He found very Material Papers, which he believd would prove of Bad Consequence to Clanranald, Barra and others.

Amongst these documents of bad consequence were two signed by MacNeil of Barra:

> I the Lord of Barra will acount for ten Pounds Sterling Recd from Lieut MacMahon for Suply to bring up my men for his Rl Hs Service

Janry the 8th 1746

S S Robt McNeil

> I the Lord of Barra do promise Lieut McMahon to be out with my men to convey Pastich of war for his Rl Hs use & will Account for what cost he might be at by my delaying of him or frachting boats for bringing my men to main land.

Robt McNeil.[21]

These documents provided conclusive evidence of MacNeil of Barra's involvement in the Rising, and were no doubt the immediate cause of his arrest and imprisonment; but letters written by his feudal superior, Sir Alexander MacDonald of Sleat, to Forbes of Culloden and to Clanranald prove that MacNeil's dealings with the Spanish ship were known to the authorities as early as November 1745. On the 30th of that month, Sir Alexander wrote to Forbes that James McDonald of Ardnifuiran had been in Arisaig

> waiting for my Vassal Barry, who took some money from the Spanish Vessel which unloaded some arms there, and promised to repair Southwards, very fast with his men. I am told these arms have been carried by boats from Barry, and lodged in the Main Land at Arisaig

More Culloden Papers (Inverness, 1929), Vol. IV, p. 155

On 20th January an anonymous correspondent wrote to Forbes that

> By advice from South Uist of the 17th instant I understand a Captain and Lieutanant Mathesons [? Mac Mahon] were then at Barra ready to carry off good quantity of money and Arms to the Mainland for the Service of the Young Pretender. The great MacNeile of Barra was likewise ready to embarque with six score men, for their escort till they join the Highland Army
>
> *More Culloden Papers* (Inverness, 1929), Vol. IV, p. 178

On 31st January Sir Alexander MacDonald wrote Forbes that 'Barray has been for some weeks in Readiness to go Southward' (*More Culloden Papers* (1929), Vol. IV, p. 202). On the 25th of the same month Sir Alexander had written a long letter to Clanranald, seeking to dissuade him from helping the Jacobites, in which he remarked that

> Barray has done all he cou'd to make me a Present of his Estate tho' I never coveted it; there is no man but knows that Arms and money were landed with him & the Government People know that he took a part of both, his Reviews and Weaponshawings are no Secret to them & he need not expect to escape a Tryal; if he is attainted it will not be in my power to give his Estate to his Son as I know the Government don't suffer to shew any favours in that way without resenting it; it is pitiful to see the poor Gentleman imposed on by a very underling Ambassador who is happy if he gets a Company of Foot when he returns as the reward of his Zeal in ruining Barray. There is but one way left to save him & that is that he bring what Arms he got directly to me, this I am afraid he'll not do & yet his people will soon be forced to give them up. As the Government looks on me as their zealous friend this thing if immediately done wou'd give me a Pretext of keeping Barray free of any Molestation, if it is delay'd it will not signifie to do it Months hence when it must be done. Wou'd it not be Charitable in you to make him meet you at Boistil's & both of you to give him your best Advice you see I wou'd gladly not gain by his ffoly. I hope in God you and your Uist men have kept your fingers clean of that Barray Cargo
>
> *More Culloden Papers* (Inverness, 1929), Vol. IV, p. 265

Sir Alexander MacDonald's advice, which was certainly disinterested insofar as MacNeil's estate would have reverted to him as feudal superior had MacNeil been attainted, was not taken. MacNeil was arrested by Captain Ferguson in April 1746; on 12th May it was reported by Ferguson to the Duke of Cumberland:

> I have as Prisoner one Mr McNeil of Barra, whom I took up on the 8th of Last Month, on my Lord Loudouns Information to me, on his haveing a designe to Raise his Men to joyn the Pretender: I presume my Lord

has inform'd Your R Highness of All the particulars, which I shall pass over, Only that I found Conceal'd 6 foot under ground in his own house three Chests of Armes A barral and A half of Gun Powder, two Boxes of Ball and some Flints, & I gott amongst his Tennants which made up in all 115 Stand of Armes which he had distrobuted amongest them; I gott Likewise in his own possession 160 Spanish Dollars; the rest which amounted to 500£ he Carried over two dayes before my Arrival to one McDonald of Buisdal his Son in Law that Lives on the Isle of South Uist, whom my Lord Loudoun & Presidient recomended to me as a person well affected to the Government, & that I showld have regard for his information: I am afried they have been both imposs'd on, for I take him to be quite disaffected ... there were about 400 men in both Islands [i.e. South Uist and Barra] had received Armes and ready to imbark for the Main (land) the first Westerly Wind, If I had not Come on the Coast as I did, & destroyed their Boat; I could not gett any of the Armes in South Uist, for I had not a sufficient force to Land & go into the Country after them ... I showld be glad to know how Your R. Highness would have me dispose of Barra & the rest of the prisoners now on Board.

Boisdale did not remain at liberty much longer than his father-in-law:

The 22nd Instant [June 1746] Captain Howe of the *Baltimore* took Alexander Mackdonald, Lord of Buisdale, on information that he had two chests of Spanish silver in his house in March last, which he confesses, and that his Son in Law [*sic*] (the La[i]rd of Barra) and the Spanish agent were in his house at the same time; which La[i]rd of Barra was lately taken by Captain Fergussone.

MacNeil was interrogated by General Campbell and sent to Inverness, and from Inverness to London, in company with other prisoners (but *not* with Flora MacDonald as has been stated) on board the *Pamela* which anchored off Tilbury on 27th August. On 1st November MacNeil and other prisoners of importance were transferred from the unsavoury quarters of the *Pamela* to the house of Dick the messenger. Here he was detained for the winter of 1746–47. On 21st April 1747, *State Papers, Domestic,* record:

The examn of Roderick McNeal Servant to McNeille of Barra.

Who saith, that he remained in the Isle of Barra the whole time of the Rebellion along with his Master Roger McNeille of Barra Esq. that his Master was not out of the Isle of Barra from the Month of August 1745 till the Month of April 1746 when he said McNeille was taken prisoner by Capt Ferguson. That his Master to his knowledge never entertained any Correspondence with the Rebels, nor ever assisted them in any Shape.

However, John McNeil examined at Mingala (the island of Mingulay) on 28th June 1746, had stated that 'He [i.e. the Chief of

Barra] was raising his men for the Pretender when taken prisoner', so the authorities knew better. Nevertheless, MacNeil was discharged on 28th May 1747. In *The Prisoners of the Forty-five* it is stated that he turned King's Evidence, but no details are given. It is certainly difficult to understand why the Government never prosecuted him. The last echo of the Forty-five in Barra occurs in 1750, when Lochgarry reported to the Prince that MacNeil of Barra would bring 150 men to aid a new rising in the Highlands (Lang, A., pp. 214–8). But this scheme was betrayed by Pickle the Spy; and in 1758 MacNeil's son and heir sailed to Canada, where he died at Quebec, leaving his son to be brought up a Protestant by the Rev. Angus MacNeil, the second son, and heir, of Donald MacNeil of Vatersay.

Fr Allan McDonald's Visit to Mingulay, June 1898

Little known, as it has no usable harbour, and can only be reached by yachts or by small boats from Castelbay in Barra, Mingulay is one of the most fascinating islands in the Hebrides, not only on account of its imposing 750-foot high cliffs with their innumerable sea birds, but from the fact that up to 1908 it was inhabited by a most interesting community, in every way as interesting as that of St Kilda; the Mingulay people had never been overawed by anglicizing schoolmasters of the early SPCK in Scotland, had preserved a most interesting store of Gaelic oral tradition, including beautiful Gaelic songs,[22] still preserved after certain families had settled on Vatersay and on Barra.

Mingulay was described by Dean Munro in 1549 as inhabited and cultivated. It is stated by the Rev. Edward MacQueen, Church of Scotland minister of Barra, to be inhabited by eight families in 1794. By the end of the nineteenth century there were eighteen families living there. The writer suspects that latterly some families preferred to live on the remote islands south of Vatersay rather than on Barra under the eyes of the agents and ground officers of the absentee proprietors who succeeded General Roderick MacNeil of Barra who went bankrupt in 1836, sold Barra in 1838, and died in London in 1863. The story of the evictions carried out on Barra in 1851 by the agents of Colonel Gordon, acting for him, can be read in Donald MacLeod's *Gloomy Memories* (see the passage quoted in Campbell, J. L. (1936), p. 221).

Mingulay was visited in June 1898 for a week by Fr Allan McDonald, priest of Eriskay, who left some interesting references to the island in the diary he was then keeping. It was a special occasion; Fr Allan was to say the first Mass in the new chapel built there and dedicated to St Columba. He describes how he was taken there from Castlebay on a calm, occasionally foggy day, the voyage taking about four and a half hours.

He stayed with Mr Finlayson, the schoolteacher, for meals, but slept in the old chapel on an improvised bed. He describes Mr Finlayson, who came from Loch Carron in western Ross-shire and must have been Gaelic-speaking, and whose grandmother had been a Catholic, as 'most entertaining and sociable'. Finlayson told Fr Allan that his great grand-uncle had been with Prince Charles in the hills after Culloden and had had to kill his dog which was with him, when he saw soldiers coming, and feared the dog might bark and give them away.[23]

Examination of the references to Mingulay in the six volumes of his *Carmina Gadelica*, shows that Alexander Carmichael certainly visited Mingulay in 1865, 1866, 1868 and 1871, probably in connection with his duties as an Exciseman, and took down very interesting traditional Gaelic folklore there; in 1871 he went there with J. F. Campbell of Islay, the collector of Gaelic folktales, and they were storm-stayed there. In his *Popular Tales of the West Highlands*, J. F. Campbell refers to a story taken down by himself on Mingulay in 1860, and to others taken down for him there by Hector MacLean at various times. In the Introduction to Vol. III of *Carmina Gadelica*, Carmichael tells how Fr Allan McDonald once went to Mingulay intending to return to Barra the same evening, but did not get away for seven weeks; he 'spent the time in religious exercises amongst the people, and in collecting old lore'. The year is not stated.

Finlayson the schoolmaster had, by 1898, been on Mingulay for thirty-nine years; he was a keen botanist and ornithologist and had corresponded with Harvie-Brown, the author of *The Vertebrate Fauna of the Outer Hebrides*. Finlayson had identified seventy-six kinds of flowering plant on Mingulay, and allowed Fr Allan to copy the list into one of his notebooks.

Fr Allan examined various archaeological remains on the island, and found 'a broken spoon of bone and lots of rough clay pots' in the ashpits of the old village that existed before the plague that depopulated the island. He did not find any trace of the existence of a Cross implied by the place-name *Crois an t-Suidheachain* (the Cross of the Sitting-down Place). He made an invaluable collection of 264 Mingulay place-names, which give a strong impression of Norse influence; in modern times only about 120 were remembered.

Fr Allan stayed on Mingulay for a week, and said the first Mass in the new chapel on Sunday, 20th June 1898. He wrote that the altar was decorated with wild flowers. On the next day the island was visited by Bishop Smith from Oban, with Fr Chisholm[24] from Barra and MacKenzie-Saville. Not being a Gaelic-speaker, the Bishop gave an English instruction, and thereafter confirmed forty-four children, most of them Campbells.

The chapel in fact had only ten years of religious use before it. In 1908 some of the Mingulay people took part in the Vatersay land raid, and the whole population was resettled there on new crofts, or on Barra, after there had been some contention between the raiders and the Congested Districts Board, which had purchased Vatersay from the landlord, Lady Gordon Cathcart, about the number of new holdings that should be made, and who should get them. When the writer visited Mingulay in June 1936, there were only two persons living there, the sheep farmer and his shepherd.

Mingulay History and Traditions

The fact is that the communities in the small islands south of Barra and Vatersay, that is of Sandray, Pabbay, Mingulay and Barra Head or Bernera, formed a most interesting outpost of Gaelic culture, and one which was far less introverted and repressed than that of St Kilda, and the transfer of their inhabitants to Vatersay and the mainland of Barra must have enriched the traditions of Barra. The writer was privileged to have known and recorded several of them, some introduced by Miss Annie Johnston, and now regrets that there never was an opportunity to work with them systematically. One of the most interesting of them was Donald MacPhee (Domhnall Ban Eileanach), living at Brevig in Barra. It must be explained that the epithet '*eileanach*' was used in Barra when referring to inhabitants of the small islands south and north of Barra, as well as of islanders generally.

Donald MacPhee was recommended to the writer in 1936 at a time when he was trying to organise a survey of the place-names of Barra and adjoining small islands; at that time he did not know that Fr Allan McDonald had made a comprehensive collection of the Mingulay place-names in 1898. Donald MacPhee proved to be most interesting on the subject of Mingulay traditions. No recording apparatus was then available for the preservation of his narrative, but he had taught himself to write Gaelic, and sent me what is translated here. Some years after I was settled on Canna, I heard that he had died, and wrote to Barra to try to find out what had become of his papers, but alas, they had been put in the fire. (Domhnall Ban Eileanach died on 26th October 1954. I am obliged to Mairi Ceit nic Fhionghuin, Secretary of Comunn Eachdraidh Bharraidh for the information.) The Gaelic of the story of the Leap of Young John, translated here, was printed in the Scottish magazine *Outlook* in January 1937.

I asked Donald MacPhee if he could tell me anything about Nic Iain Fhinn, the 'daughter of fair-haired John' the famous Barra poetess who won the bardic contest against the South Uist bardess in the famous extemporised waulking song, *Cha deid Mór a Bharraidh bhrònaich*, 'Mor will not go to miserable Barra' – Mor was a daughter of MacDonald of Clanranald; she was a genuine person who lived in the middle of the seventeenth century. Donald MacPhee wrote to me in Gaelic, saying:

> Tradition tells us that Nic Iain Fhinn was a midwife and a nurse for the MacNeils of Barra before they left Castle Kismul which was early in the

eighteenth century. She had the gift of composing poetry, but her songs are lost except for a few that were written down.[25]

It is said that Nic Iain Fhinn was born at Cliat in Barra, and that Anna MacNeil, daughter of Ruairi son of Donald MacNeil, who was a famous midwife in the islands, was related to her. Anna was born on Mingulay, and lived to a great age – a hundred and five. She died on Sandray in 1910; she was the last person buried on Mingulay. Her father was born at Cliat. Ruairi son of Donald MacNeil was a young lad when 'Eoligary Castle' was built, that was at the beginning of the nineteenth century.[26] Ruairi[27] was married on Mingulay; his wife's name was Fionnaghal daughter of Eoin son of Diarmaid, they had a big family. Ruairi was a famous cragsman; he never wore a shoe, nor a bonnet; he was *spògach uinneineach* in a praiseworthy sense, stout-footed, thick ankled, for going on the cliffs to get sea birds and their eggs like Anna's ancestress Nic Iain Fhinn; she was a MacNeil.

Fionnaghal the wife of Ruairi was herself a midwife, famous on Barra and on South Uist. This Ruairi, son of Donald, was a wise, strong, intelligent man. He reached a great age, nearly a hundred and twenty. He was buried on Mingulay like his wife and many of his relations.

Visits by Ministers

In Ruairi's time ministers of the Free Church and of the Established Church of Scotland used to come to the smaller islands south of Barra to teach and to preach, and especially to Mingulay. One particular day at the beginning of summer, authorities came to test the school on Mingulay. Amongst them were three ministers. They saw an old man digging with a spade. A young minister said to the others 'I'll go an instruct the old fellow'. One of the other ministers said 'My advice to you is to stay away from him'. 'Let him choose, I'm going over to teach the old man'.

The young minister greeted Ruairi, and Ruairi greeted him. The minister said 'Do you know, my man, what hell is?' Ruairi put the handle of the spade under his arm. He replied 'Hell, my man, hell is deep and difficult to measure, but if you keep on going, you'll find the bottom'.

Ruairi, MacNeil of Barra, and the minister

Ruairi, son of Donald, went to Mingulay when MacNeil of Barra, the laird, evicted all the people from Eoligary. At that time MacNeil was living at Vaslain[28]; before 'Eoligary Castle' was finished. MacNeil's brother was then tacksman of Scurrival; Angus the son of the tacksman was away in Edinburgh, learning to be a minister. There was only one priest on Barra at that time; he was frequently going to the smaller islands and around the villages of Barra. The son of the tacksman of Scurrival came home to Barra from Edinburgh, fully qualified. It happened that that week the priest[29] was on Mingulay. MacNeil of Barra ordered his own people at Eoligary to be at the young minister's sermon the next Sunday. All of them, and the crofters, went there, except one man called Currie – MacMhuirich, who had often been MacNeil's adviser.

When the priest came from Mingulay, he heard that all the people, the Eoligary people, had been at the minister's sermon, except Currie. The priest rebuked the people angrily, telling them that before the year was out, every one of them who had been at the sermon, would be sent away, except for Currie alone. MacNeil also heard that Currie was not at the sermon. He sent for Currie and for the minister, and asked the minister to give Currie a good sermon. The minister gave an impressive practical sermon to Currie. Currie said, 'If the minister is good, he's a good man.' Said MacNeil, 'That doesn't tell me if the sermon was a good one or a bad one.' Currie said 'Now and again; that's enough!'

Before the year was out, MacNeil sent all the crofters and people of Eoligary away, except for Currie; the priest's words came true.

Fr Angus MacDonald

Later, there was a priest on Barra called Fr Angus MacDonald (1805–25), at the time of General MacNeil, the last MacNeil of Barra (and his father). Fr Angus was a famous priest, all the people loved him. MacNeil himself respected him, and gave him a glebe like the one which he gave to the minister. Fr Angus was a bard; a cancer grew on his chest, and he sent for Doctor MacLeod, the Dotair Ban (the fair-haired doctor), from Uist; Dr MacLeod cut off the tumour, and cured him.[30]

The Bishop sent to ask Fr Angus to go to be head of the Scots College in Rome. Fr Angus was the best Gaelic scholar in the diocese at that time. The people gathered at the church the next Sunday, when they heard that the priest was going to leave; they agreed that they would not let him leave, that they would put a stone through the side of the boat which was going to take him away. The Bishop had to come to Barra for Fr Angus, and take him away. Fr Angus went to Rome as head of the Scots College. It is said that the cancer returned again, and was the cause of his death (in 1833); he was buried in Rome.

Young Iain's Leap on Mingulay

On a stormy winter night 250 years ago, a Spanish ship laden with a cargo of codfish came ashore on Traigh Uais on the west side of

Barra, driven from the open sea by a fearful gale, with her sails in shreds. She stopped on the sandy beach with great waves breaking over her. The local people collected towards the shore. They could see her crew on her masts, in great danger of being drowned without a chance of being saved. The folk on shore saw that they might try to get a light line on board, though the boat was a long way from them.

They got three lengths of sixty fathoms each of heavy rope and coiled them in reels on the shore. If they could tie a pebble to a light line, they could tie the heavy rope to it, by which means the whole crew could be brought ashore one by one. It was the more able young man in the party who had to throw the stone.

This was young Iain MacNeil, a son of MacNeil of Barra the laird; he was the strongest man of the party. Young Iain threw the stone, and it reached the ship, and the crew got hold of the line; but the line hit the son of the skipper and killed him. All the crew got to land safely. The skipper demanded that the law should deal with the man who had thrown the stone, and punish him. Since the law was in the hands of the Laird, he would have to put the man who had thrown the stone to death, in spite of everything[30a] there would have to be a death for a death. MacNeil would not do this; they fell out so badly, that MacNeil ordered that neither the skipper nor his men should be taken into any house on Barra.

The crew camped that night at the foot of the little hill at Eoligary. The next day they crossed the sound to Uist. The skipper complained to Clanranald, the Laird of Uist, that Young Iain the son of MacNeil of Barra, had killed his son, and that he had got to get a hold of Young Iain to make him pay for it.

Young Iain was on the run, not knowing when his enemy might come on him. What he did was to go over to Mingulay with his friends; he had no worry that his enemy could get a hold of him there. He spent the winter on Mingulay, with his friends. Every day he would be fishing and fowling around the island. On a certain day he and other lads were on Druim na h-Aoineig, and they came to the cliff there called Biolacreag, near Garadh na h-Aoineig, opposite Tom a' Mhaide. There are 700 feet from the top of this cliff to the sea, it is fearful to look down to the sea there.

The lads asked each other 'who will leap over to the pinnacle?' No one but Young Iain dared to jump over to it. Young Iain jumped over to the pinnacle and back again from side to side, and the pinnacle was called Leum Iain Òig, Young John's Leap, ever after.

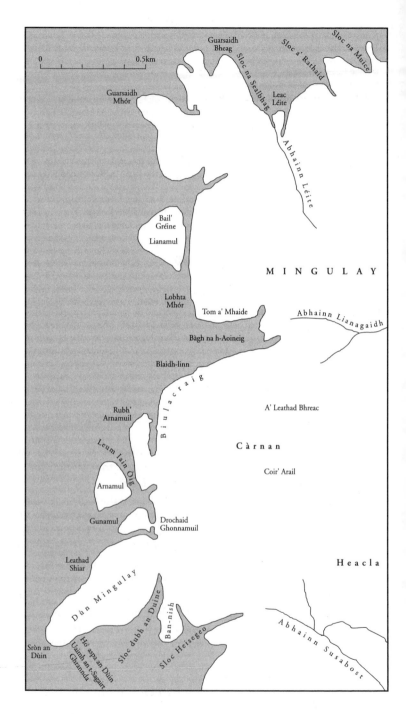

The west coast of Mingulay with the place-names augmented from research and showing the site of 'Young John's Leap' as preserved in oral trdition.

112

Young Iain and the Kintail Traitor
.

Young Iain was always fishing with lines on the Oitir Mhór[31] along with the Eoligary people. There was then a stranger staying at Eoligary, a Kintail man who had been expelled from there for thieving and for bad neighbourliness. This man was called the Kintail Traitor.[32] He had come to Barra, and MacNeil of Barra had taken pity on him, and had given him a croft at Eoligary. This spring the Eoligary crofters were short of barley seed and of seed potatoes, and so was the Kintail Traitor. The Kintail Traitor went over to South Uist to ask for seed from Clanranald. Clanranald told him he could get all the seed he wanted for nothing, if he could get hold of Young Iain. Clanranald had been telling the Captain of the King's ship, at Lochboisdale, the story of how Young Iain had killed the skipper of the Spanish ship.

The Kintail Traitor answered 'If you give me the seed for nothing, I'll try to put Young Iain in your power. On the first fine day I'll take Young Iain to fish on the Oitir Mhór in my own boat. You give a warning to the Captain of the King's ship.'

The Kintail Traitor got all the seed he wanted from Clanranald for nothing. The first stormy day he went to Young Iain and asked him to go along with him to set lines on the Oitir Mhór. Young Iain replied 'are you out of your mind, man, wanting to go to set lines on the Oitir Mhór on such a day, with a northwesterly gale? But if you row your side of the boat to land, I've no fear at all that I'll not row my side of her to land, even if she were twice as big.'

With the treachery that was in the Kintail Traitor's heart, he had put pine thole-pins in the gunwale of the boat, and in the thole-cleats. When they had finished setting the lines, the King's ship appeared around Rubha na h-Ordaig, the Promontory of the Thumb, the south-east point of South Uist. Young Iain asked for the oars to be put out; they put the oars out. The King's ship was coming on well. The pine thole-pins began to break one by one; even iron ones would not have stood for Iain when he saw the pursuit approaching; he was a strong well-set fellow.

The King's ship came alongside the boat, and Young Iain was taken out of her. The Kintail Traitor and his boat were left at Lochboisdale by the Captain of the King's ship, who took Young Iain with him to Edinburgh, where Young Iain was condemned to death by the Edinburgh court. They ordered him to be burnt, and a big fire was made and Young Iain was stripped in order to be thrown into the middle of it.

A big crowd collected around. There was a lady amongst them. She asked the lawmen to give her that fine fellow and not to burn him. The lawmen gave her leave to take him away, and she took him with her, and kept him for three days; then she sent him back to the lawmen again. They ordered him to be put in a barrel with spikes through it, and to be let rolled down the hill in Edinburgh. This was done, and Young Iain suffered the death of an innocent martyr on account of the crew of the Spanish ship which was saved on the Traigh Uais on the west side of Barra. Young Iain was buried in Edinburgh, and the son of the Spanish skipper was buried in the Barra graveyard at Eoligary.

1. Dr John Lorne Campbell of Canna, scholar, folklorist and farmer.
Photo. Tom Weir.

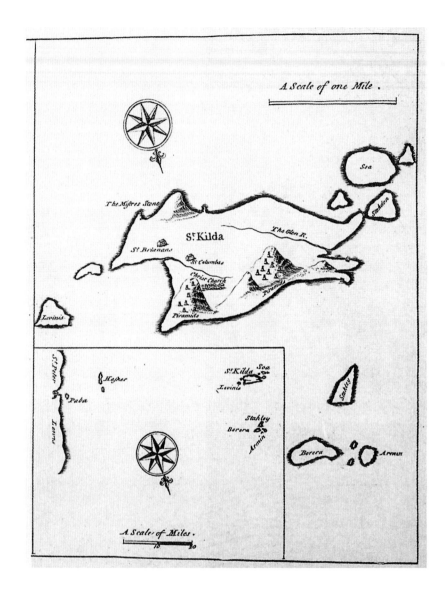

2. Map from Martin Martin's 'Late Voyage to St Kilda' of 1698.
Prominence is given to three church sites round the settlement in Village
Bay. Canna Collections.

3. Peigi and Mairi MacRae, North Glendale, South Uist, shearing oats on their croft. Photo. Margaret Fay Shaw.

4. Seonaidh Caimbeul (1859–1944), South Lochboisdale, South Uist, bard and storyteller. A collection of his songs, *Orain Ghaidhlig le Seonaidh Caimbeul*, was published by John Lorne Campbell in 1936. Photo. Margaret Fay Shaw.

5. Father Allan McDonald (1859–1905), poet and folklorist, and parish priest of South Uist and Eriskay. Photo. W. B. Blaikie, Canna Collections.

6. *Bannal* or group of women fulling cloth on the 'waulking board' in Eriskay, 1898. This work was the occasion for the complex work- or chorus-song, the *òran luadhaidh*. Photo. W. B. Blaikie, Canna Collections.

7. Stone cell of the early Christian monastic settlement of Sceilg Mhichíl, Co. Kerry, similar to beehive dwelling structures surviving on Eileacha Naomha, the 'Holy Rocks' of the Garvellachs, and in Canna.

8. Aonghas Beag, Angus MacLellan (1869–1965), South Uist. His vast store of traditional stories, ballads and personal reminiscences was recorded by John Lorne Campbell and Calum MacLean. Photo. Margaret Fay Shaw.

9. Kelp burning at Gribune Head, Mull, from William Daniell, *A Voyage round Great Britain*, London 1814.

10. 'Kyloe' or Highland cow from the Hebrides, drawn in the early 19th century by the Scottish artist, James Howe. The breed was largely displaced by sheep and lamented by the poets (see page 212).

BLACK-FACED or SCOTS RAM

11. Coarse-woolled blackfaced sheep of the Scottish Borders, drawn about 1798, of the improved breed whose introduction into the Highlands and Islands heralded the Clearances and drew the vituperative protests of the poet against '*na caoraich cheannriabhach*' (see page 211).

John MacNeil, 'Shepherd Duncan on Barra Head'

Recorded at Northbay, Barra, on 7th April 1951; Gaelic transcribed by John MacLean MA and translated by John Lorne Campbell. Gaelic printed in *Gairm* 2: 271.

There are always arguments, especially between myself and Angus, son of Iain son of Angus son of Murdo here, who will be telling me that it is much easier for men to make a living now than it was in the time of his grandfather or perhaps of his great-grandfather, and I am always opposing him. However, that wouldn't make him yield. Eventually it occurred to me to put the case of this able fellow before him. This was Shepherd Duncan on Barra Head, who came here to Eoligarry as gardener to Dr MacGillevray. He spent a time there, and when it came to him to want to start a household, he wouldn't get a house or a holding from him, he couldn't work for Dr MacGillevray any longer, so he set out on his own.

Barra was only a small place, and it wasn't easy for him to get land where he wanted to; that's what sent him so far away as Barra Head. He reached Barra Head, then, he was a land worker himself, a well-found person. He had come from Appin, a strong, healthy fellow, a really kind man who was always ready to give a hand to a friend who was in need; he proved that in more than one way during his lifetime on Barra Head.

Anyway, he started a household, even though the place, Barra Head island, was small. He got a part of it; the place suited him and the soil suited him; he told himself that he was believing what the bee had said to the fly:

'I always believed, and that's the truth,
That diligence brings forth good fruit.'

He began to cultivate the land. He married;[33] his family was coming on for him, he raised a family there. There were eight or nine of them, and there wasn't a family like his to be found in the Long Island.[34] Not one of them was less than six feet tall, some of them were more than seven feet; and he never spent a halfpenny in a shop while he was rearing them, but what he took out of the land while he was cultivating it on Barra Head. He never put a rag of clothing on them that came from any shop or market, but what his wife was making in the little island, on Barra Head, and as for shoes, there was no need for them, they were doing all right barefooted.

And that family grew up as pleasing and as well taught as any family between the Butt of Lewis and Barra Head, I'm sure; when they had grown up, they were as wise, as skilful, and as diligent, as they had seen their father to be as long as he was facing the world while he was being a father to them, until they set out for themselves. And they were so diligent and so hospitable, that they built their father's house. I heard of people talking about them say there was no house nor home in the Long Island as hospitable, and it being in such a remote place.

Anyway, they got on so well here that they acquired as big, fine, sufficient boat as there was between Aberdeen and the Western Isles for fishing herring, ling and cod, and every other kind of fish. They got every kind of fishing gear that fishermen need, including a trawl; and this year and winter being fairly good, and fish plentiful around Mingulay and Barra Head, they began trawling for saithe and lythe and fish of that sort off the east shore of Mingulay. They had plenty of salt; they began to salt fish on the rocks of the shore when they ran out of barrels, and filled them, and when the fish were salted, they dried them, and they were piling them there on top of each other, splendid and hard. And at the first coming of spring, in the first days at the beginning of spring, they came to Castlebay to get the boat – it had to be kept safe there, there was nowhere for the like – and then they took the boat over to Barra Head.

They filled the boat with the fish there, and they put two sails on her on the morning that they saw it suitable to go to Loch Swilly in Ireland. Big Peter his brother[35] was along with them, and was selling the fish. They used to spend two or three weeks away, and then come home, and then put ashore on Barra Head as much as their father needed of potatoes and every kind of seeds, flour, bacon, meat – everything the house needed – and bottles of porter, beer and whisky, and left that safe indoors, and that very same night they would hoist the same white-topped sail and would take her where neither wind nor weather would trouble her, and would go on their dinghy back to Bernera. And when they reached their house and had set the family in order, Shepherd Duncan's family was the only one there – there was no one else there at all.

They would set the big table, and put on it all sorts of food which wasn't easily to be seen in any other house throughout the Isles, but there alone, and when they all were seated around it, Donald[36] put – he was the oldest of the family, taking charge of everything, and well he could, he was an able, worthy person who knew his business, and knew well how he should go about everything for his own need or for anyone else's ...

He put his hand on his chest and took out a red napkin; he would open it, spread it on the table, and count out 120 gold sovereigns – a notable big sum in those days; when he did that, he would collect them with his hand into piles, and he took a handful out with his fingers like this, and put it aside, and say, 'this is needed to keep the work going' and push the rest over and say to his mother 'take care of that'.

After a day or two, they would go over to Castlebay with the boat, leaving good weather and good day with those they belonged to, and reach Castlebay. They would fill the big boat with lobster creels, and take the dinghy along with them, and reach Heisgier of North Uist, where they would start fishing lobsters. When they had been at that for a while, and had sent the lobsters to market after having done well at them, they would take long lines on board, and before the year was past, a man could indeed say – Calum MacAulay[37] said it to me himself – that there was no house from the Butt of Lewis to Barra Head that was so well provided as the house of Shepherd Duncan on Barra Head!

And he was a stranger who didn't belong to the place at all! Without doubt, he was not the only one at that. There were people on Barra at the time who were just as diligent as the Sinclairs; for all that, that man (Angus son of Iain) tells me and other people that it wasn't easy to make a livelihood at that time. It was easy to make a livelihood at that time if men did their very best, as the Sinclairs did. They won't do that; they are getting many things easily now; and I'd be surprised if that is going to go on, there won't be a stop put to it some time. But I hope it won't get any worse in my time, for as long as I live, anyway. But that's the truth, and that's what I heard of the story of Shepherd Duncan.

Iain Nill Mhoir (The Coddy): 'Well, it can't get any worse than it is; for the fishing, it can't get any worse.'

Iain Nill Dhomhnaill (John MacNeil): 'You are not going to scold me now, John, after that?'

The Coddy: 'I'm not, I'm not, I'm agreeing with you.'

John MacNeil: 'The livelihood there was then, people were satisfied, they were getting food, they had food. They weren't buying clothing anywhere at all.'

The Coddy: 'They weren't.'

John MacNeil: 'The man went to the island himself, there was nothing there but the island itself and himself.'

The Coddy: 'Since the trawlers first began – I myself heard my father saying, standing on the floor, if this was going to go on – the destruction,[38] the trawlers coming and scraping the shores – that the day would come when fish would be imported into Barra and sold there, not being caught there and sent away to market.'

Note

I am much indebted to Mairi Ceit Nic Fhionghuin, Secretary of the Barra Historical Society, for the following information about Shepherd Duncan (Sinclair); he was:

> The son of Donald Sinclair from Appin, and Mary MacLachlan, on the estate of Barra. Initially he worked at Vatersay, then Glen, and finally on Bernera.
>
> In 1832 Duncan, who was a Protestant, married Mary MacNeil (1816–1885) (*nighean Iain Ruairi*), Mingulay. Duncan remained a Protestant, but his children were brought up as Catholics. When he died, he was taken for burial to the Church of Scotland cemetery at Cuithir, Barra.
>
> The ruins of the Sinclair family's house on Bernera are to be seen to this day.

The fact is that going to Barra as a shepherd in 1832 meant facing an uncertain future. By then (General) Roderick MacNeil, the last MacNeil of Barra in the direct line, was in considerable financial difficulties; his father had died in 1822 just when the price of kelp, an important export, had started to fall; his heir had succeeded to an estate embarrassed by settlements made on his mother, his younger brother and five sisters. On 4th March 1831 the parish priest, Fr Neil MacDonald, wrote to his successor, Fr Angus MacDonald who in 1825 had become head of the Scots College in Rome, telling him that the General and his agents had been going through Barra taking up cattle from the small tenants in lieu of rent, and that the General had given orders 'that every sheep on Barra should be killed. The whole have been killed with the exception of a very few kept by the North Uist people [incomers] who resisted him in all his unheard of measures, for which, it is reported, they are to be sent off.' In 1836, General MacNeil became bankrupt, and Charles Shaw in Edinburgh, agent for the Trustees, reported that he advised 'sending two thirds of the population to America, so that land can be let for grazing' (Campbell, J. L. (1990), pp. 73–74). In 1883, Dr D. W. MacGillevray, then the tenant of Eoligary Farm, said he had been there for about thirty-five years, and had herds working for him, and had known General MacNeil well. (*Minutes of Evidence of the Crofters Commission*, p. 682.)

Mgr MacNeill of Morar
.

Various obituaries described the career of the late Mgr Canon John MacNeill as parish priest, army chaplain and County Councillor. Little has been said of his original background which was in the remotest parts of the Catholic Hebrides. Bernera, where Mgr MacNeill was born; Mingulay, where his father went to school; and Sandray, where his mother was born, are all totally depopulated today.

The late Mgr Canon John MacNeill was a distinguished person in many ways, and a true representative of the old Highland tradition. He was born on the island of Bernera, southernmost of the Barra group, where Barra Head lighthouse is situated. The group of small islands which stretch for about fifteen miles south of Barra and include Bernera, Mingulay and Pabby, were formerly part of the endowment of the Bishopric of the Isles and used to be known as the 'Bishop's Isles'.

Mgr Canon MacNeill was the eldest son of Michael MacNeill (Micheal Iain 'ic Aonghais 'ic Neill), and of Sarah MacKinnon (Mór Eachainn 'Ill' Easbuig). His mother came from the island of Sandray, also south of Barra. His grandfather, John, lived on Bernera all his life, and had three sons and a daughter, all of whom were exceptional in mental powers and diligence.

Michael, the eldest, went to school on Mingulay, the larger island adjacent to Bernera, where Mr Finlayson was schoolmaster for many years (he later communicated Mingulay place-names and plant names to Fr Allan McDonald of Eriskay). During Michael's weekends at home he taught his brothers, Neil and Allen, all he had learnt.

Bernera at that time was divided into five crofts, one of which was allotted to the lighthouse, the others to different families. When Michael MacNeill and his brothers had grown to manhood it was the time of the big fishing boom in Barra, and these young men began to engage boats, and buy their fish, and cure it for export, as is still done in North Norway, Iceland and the Faroes, where encroaching trawlers have been kept at bay, unlike the Hebrides.

They did well, and eventually when the future Mgr Canon MacNeill was about seven years old, the family came over to live in Castlebay, where Michael MacNeill built the house and shop which is now the bank building there. Before leaving Bernera, Michael had engaged a man known as Domhnall Ruadh Sgoileir to give his children their first education, so that when they joined Castlebay School, they were in no way behind, and were soon far ahead of their contemporaries.

John MacNeill went on to Blairs from Castlebay School to be educated for the priesthood. After his ordination, he was first appointed to the parish of the Small Isles, and then to Eriskay, where he succeeded Fr Allan McDonald late in 1905, on Fr Allan's lamented early death.

Mgr Canon MacNeill was a Highland gentleman in the best and most authentic sense of the word. His mother was a sister of Ealasaid Eachainn and Peigi Eachainn, who were great singers of Barra folksongs and bearers of Barra traditions; some of which have fortunately been taken down by Miss Annie Johnston. Michael MacNeill himself had a keen interest in the traditions of Barra, and his house was a centre for songs and stories: he corresponded with MacNeills in Cape Breton about the history of the island and of the clan to which they belonged. He is still remembered as a devout and upright man.

Mgr MacNeill himself was thus well acquainted with the background of oral Gaelic literature that is an education in itself, and in private he strongly encouraged attempts to record and preserve it. In public life he was a staunch defender of the islands and their interests on Inverness-shire County Council for many years, even when representing a mainland district. His passing was a great loss, not only to the Catholic community of Inverness-shire, but to the whole Highlands and Islands.

Notes and References to Section 4

[1]Transcript of late Rt Rev. Mgr Cameron, cited in Giblin, C., *Irish Franciscan Missions to Scotland 1619–46*.

[2]Translation by Dom Denys Rutledge O.S.B., to whom I am much obliged; cited in Giblin, C., *Irish Franciscan Missions to Scotland, 1619–46*.

[3]'Noisy' or 'turbulent' Roderick.

[4]According to Barra tradition he was called Uibhisteach because he was born in South Uist, where his mother, a Clanranald, had relations.

[5]Register of Deeds, 10th January 1595–6: Actions and Decreets, 193: 424 and 175:35. I am obliged to my brother, Mr Colin Campbell, for this information.

[6]In *Register of the Privy Council,* Vols VIII and IX *passim,* with reference to the Dynes Case.

[7]It is possible that it was a brother of MacNeil of Barra who was killed at Glenlivet in 1594. His name is given as Gillean in *Macfarlane's Genealogical Collections* (Clark, J. T. (1900), I, p. 257).

[8]This reference to both Neil Og MacNeil and Auchinbreck is omitted from the index of the *Book of Dunvegan.*

[9]See *Innes Review,* Vol. V, 33.

[10]The document in which this list occurs is called 'A Representation of the most deplorable state of severall paroches in the Highlands both in the Western Isles and Continent within the bounds of the Synod of Argyle in

which places the Reformation never obtained, 1703.' It is printed in the *Maitland Miscellany*, III, 424–31.

The list itself appears to have been overlooked by the author of *The Clan MacNeil* (New York, 1923), as he states (p. 149) that the laird in question, Roderick MacNeil of Barra (claimed as 38th chief) and his heir were 'nominally Protestants', gives the number of his children as four instead of five, and makes no mention of his brother Murdo. Donald MacNeil of Vatersay's two sisters are not mentioned either.

[11]SPCK Committee's Minute of 4th January 1728.

[12]The MacLeods of Greshornish were cadets of the MacLeods of Harris (Dunvegan), being descended from the youngest son of Rory Mór MacLeod, who died in 1626. See *Innes Review*, Vol. IV, 46, 110, and I. F. Grant, *The MacLeods* (London, 1959), p. 235. The MacLeods of Greshornish were certainly Protestants at this time.

[13]The MacNeils of Vatersay appear to be descended from Niall Uibhisteach, the rightful heir to Barra who was dispossessed around 1615. See above p. 91; and Cathaldus Giblin, O.F.M., *Irish Franciscan Mission to Scotland* (Dublin, 1964), p. 76.

[14]This appears to refer to the visit of Bishop James Gordon in 1722. See his report to Propaganda, written on 15th October 1723, and printed as Appendix X to the fourth volume of Bellesheim's *History of the Catholic Church of Scotland* (London, 1890). In this Bishop Gordon stated that in the Highlands and Western Islands he had 'administered the sacrament of confirmation to 2,090 persons, the majority of the adults being converts, and among them many notabilities. In each of the islands and districts which he visited, a certain number of heretics made profession of the Catholic faith before his departure, or some similar occurrence took place... He went to some places, and bestowed there the benefit of confirmation, where no bishop had ever been before ...'

[15]This refers to the £1000 a year originally bestowed by King George for purposes similar to those of the Society.

[16]i.e. the people had gone with their cattle to the summer shielings in the hills. Even after the passing of the Scottish Education Act of 1872, summer herding was still a cause of poor school attendance in the islands, see F. G. Rea, *A School in South Uist*, p. xx (London, 1964). May and June were the time of maximum scarcity in the isles, when the preceding year's harvest was nearly exhausted, and before the new one had grown.

[17]Old Style.

[18]The Culloden Papers prove that the authorities were already aware of what was going on. See quotations below.

[19]Admiralty Papers.

[20]This Hector MacNeil was probably the unnamed elder son of Donald MacNeil of Vatersay mentioned in *The Clan MacNeil* (p. 96) as having died unmarried. He was probably one of the prisoners who died of typhus. His name is not included in Seton, B. (Ed.) *The Prisoners of the Forty-Five* Vols. I–III, Edinburgh: Scottish History Society, 1928–29.

[21]Copies, not originals, in the Admiralty Papers. The copyist has written 'Robt.' in error for the unfamiliar (to him) 'Rodk.' (Roderick).

[22]Readers can be referred to the three volumes of *Hebridean Folksongs* for examples of these recorded from Anna Raghnaill Eachainn, Màiri Iain Choinnich and Ealasaid Iain Dhunnchaidh, all of Mingulay background.

[23]I have not yet been able to find confirmation of this story in the literature of the 1745–46. It might well have happened in Glenmoriston, in which case the great grand-uncle might have been a Grant or a Chisholm. The Chisholms were a Catholic clan. It is tempting to think that Mr Finlayson might have been connected with John Finlayson who was in Prince Charles's artillery and who made a map of the battlefield at Culloden, but he came from Edinburgh and was taken prisoner after the battle.

[24]Who had built the new chapel on Mingulay.

[25]Others were the Barra part of *An Spaidearachd Bharrach*, 'The Barra Boasting', and the well-known song '*Latha dhomh bhith am Beinn a' Cheathaich*, 'One day on the Misty Mountain'. See songs Nos. XXXVII, LXVII and LXVIII in *Hebridean Folksongs*, and the Notes thereon.

[26]It was a little earlier; Edmund Daniel Clarke visited Eoligary House in 1797.

[27]It is possible that Ruairi was the 'Roderick MacNeill' on Mingulay from whom both Alexander Carmichael and J. F. Campbell took down folklore in 1871. See *Carmina Gadelica* Vol. III, p. 110.

[28]Donald MacPhee wrote 'Vatersay', a slip for Vaslain.

[29]According to *The Clan MacNeil*, the Rev. Angus MacNeil of the *Vatersay* family was the minister of Barra from 1771 to 1774. The priest at that time was Fr Alexander MacDonald, 1765–1779. It is certain that the MacNeils of Vatersay were then Protestants; see 'The MacNeils of Barra in the Forty-five' above pp. 96–104. The Vatersay branch of the family may have felt that they had a claim to the estate as descended from Niall Uibhisteach, the dispossessed heir of 1615.

[30]Fr Angus made a Gaelic poem about his operation and in praise of Dr MacLeod, beginning *Dà mhios dhiag agus ràthaich/Bho 'n thàrmaich an cnap*, 'Fifteen months ago the lump gathered'. See Henderson, *Leabhar nan Gleann*, pp. 151–3, and Colm O Lochlainn, *Deoch-Slainte nan Gillean*, p. 57. Fr Angus MacDonald also wrote three poems on the last two MacNeils of Barra, and the hymn *Laoidh*; Fr Allan McDonald copied the poem to Dr MacLeod, and one of the MacNeil poems, into his second folklore notebook, where they are items 79 and 80. In his letter of 12th January 1830 to Fr Angus, his successor Fr Neil MacDonald alludes to the MSS of Fr Angus's poems having been given to John, son of Iain Campbell in Mingulay.

[30a]Gaelic proverb *Clacha dubha an aghaidh sruth*, 'Black stones against a stream', i.e. in spite of all obstacles.

[31]The shallow water off the north-east of Barra.

[32]The MacNeils of Barra had been in trouble with Roderick MacKenzie, Tutor (*Taoitear*) of Kintail in the early part of the seventeenth century; he

had captured Ruairi an Tartair, MacNeil of Barra, and taken him to Edinburgh, by the means of wine; but Ruairi an Tartair was not put to death there. See *Tales from Barra, told by the Coddy*, pp. 33, 34. Roderick MacKenzie was rewarded for this by being given the feudal superiority of the Isle of Canna, which later passed to the MacDonalds of Sleat.

The Iain Og, 'Young Iain', of Donald MacPhee's story may well be the 'John Og' who was a son of Ruairi an Tartair, and MacLean of Duart's sister according to *The Clan MacNeil*, and was involved in the piracy on the merchantman captained by Abel Dynes, who was taken to Linlithgow to go to Edinburgh by Clanranald early in 1610, and imprisoned in the Tolbooth, where he died, *op. cit.* p. 69. If so, the allusion to seed potatoes in the story is an anachronism.

[33]His wife was Mary MacNeil from Mingulay.

[34]The whole chain of the Outer Hebrides.

[35]Peter Sinclair, 1850–1917.

[36]Donald Sinclair, 1838–1910.

[37]Skipper of the boat that served the lighthouse at Barra Head.

[38]i.e. of immature fish.

Section 5

·

Recollecting History in the Small Isles:
Eigg, Rum and Canna

·

The Massacre in the Cave called Uaimh Fhraing

The earliest reference to this grisly event is to be found in the 'Description of the Isles of Scotland', written apparently as a report to King James VI of Scotland, before 1595, but not printed until it appeared in W. F. Skene's *Celtic Scotland* (Volume 2, 1880, p. 433); the references to Eigg and to Angus John McMudzartsonne are not indexed. The section on Eigg reads as follows:

> Eg is ane Ile verie fertile and commodious baith for all kind of bestiall and corn, speciallie aittis [oats] for eftir everie boll of aittis sawing [sowing] in the same ony yeir will grow 10 or 12 bollis agane. It is 30 merk land, and it pertains to the Clan Rannald, and will raise 60 men to the weiris [wars]. It is five mile lang and three mile braid.
>
> Thair is mony coves under the earth in this Ile, quhilk the cuntrie folk uses as strenthis hiding thame and thair geir thairintill; quhairthrow it hapenit that in March, anno 1577, weiris and inmitie betwix the said Clan Renald and McCloyd Herreik [Harris], the people with ane callit Angus John McMudzartsonne, their capitane, fled to ane of the saidis coves, taking with thame thair wives, bairnis, and geir, quhairof McCloyd Herreik being advertisit landit with ane great armie in the said Ile, and came to the cove and pat fire thairto, and smoorit the haill people thairin to the number of 395 persones, men, wyfe, and bairnis.

There is another early reference to the massacre in *Ane Descriptione of Certaine Pairts of the Highlands of Scotland*, written around 1630 by someone with a good deal of local knowledge, but not printed until 1907, when the Scottish History Society published the second volume of *Macfarlane's Geographical Collections*. It reads:

> This Illand of Eigg is thirtie merk lands, thrie mylls in length or thereby and two mylls broad. They perished and destroyed with the smoak of the fyre the number of both of men and woemen an barnes within ane Cove or den that is in this Illand of the Inhabitants by McLeod of Harie being in warrs against him for that tyme, and taking this place for their safetie and refuge.[1]

There is no gap in the printed text between 'number of' and 'both', but it is clear that there should be; a number has not been filled in. As regards the statement printed by Skene, one thing is

127

certain – the date given, 1577, must be wrong. Tradition unanimously attributes the massacre to Alasdair Crotach, 'Humpbacked Alasdair', the eighth chief of the MacLeods of Harris and Dunvegan; and Alasdair Crotach died in 1547.[2] On this point Canon R. C. MacLeod of MacLeod who gives the MacLeod version of the story in his *The MacLeods of Dunvegan,* and the Rev. Donald MacLean, minister of Eigg from 1787 to 1810, are in complete agreement. While the Skye version given by Canon MacLeod, judging from the Gaelic quotations in it, must have been cast in the form of a traditional Gaelic story, the Rev. Mr MacLean's account is perfectly clear and straightforward:

> The cave on the south west side of Eigg, called Uaimh Fhraic (the Cave of Francis), is remarkable not only for its form, but also for the murder of this island by Alistair Crotach, Laird of M'Leod. The entrance of this cave is so small, that a person must creep on four for some 12 feet; it then becomes pretty capacious, its length being 213 feet, breadth 22 and height 17.
>
> With regard to the murder abovementioned, it is said that some of M'Leod's vassals, returning from Glasgow, touched at the harbour of Eigg. Some Eigg women were then tending cattle in Eilean Chastell, the small island which forms this harbour. The strangers visited, and maltreated the women. Their friends having got information, pursued and destroyed those strangers. This treatment of his vassals, M'Leod considered to be an insult, and came in force to avenge their death.
>
> The inhabitants, apprised of their danger, flocked to this cave for concealment, excepting three, who took other places of refuge, and a boat's crew then in Glasgow. M'Leod, after landing, having found no inhabitants, believed that they had left for the mainland, and resolved to return immediately to Sky.
>
> The people in the cave, impatient of their confinement, sent a scout to reconnoitre, who imprudently shewed himself upon an eminence, when he was readily observed by the enemy, then actually under sail for Sky. Unfortunately for the inhabitants, where was new laid snow upon the ground. M'Leod relanded, and traced the scout to the cave's mouth: he offered upon delivering up to him the murderers of his people, to spare the other inhabitants.
>
> The terms were rejected, upon which M'Leod smoaked them all to death. In the confined air of this cave, the bones are still pretty fresh, and some of the skulls entire, and the teeth in their sockets. About 40 skulls have been lately numbered here. It is probable that a greater number was destroyed; if so, their neighbouring friends relations may have carried them off for burial in consecrated ground.

Canon MacLeod says that Alasdair Crotach's son William was present, and was left by his father to complete the work of collecting combustibles and setting them on fire in the mouth of the cave. It is significant that he was thereafter known by the nickname of Uilleam na h-Uamha (William of the Cave). William died in 1551. Apparently his foster-brother was one of the persons killed or ill-treated on Eigg by the MacDonalds.

Canon MacLeod thought that the massacre on Eigg must have occurred between 1500 and 1520. Also in favour of a considerably earlier date than 1577 is the fact that, in 1588, Sir Lachlann MacLean of Duart with the assistance of a hundred Spaniards from the Tobermory galleon, was accused of having despoiled, burnt and depopulated the islands of Eigg, Rum and Canna. Perhaps the date of the cave incident was entered in the official 'Description' as 1577 to take some of the heat off MacLean, who was on friendly terms with Queen Elizabeth whom James VI of Scotland wanted to succeed; or perhaps a copying mistake has been made by some transcriber, who may have copied something like 1517 in an old manuscript as 1577.

In any case there is no allusion to the massacre in the report of the Irish Franciscans who visited Eigg in 1625 and found 200 persons (presumably adults) living on the island, including an old lady who remembered having heard Mass there in her youth; nor is there any mention of it in the Book of Clanranald, the records kept by the MacMhuirichs. In oral tradition there are some suggestions of trouble about a marriage, or over the treatment of a wife, see the song *'S trom an direadh*, 'Sad is the Climbing', and the Notes thereon, in *Hebridean Folksongs* Vol. II, No. LX. Hugh MacDonald, who does not mention the massacre in his *History of the MacDonalds*, says that:

> Alexander MacLeod of Harris, having married the Laird of Moidart's daughter sent her home some time thereafter, but the Laird of Moidart afterwards apprehending him in Egg (*sic*) hanged MacLeod's brother and kept him prisoner for seven years at Castle Tirrim in Moidart where he got his back broke which made him hunch backed all his lifetime.

There is nothing about this in Canon MacLeod's account, where the damage to the back is ascribed to a knife wound in a personal fight with a member of the Clanranald clan.

The Swiss geologist Necker de Saussure, who visited Eigg in September 1807 during his tour of Scotland in search of geological specimens, stayed first with a MacDonald, an old soldier who had been at Culloden as a boy, carrying a gun for his father (1746) and had later been at the siege of Quebec, was told the story of the cave, which must have been confirmed by the Rev. Donald MacLean with whom de Saussure spent one or two nights. He gives the story

(Vol. 2, p. 464) and then goes on to describe his own visit to the cave, which I translate from the French:

> At first we didn't see the entrance to the cavern at all; it was concealed by bushes and brambles. The entrance is so low that we had to crawl on our bellies to go in; but after we had advanced a little in this way, we found ourselves in an extensive and lofty grotto.
>
> Having a torch, we penetrated as far as we could in this long narrow cavern. Distrustful of tradition, we had considered the story of MacDonald [his first host on Eigg] to be fabulous, but the sight of the grotto's walls still smoke-blackened, and above all the sight of a quantity of skulls and of human bones lying on all sides of the ground, was a too striking proof of the truth of the fact.
>
> The effect produced on us by the unexpected discovery of these death-heads, the horror that assailed us at such a sight, can be better felt than described.
>
> The same cavern offered us an object of attention of another class. Generally one is tempted to attribute the formation of caves on the shore to the action of the sea; but that explanation cannot fit the form of this one. Indeed it only presents to the sea side a hole three feet in diameter at the most; whereas in the interior of the rock it is more than 30 feet high. Therefore the sea didn't excavate it. Rather it is to be assumed that this cavern was formed at the same time as the rock which encloses it, that it is a natural space created during the consolidation of the '*wakke*'[3] by the release of gas or of acqueous vapour.
>
> On our return to MacDonald's cottage, we found the Rev. Mr MacLean the minister of the Isle of Eigg there; he was awaiting us to invite us to dinner with him, and to come to stay at the manse for the time we counted on passing on the island. We accepted this obliging invitation with the more pleasure, as the cottage in which we had slept did not offer a very tempting resting place.

Necker de Saussure visited the cave on Eigg on 11th September, at a time when the entrance would have been better concealed by bracken and brambles than it would have been in March (whatever the year) in the 'Description of the Isles' quoted by W. F. Skene.

Necker de Saussure meets Ranald MacDonald
.

After an abortive attempt to sail from Eigg to Rum on 10th
September 1807, in the course of which the boat, crewed by two
'mariners' from Eigg, was nearly dashed against the rocks in the
sound between Eigg and the small island of Eilean a' Chaisteil,
Necker de Saussure went back ashore on Eigg, and took the chance
of going over to the west side of the island to visit Ranald MacDonald,
son of the famous Jacobite poet Alexander MacDonald, (Alasdair
mac Mhaighstir Alasdair) at the farm of Laig, of which Ranald was
the tenant, a farm well known in Hebridean tradition, which Ranald
had tenanted since before 1766 (MacDonald, A. and MacDonald,
A. (1907), Vol. III, pp. 288–9). Necker de Saussure wrote in French:

As soon as we had landed, we resolved to use the rest of the day to visit
the farm called Laig, in the west part of Eigg, where their lives a tenant
of the Clanranalds, also called MacDonald. We had been given a letter
for him exhorting us to see him as representing the type of the old
Scottish Highlanders whose habits and customs he has maintained.

It was there that we first experienced the cordial welcome which
this old man made us. He kept us to dine, but before the table was
served he made us drink whisky with him, toasting each other. We then
followed him to see a little plantation of trees, which he had recently
made; these are the only trees on the island, and he hopes to bring
them to something. It is true that the situation is very favourable, the
farm is sheltered from the north, east and south winds from the sea by
high hills. The little plain of Laig is open to the setting sun, being on a
beach bathed by the arm of the sea which separates Eigg from Rum.
From there we could see with longing the pointed mountains of that
island, which we had vainly tried to reach.

Dinner was simple, but was extremely good; we hadn't eaten bread
since we left Ulva; accustomed as we were to the rye scones which we
had found there, we lacked nothing. Our host told us several interesting
details about the Pretender, of whom he spoke with emotion. It seemed
extraordinary to us to hear him, in naming the Duke of Argyll or the
Earl of Breadalbane, call them simply Argyle and Breadalbane. For
him this wasn't a sign of familiarity or of scorn, in this he followed the
old Scottish custom, which is that of giving noblemen, landowners
and farmers the names of their properties, of their domain, or of their
farms, without adding to them their family or any other title. It was
this that I had heard the boatmen of Mr MacDonald of Staffa, when
either talking of him or speaking to him, call him 'Staffa' as the most
respectful title.

When our host mentioned the Campbells we could discover yet in
his talk some trace of the animosity which used to exist formerly between
his clan and theirs. But to hear him, all the peers of the Kingdom were

nothing compared to his chief Clanranald,[4] whose name returned at every moment in his conversation. Altogether nothing was more singular than the way of living of this good old man; he had the tone and the manners of an epoch belonging to the past, to a generation that had almost disappeared.

After dinner, following the custom, he gave toasts; the first was to the King, the second, filled to the brim, to Clanranald. He diverted us much by singing plenty of Gaelic songs; and as he passed as knowing bagpipe airs as well as a piper, we begged him to give us some examples of them. He then sang several pibroch tunes with all their passages and their difficulties, imitating with his voice the sound of the bagpipes in the most pleasing manner.

The most curious thing which we saw in his possession was a Gaelic manuscript, which he told us had been written by his grandfather,[5] it was the only manuscript of the kind that I have yet seen, written in peculiar characters, which have not been used for a long time. I could not know what the manuscript contained, but at least I was assured that it was Gaelic.

When we departed, good old Laig accompanied us to the door of his house. There filling a glass he drank to our health, then passed it successively to each one of us, and we emptied it in witnessing his hospitality. This little ceremony is a very old ceremony called 'door drink' (*Deoch an Doras*), and which is analogous to that of the vin d'etrier (stirrup cup) of our fathers. It is now altogether out of use, for I never saw it practised except by Laig; it is nevertheless still well known to the people of the mountains and the islands of Scotland.

After having taken leave of our excellent host, we recovered our way as well as we could do in the dark, and we only got back to the manse at suppertime.

Later on, Necker de Saussure writes that:

Mr MacDonald of Clanranald, the proprietor of Eigg, does not possess any habitation there where he can reside. An agent (*regisseur*) manages this domain for him, and receives the annual rents of the big farmers – *taxemen* (*sic*) who here, as in all the Highlands, hold directly from the proprietor the lands which they get worked by the *cottagers* or land workers, to whom they sublet a cabin and some acres (*arpens*) of land for their own use.

Necker de Saussure continues by saying how the parish comprises Canna and Muck as well as Eigg, and praises the Rev. Donald MacLean for the courage with which he confronts the difficulties of travel where storms are so frequent and the seas are so rough. He goes on to say:

I learned with astonishment that nearly half of the inhabitants of Eigg are Catholics. They have a priest of their religion and a church which is consecrated to them. This priest is a Scot who studied in France.[6]

Although the followers of both cults live on good terms together, I found it curious to listen to several animated discussions about the sectarian controversy of this little island. It is a subject of conversation which is treated with vivaciousness and warmth, but without bitterness and without too much intolerance. One is surprised to hear arguments renewed and a kind of dialectic which in all the rest of Europe have rested buried in the most profound oblivion.

Later on, writing of Gaelic-speaking Scottish Highlanders in general, Necker de Saussure says:

Apart from superstitions widespread amongst all the European nations, the Scottish Highlanders have many particular to themselves. They have inherited from the Catholic religion a kind of veneration for places formerly consecrated by this cult, and they go on pilgrimages to certain springs and to certain caves which still carry the names of men and women saints, to find the cures for their ills there (Vol. III, p. 231).

Ranald MacDonald and the Eigg Collection, 1776

Ranald MacDonald (known as *Raonull Dubh*) was the only son of Alexander MacDonald, the Gaelic poet, and his wife, Jane or Jean MacDonald of the Dalness family of Glenetive. He was born probably around 1728 or 1729. In the present state of research little is known of his early life though we may infer that his parents' movements and the career of his father would provide some indications. He must have been at least fifteen years of age therefore when the family were living at Coire a' Mhuillinn and he substituted for his father as the SPCK schoolmaster in Ardnamurchan in 1744. Alasdair Mac Mhaighstir Alasdair (Alexander MacDonald) had been the SPCK schoolteacher and catechist in Ardnamurchan since 1729 and had been reported as having been absent from his charge, probably when he was helping to rally support for the Jacobite cause. His son Ranald is described in 1807 by Necker de Saussure, the Swiss geologist, as a vigorous old man who sang Gaelic songs and pibrochs. He must have died within the next few years and possibly about 1809.

Ranald MacDonald was the compiler in 1776 of the first printed collection of Gaelic songs, based largely probably on collections made by his father, which was then printed in Edinburgh and which he titled *Comh-chruinneachadh Orannaigh Gaidhealach le Raonuill MacDomhnuill Ann 'N Eilean Eigg, Vol. I*, now referred to as the 'Eigg Collection', 'all set to music and composed in the last 200 years'. Writing to Johnson from Edinburgh in February 1775, after their famous visit to the Western Isles, James Boswell mentions Ranald in slightly patronising tone:

> There is now come to this city, Ranald MacDonald, from the Isle of Eigg, who has several MSS of Erse poetry, which he wishes to publish by subscription ... This man says that some of his manuscripts are ancient; and, to be sure, one of them which was shewn to me does appear to have the duskiness of antiquity.

His English Introduction makes it clear that his book was the first produced under the influence of the revival of the interest in Gaelic verse aroused by the publication of James Macpherson's *Ossian* in the 1760s. Ranald dedicated his book to James Grant of Corriemony (1743–1835), advocate and author, who himself later wrote 'Thoughts on the Origin of the Gael' (1814) and discussed the Ossianic question. Lord Kames and Dr Blair were also noted in the Preface as persons who believed in the authenticity of Ossian, Blair's 'Critical Dissertation on the Poems of Ossian, the Son of

Fingal' having been first published in 1763 and thereafter providing a touchstone of critical support. The projected second volume of the 'Eigg Collection', which was, he wrote, to contain 'poems of much older date than these of the first', might well have included genuine Ossianic ballads such as were later collected and printed by John Francis Campbell of Islay. The introductory essay in an appropriately rhetorical tone gives significant insights into contemporary attitudes:

> The Gaelic language, now struggling for existence in a narrow corner, was once the mother tongue of the principal states of Europe. It was in particular, and for a considerable length of time, the only language spoken by our ancestors, the ancient Caledonians. The concise and nervous expression of this language, its passionate and elevated tone, display, in lively colours, the national spirit of Caledonia, that spirit which has effectually repelled the invasions of those who had torn the rest of Europe to pieces.

The author attributes the decay of Gaelic to political causes on which he offers no further explanation which would be needless within thirty years of the Battle of Culloden and within the period when proscriptive legislation was still on the statute book. But following the publication of Ossian and in oblique reference to it, he could remind his readers of newly discovered virtue and value of which he was clearly one of the surviving custodians:

> a few years ago, some fragments of the best and most ancient Gaelic Poetry were offered to the public in an English translation, inspired with a considerable share of the majesty, simplicity and elegance of the original composition ... Independent of the beauty of their composition, they served to exhibit a picture of human manners so exalted and refined

In 1776, Ranald MacDonald was living in the Isle of Eigg as tacksman or tenant of the farm of Laig, the lease of which he had got from MacDonald of Clanranald, known as 'Old Clanranald', before 1766, the year in which the chief died. Ranald is said to have been tenant of the Inn at Strath Arisaig for some years before moving to Laig.

In his book he refers to having been 'at much labour and expense, during the course of two years, in collecting the poems now offered to the public'. It is clear from the variations in orthography that Ranald must have got them from a variety of sources. Dr Colm O Baoill of Aberdeen University has shown that five of the songs have every appearance of having been copied from the collection of Dr Hector MacLean of Grulin, Isle of Mull, a collection which was then taken to Nova Scotia in 1819 by the Tiree bard, John MacLean

(1787–1848), and is now in the public archives of Halifax. The interest of Ranald MacDonald and his father in MacLean poetry was probably based on their personal acquaintance with the Rev. John MacLean, minister of Kilninian (that part of Mull nearest to Ardnamurchan) from 1702 until 1752. Alexander MacDonald's poem in praise of the Gaelic language was clearly influenced by the Rev. John MacLean's eulogy addressed to Edward Lhuyd which had been printed in the folio volume of *Archaeologia Britannica* in 1707.

The 'Eigg Collection' contains 106 Gaelic poems totalling 9681 lines of Gaelic verse and also includes some translations. Among the most important poems were seven by, and three later attributed to, Ranald's father; of these ten, seven were not included in Alexander MacDonald's own edition of Gaelic poetry of 1751. Of these, the most important is the dramatic 566 line poem on the voyage of Clanranald's galley or *Birlinn* from Loch Eynort in South Uist to Carrickfergus in Ulster; there is also a manuscript version of this in the Library of the Royal Irish Academy. Beside his father's songs, the collection includes some elegies by the MacMhuirich bards to Clanranald, and songs by Mary MacLeod, Iain Lom MacDonald of Lochaber and John MacCodrum of North Uist.

The Swiss geologist, Necker de Saussure, who visited the Isle of Eigg in 1807 had an interesting encounter with Ranald MacDonald, owing to the former having been storm-stayed in Eigg when wanting to cross to the Isle of Rum. De Saussure had been advised to see Ranald 'comme le type des anciens montagnards de l'Ecosse, dont il a conservé les moeurs et les usages'. He wrote that nothing was more singular than this good old man's way of life; it was the tone, the manners of an already long past epoch, and of a generation which would soon disappear. Ranald showed de Saussure a Gaelic manuscript which had belonged to his grandfather. De Saussure wrote that Ranald had planted the only trees growing on the Isle of Eigg, and describes how he sang Gaelic songs some of which imitated bagpipe music.

Ranald was the only one of eight tenants living in Eigg who had paid rent to 'Old Clanranald' who had died in 1766. His son Angus succeeded him in the farm of Laig and he in turn was succeeded by his son Allan in 1833.

Editions of the 'Eigg Collection' appeared in 1782 and 1809 (in Glasgow), the latter edited by Peter or Patrick Turner who published his own collection of Gaelic poetry in 1813. Turner was a well-known collector of Gaelic manuscripts and could also have acquired Ranald MacDonald's manuscripts. Ranald's name is not amongst the list of the subscribers to Turner's book and this suggests that he had died before the book was projected. Turner's own manuscript collection occupies 172 pages in Rev. Alexander Cameron's *Reliquiae Celticae*.

Editor's Note

It is conceivable that the 'Mr MacDonald' described so intriguingly by Necker de Saussure when he was storm-stayed in Eigg in September 1807 was Angus, the son of Ranald rather than Ranald himself who had been born about 1728 or 1729. He, the Tacksman of Laig, was 'a tenant of the Clanranalds... called MacDonald' and showed the writer 'a Gaelic manuscript which he told us had been written by his grandfather'. Undoubtedly by the standards of the time, Angus was himself then advancing in age and we might expect him to show off work in manuscript by his grandfather, Alasdair Mac Mhaighstir Alasdair. Angus is named in a Clanranald Rental of 1813 (National Archives of Scotland [NAS] GD 201/1/351/14) but in the Judicial Rental of the Clanranald Estates of 1798 the tack is held by his father: 'Ranald MacDonald, Tacksman of Laig at a Yearly Rent of £41 8s 9d in virtue of a tack entered into between the late Clanranald and the deponent of 11th April 1786' (NAS GD 128/ 49/3/8 Fraser-Mackintosh Papers). The survival into advanced old age of Raghnall Dubh – known also to Eigg and Moidart tradition as 'Raghnall Giobach' ('Ragged Ranald'?) – to be described in personam in September 1807 is confirmed by a document in the papers of the Highland Society of Scotland; the Society received a prospectus for Ranald MacDonald's Eigg Collection dated June 1808 in which the book is called a 'Volume of invaluable and select ancient Gaelic Songs, Iohrams, and Boat Songs... by Mr Macdonald of Laig, Island of Eig' and the complier describes himself as 'being now nearly eighty years of age' (see Ronald Iain Black, 'The Gaelic Academy: Appendix: The Ingliston Papers', in *Scottish Gaelic Studies* Vol. XV (1988), pp. 103–121, and especially p. 109).

What Became of the Native Deer?

Early accounts of the Isle of Rum are to be found in Dean Monro's *Description of the Western Isles of Scotland* (1549); in the *Description of the Isles of Scotland*, probably a report written for King James VI around 1595, printed by W. F. Skene in Vol. III of his *Celtic Scotland*; in *Ane Description of Certaine Pairts of the Highlands of Scotland*, printed in Vol. II of *Macfarlane's Geographical Collections* (the date of this description is around 1630); and in Martin Martin's account of Rum in his *Description of the Western Islands of Scotland* (1697). Martin Martin saw his book through the press; the earlier accounts consist of transcriptions from MSS, which sometimes contain errors, like 'Britane' for 'Beltane' in one version of Monro's book, 'Ronin' as the name of the island is a pretty obvious one for an occasional way of writing 'Roum' for 'Rum' (ou = long u in Scots). The information contained in these various accounts may be summarized as follows:

1. Rum is a big island (though its dimensions are much understated by Martin and in the 1630 account); it is also very mountainous.
2. It was largely uncultivated; there were only two agricultural townships on the island, one at Kilmory on the NW side, the other in Harris glen on the SW side. These contained only ten merklands[7] and the whole island could only raise six or seven men for the wars; whereas Canna had six merklands and could raise thirty men, and Muck had four merklands and could raise sixteen men, more than twice what Rum could.
3. Rum possessed a large number of small deer, which were caught and killed by being driven, presumably by deer hounds, into traps called 'taynschells' in the literature, formed by gradually narrowing stone dykes built in some of the glens, as described in the *Old Statistical Account*.
4. Certain fat sea birds the size of doves came in to the hills in spring to nest, and were considered good to eat, although the flesh was strong or 'wyld' (possibly Manx shearwaters).
5. The island belonged to the MacLeans of Coll, whose patronymic is given by Monro as 'M' Kenabrey' (Gaelic for Mac Iain Abraich = son of Iain from Lochaber). Martin Martin gives the local story, that the descendants of Lachlin, a Cadet of this family, are liable to a sudden death, or death by illness, if they shoot a deer in the mountain called Finchra in Rum – some striking coincidence at some time must have given rise to such a story. Martin says that the inhabitants were Protestants, but they were

still Catholics at the time he wrote, and the story of *Creideamh a'*
Bhata bhuidhe and the conversion of the community is related
in the chapter on the British Fisheries in *Canna. The Story of a*
Hebridean Island.

Martin writes that 'The Mountains have some hundred (*sic*) of
Deer grazing in them' (p. 173). Elsewhere he writes that:

> The Eagles are very destructive to the Fawns and Lambs, especially the
> black Eagle, which is of lesser size than the other. The Natives observe,
> that it fixes its Tallons between the Deers Horns, and beats its wings
> constantly about its Eyes; which puts the Deer to run continually till it
> falls into a Ditch, or over a Precipice, where it dies, and so becomes a
> prey to the cunning Hunter. There are at the same time several other
> Eagles of this kind, i.e. the White tailed eagle which fly on both sides of
> the Deer; which fright it extremely, and contribute much to its sudden
> Destruction.

This is in the section of his book about North Uist (p. 70). He
adds, 'The Forester and several of the Natives assur'd me, that they
had seen both sorts of Eagles kill Deer in this manner.' At Coleraine
in the north of Ireland in 1700, Edward Lhuyd noted (amongst
other things) from the Rev. John Beaton of the famous medical
family on Mull the same information about Eagles killing deer.[8]
In 1772, Thomas Pennant made a Tour of the Hebrides, visiting
Rum and Canna, but not Eigg or Muck, and wrote what is the fullest
account of Rum, before the nineteenth-century evictions, that we
possess. Pennant stayed in the only house in the village at Kinloch
that had windows. He wrote that the chief activity of the Rum people
was raising black cattle to be sold to graziers. The mutton of the
small local sheep was 'the most delicate in our dominions', and he
said that there was:

> Very little arable ground except about the nine little hamlets that the
> natives here have grouped in different places, near which corn, i.e. oats
> and barley, is grown in diminutive patches, for the tenants here have
> run-rig[9] as in Cannay. The greatest farmer holds land rented for £15/
> 12/- a year and pays that in money, i.e. not by services. The whole island
> is rented at 2000 merks.

He adds in a footnote that a merk = 13 $^3/_4$ pence, that is to say,
that the total rental of Rum was approximately £275 a year. He said
that no hay was made on the island, but special spots of grass were
preserved for winter grazing, with a *Fear cuairtich* (watchman)
appointed by each farm to preserve the grass and the corn; in return
he was allowed as much grass as was needed for four cows, and as

much land as one horse could till and harrow. As regards horses, or rather ponies, there was an abundance of mares, and as many stallions as necessary; the geldings were kept for market, but the fillies were never sold. A few goats were kept, but very few poultry, owing to the scarcity of grain. As for deer:

> These animals once abounded here, but they are now reduced to eighty by the eagles, who do not only kill the fawns, but the old deer, seizing them between the horns, and terrifying them till they fall down some precipice, and become their prey.

Pennant names a number of birds observed on Rum, the first being 'Ring-tailed eagles'. He gives some interesting statistics which are best discussed in conjunction with those quoted by the next author, the Rev. Donald MacLean, who wrote about the parish of the Small Isles, Eigg, Rum, Canna and Muck, in Volume XVII of the *Old Statistical Account* published in 1794. But now the deer are gone. The decline in the deer can be set down as follows:

1545	Abundant small deer
1595	Many
1630	Very many
1697	100
1772	80
1794	None.

MacLean gives a very interesting description of the 'taynschell', or medieval deer trap, that had formerly been used, and refers to eagles as a cause of the decline.

> In Rum there were formerly great numbers of deer; there was also a copse of wood, that afforded cover to their fawns from birds of prey, particularly from the eagle: while the wood throve, the deer also throve; now that the wood is totally destroyed, the deer are extirpated.

He does not say where the wood was, or how large it was, or what kind of trees were in it. Judging by pollen analyses made in Canna, they would probably have been Scots pines, birches, alders, rowans, aspens and willows, such as exist in the traditional wood on the north side of Soay Sound in Skye. MacLean continues:

> Before the use of firearms, their method of killing the deer was as follows: on each side of a glen, formed by two mountains, stone dykes were begun pretty high in the mountains, and carried to the lower part of the valley, always drawing nearer, till within 3 or 4 feet of each other.

From this narrow pass, a circular space was inclosed by a stone wall, of a height sufficient to confine the deer; to this place they were pursued and destroyed. The vestige of one of these enclosures is still to be seen on Rum.

Firearms came late into the Highlands; in 1601, the battle of Carinish in North Uist was fought with bows and arrows, and won by superior marksmanship. The deer were presumably pursued by deer hounds; the account recalls the days of Fionn Mac Cumhail and his dog Bran in the old Fingalian stories.

Population statistics

Source	Souls	Children Boys	Girls	Adults	Families	Villages
Rev. M. McAskill, 1768	302					
Thomas Pennant, 1772	325	102	76	149	59	9
Rev. D. MacLean, 1794	443	(55.7% of whole parish younger than 20)				
Hugh Miller, 1828	1 sheep farmer and a few shepherds					

The tragic story of the depopulation of the Isle of Rum can be read in Alexander MacKenzie's *The Highland Clearances* and in Noel Banks's *Six Inner Hebrides* (1977). The native human population followed the native deer into oblivion; the native eagles which had preyed on the native deer were destroyed by the gamekeepers of the wealthy non-native proprietors who succeeded the sheep farmers, and made Rum a private kingdom from which visitors were excluded apart from the proprietors' private guests, until Rum was bought by the Nature Conservancy (now Scottish Natural Heritage) in 1953; they brought in a small population, and later re-introduced a few sea eagles. The deer now on Rum are the result of a re-introduction from the mainland made about 150 years ago.

Canna is St Columba's Hinba

Few other early Scottish historical questions have given rise to so much speculation and argument as that of the identity of the island called in Adamnan's *Life of Columba* – *'Hinba'*. Almost any modern guidebook to Iona is likely to repeat the error of W. F. Skene in identifying it with *Eileann na Naoimh* (*sic*) (the Island of Saints) in the Garavellochs, lying between Luing and Mull in the Firth of Lorne, Argyllshire. The fact is that, as Professor W. J. Watson pointed out, the correct Gaelic name of these islands is Na h-Eileacha Naomha, which means 'The Holy Rocks', which he says, was 'beyond reasonable doubt the site of Brendan Moccu Alti's monastery of Ailech, founded probably some time before Columba had come to Iona (Watson, W. J. (1926), p. 81).

What do we know about Hinba? From allusions in Adamnan's book we learn that (1) Columba was fond of it; (2) there was an adequate harbour there, a sea inlet called a *Muirbolc Már* in Old Gaelic, a 'big sea-bag'; (3) there was a monastic settlement there; (4) it was inhabited; (5) Columba had a revelation of the spiritual secrets and of the meaning of difficult passages of Scripture there, and regretted that his foster-son Baithin, who was his cousin and his successor as Abbot of Iona, was not with him and able to write these things down, but 'Baithin however could not be present and able to write these things down, being detained by winds in the Egean Island', i.e. the Isle of Eigg.

The question of identifying Canna with Hinba involves topology, archaeology and geology. Skene dismissed the suggestion of Canon Reeves that Canna might be Hinba, summarily, saying that Canna could not have been Hinba because its only archaeological remains were the ruin of a small church;[10] Skene dismissed the possibility that Columba and Baithin could have come north together with Columba staying in Canna and Baithin going on to Eigg to rejoin Columba on Hinba later, because 'if Hinba is Canna, Egg (*sic*) lies very far to the eastward of it' (Reeves, W. (1874), p. 318). Eigg is, in fact, about fifteen miles southeast of Canna; in 1939 on a good day the writer took a party by a slow converted lifeboat to Mass in Eigg from Canna and back again on the same day. What would have been more reasonable than for Columba and Baithin to come north together, one to go to Canna and the other to Eigg, arranging to meet on Canna again? How could anyone have conducted a mission from Iona to the Small Isles and Skye by small boats without using Canna Harbour, which is far the best harbour in the district, as yachtsmen well know?

Considering Canna Harbour, the geological fact is that, in Columba's time, Canna and the adjoining Sanday may well have been joined by sandhills, since eroded by the prevailing southwest winds, and the rising rides, which at this point where Canna and Sanday are separated by a narrow channel come from the west, not the east. Anyone can stand on the footbridge on a bright day at the right time and can see the sand grains moving eastwards in the current; the writer has also observed these things while waiting for the tide to rise sufficiently to take a 15-foot dinghy through the channel beneath the bridge, and has observed the sand banks revealed at low tide in the harbour increase over fifty years, though by how much would be difficult to say accurately. The sand comes from the Tràigh Bhàn at the northwest end on Sanday; the sea bottom northwest of it is sandy for a considerable distance.

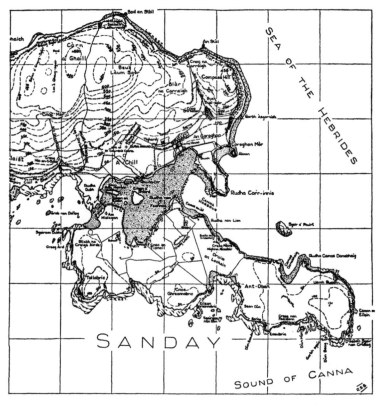

Reproduction of O.S. map of Canna Harbour. Scale, three inches to the mile.
The reader should visualise the map as showing the harbour as navigable at all states of the tide, as it very probably has been in St Columba's time, before silting.

The map printed here shows that Canna Harbour, *was navigable at all states of the tide before most of it had become silted up*, was then two-thirds of a mile from end to end, and could certainly have been considered a 'big bag' from the point of view of a small boat, especially as the entrance could not be seen from within the inner harbour.

Martin Martin, who gives a vivid description of Iona as it was in his time (1690s) records the traditional size and appearance of the boat which brought St Columba and his followers to Iona, saying that:

> The Dock[11] which was dug out of Port *Curich* is on the shore, to preserve *Columba's* Boat called *Curich*, which was made of Ribs of Wood, and the outside cover'd with Hides; the Boat was long, and sharp-pointed at both ends; Columbus is said to have transported eighteen Clergy-men[12] in this Boat to Iona.

So strongly was the memory of St Columba preserved in Canna, that the Irish Franciscans who came to Canna in the autumn of 1625 reported that Canna was

> Once held by St Columba, whom all the inhabitants ... hold in veneration, like a second God. The place itself is most pleasing and charming.

They added that by his blessing Columba had freed the island from all venomous reptiles. The belief of the inhabitants that Canna was 'once held by St Columba' is a powerful piece of evidence that Canna is Hinba. Skene, who dismissed the idea, had apparently never visited Canna and did not know anything about the monastic remains at Sgor nam Ban-naomh, or anything about the remarkable selection of early carved stones of Christian origin which have been found on the island. Yet modern writers still continue to repeat Skene's mistaken judgements in the matter. It is to be hoped that the comprehensive archaeological survey of Canna, which has been undertaken as a long-term project under the aegis of the National Trust for Scotland, will provide further confirmation of the writer's belief that Canna is Hinba.

Notes and References to Section 6

[1] *Scottish History Society*, Vol. 52, p. 176.

[2] John Muideartach who died in 1574 had four sons by two wives and four more by 'a daughter of Charles son of Neil', of whom the last was called Angus. He could have been Clanranald's tacksman or baillie in Eigg. See 'The Book of Clanranald' in *Reliquiae Celticae* Volume II, pp. 170–1.

[3] Wakke or wacke. A German term 'applied to a soft and earthy variety of

basalt, or to the greyish-green to brownish-black clay-like residue resulting from the partial chemical decomposition in place of basalts, basaltic tuffs, and related igneous rocks'. W. Humble, *Dictionary of Geology and Minerology*, 2nd edition, 1843.

[4]Actually the Clanranald in 1807 was young Ranald George, son of John Moidartach and of Katherine MacQueen, the daughter of Robert MacQueen the Lord Justice Clerk. He was the first Clanranald to bear the Christian name of 'George', and the first to be educated at an English 'public school', Eton. Not surprisingly he got caught up in a fast extravagant fashionable English set; he was caricatured in London dancing the quadrille partnered by Lady Worcester, whose hand he is kissing. The inevitable consequence was the sale of the traditional Clanranald estates one after another from 1813 on. Eigg and Canna went in 1827, South Uist and Benbecula in 1838. Only Caisteal Tioram, the ancient stronghold of the family in Moidart, was left.

[5]This was the Rev. Alexander MacDonald, non-jurant minister of Islandfinnan in Moidart, whose second son, the famous Gaelic poet, was known to have been able to write in the old Gaelic characters.

[6]The priest on Eigg at this time was Fr Anthony MacDonald, who was in charge of the parish from 1791 to 1834. Necker de Saussure writes that there were all but 300 Catholics living on Canna. It is a pity he never met Fr Anthony MacDonald; it would be interesting to have de Saussure's impressions of him.

[7]An ancient tax valuation based on the amount of livestock the holdings could carry, and assessed in terms of the *merk*, a silver coin valued at 13s. 4d. Scots.

[8]See J. L. Campbell and D. Thomson, *Edward Lhuyd in the Scottish Highlands*, p. 65, amongst other notes in Welsh, translated by Professor Derick Thomson.

[9]A system whereby the hill grazing was held in common, and the arable held in strips which were periodically re-allocated to the different holders.

[10]Skene's appendix to Canon Reeves' edition of Adamnan's *Life of St Columba*, 1874, p. 319.

[11]1716 ed., p. 263. 'Dock' here = 'the bed in the sand or ooze in which a ship lies at low water' (O.E.D.).

[12]i.e. monks.

Section 6

.

Poetry and Song: Alexander MacDonald

.

Alexander MacDonald, c. 1698–1770

Alasdair Mac Mhaighstir Alasdair, the famous Jacobite poet of the 1745 rebellion, was connected with the Hebrides as a member of the Clanranald branch of the MacDonalds; born at Dalilea in Moidart, son of an Episcopalian minister, he held the rank of Captain in the Jacobite army, and was charged with teaching Prince Charles Gaelic. He was Baillie of Canna in the spring of 1751 when his famous little book of Gaelic poems, entitled *Ais-eiridh na Sean Chánoin Albannaich; No, An nuadh Oranaiche Gaidhealach*, was published in Edinburgh. It was thought that there might be another Rising in 1751, and this book was clearly intended to encourage one. Its title means 'the Resurrection of the Ancient Scottish Language'.

The book was dedicated to Walter Macfarlane, the antiquarian whose *Genealogical* and *Geographical Collections* were later to be published by the Scottish History Society (Mitchell, A. and Clark. J. T. (1906–8)). The first poem in the book is the author's praise of the Old Gaelic language. This is quite clearly written in the same style as the Rev. John MacLean's on the same subject praising Edward Lhuyd for awakening the Gaelic language in Scotland from its grave, printed with others in praise of Lhuyd at the beginning of Lhuyd's *Archaeologia Britannica* in 1707. MacLean was minister of the parish of Kilninian in Mull for the first half of the eighteenth century, at the same time that Alexander MacDonald was working on translating a Latin-English wordlist into his *Galick Vocabulary*. It is quite possible that MacDonald consulted both MacLean and the *Archaeologia* in the course of doing this work, thereby extending his own vocabulary. Kilninian in Mull is not far from Ardnamurchan where MacDonald was stationed as an SPCK catechist in the 1730s (see also J. L. Campbell's book, *Highland Songs of the Forty-Five*, 1984 edition).

Portrait of a Traditionalist
•

Published in *Scots Magazine*, October 1935, pp. 61–76

The author of *The Birlinn of Clanranald* is already sufficiently well known as the most important eighteenth-century Scottish Gaelic poet, but he has not yet received due attention as a historian of the 'Forty-five and as one of the most interesting personalities, outside the immediate circle of the leaders, concerned in the Rising. This is partly due to the fact that his authorship of the anonymous 'Journall and Memoirs of Prince Charles's Expedition into Scotland, &c., 1745-6, by a Highland Officer in his Army' (printed in the *Lockhart Papers*, Vol. II., pp. 479–510) has only recently been established by Mr Compton Mackenzie, after Lang had wrongly attributed it to Morar, and Blaikie to Kinlochmoidart. The internal evidence for MacDonald's authorship will be considered later. It is almost incontrovertible. Apart from this 'Journall', MacDonald is also the part-author of an account of Prince Charles's wanderings after Culloden, of which he, Glenaladale (his cousin), and Young Clanranald (his close friend, whom he warmly praised in one of his poems) each wrote a part, and which MacDonald himself presented to Bishop Forbes, compiler of *The Lyon in Mourning*, in 1747. In 1751 he sent to Forbes an account of the atrocities committed in the islands of Eigg and Canna by the Hanoverians under Captains Scott and Ferguson and Lieutenant Thomas Brown. Thus it is clear his writings cover every phase of the Rising, and many a historian of the 'Forty-five has been unwittingly much in his debt.

Alexander MacDonald, known in Gaelic as Alasdair Mac Mhaighstir Alasdair, was born around or before the year 1700. Some of his biographers have suggested a date ten years earlier, but it is difficult to accept this for two reasons. Had he been born in 1690, the probability is overwhelming that he would have taken part in the Rising of 1715; but this Rising is never mentioned in his poems. In the second place, it seems unlikely – though, of course, it is not impossible – that the fiery verses with which MacDonald welcomed the Prince were the composition of a man fifty-five years of age. The date of his birth is a mystery, though an examination of the records of Glasgow University, which he is said to have attended, might provide an indirect clue.

MacDonald was the second son of the Rev. Alasdair MacDonald, non-jurant minister of Island Finnan in Loch Shiel in the former parish of Ardnamurchan. He was also a first cousin of Flora MacDonald and cousin of MacDonald of Glenaladale, both to become celebrated for the parts they played in the 'Forty-five. With such a background it is not surprising that, when the news came, MacDonald supported the Jacobite cause; there are however, earlier signs of his partisanship, though this was not at first openly apparent.

MacDonald is first mentioned in contemporary records as a SPCK schoolmaster and catechist in Ardnamurchan in 1729. Mr William Mackay published in the *Transactions of the Gaelic Society of Inverness* (Vol. XI, p. 171) extracts from the records of the Presbytery of Mull bearing on this period of MacDonald's life. Apart from teaching in various villages, MacDonald was involved indirectly in two ecclesiastical scandals, the first in 1734 and the second ten years later. In the first case he had successfully prosecuted a call to a certain Mr Daniel MacLachlan. MacLachlan survived a preordination charge of drunkenness, swearing and singing indecent songs; but two months after his induction, he deserted his parish and shortly afterwards created a tremendous scandal by publishing in London a pamphlet entitled 'An Essay upon Improving and Adding to the Strength of Great Britain and Ireland by Fornication', in consequence of which he was excommunicated, arrested and imprisoned. In 1744 MacDonald was involved in an even more extraordinary clerical affair, being concerned with one John Stewart, a Mull drover, in giving information against Francis MacDonald, Presbyterian preacher in Strontian and formerly Roman Catholic priest in Moidart, who was charged before the Presbytery of Mull by Dr Hugh MacDonald, Vicar Apostolic of the Highlands (Morar's brother), and Kinlochmoidart (who was also a Catholic) with having committed incest with his sister, as well as with other crimes. This case, which caused the Presbytery no small perplexity, was eventually compromised by the removal of Francis MacDonald to Skye.

In associating himself with this action, MacDonald must have risked the displeasure of contemporary orthodox Presbyterians, and while it is true that the obscene nature of some of his less reputable poems suggests a preoccupation which may itself be enough to account for his activities in this case, there are strong grounds for thinking that MacDonald was moved by secret political and religious sympathies. Mere moral indignation is unlikely. A hint of these sympathies can already be found in his *Galick and English Vocabulary* (which is really an English-Gaelic vocabulary based partly on wordlists in some Latin grammar). This was written for the SPCK and printed in 1741. MacDonald must not be judged by his servile dedication to the Marquis of Lothian; for the salary then paid to him by the Society and the Committee for managing the Royal Bounty together was only £15 a year. Much more significant is the inclusion in the list of Saints' Days of 'King Charles Martyrdom, January 30th' and 'K. Ch. 2d's Restoration, May 30th', not orthodox festivals for a Whig textbook. At Whitsuntide 1745, MacDonald finally deserted his school, and between this time and the landing of the Prince (25th July) apparently became formally converted to Roman Catholicism. The exact date of his conversion is not known. Then, when the *Du Teillay* anchored in Loch nan Uamh, he was among the first to greet his Prince. Here we come to his anonymous 'Journall' and the proof of his authorship.

The proof is circumstantial, but it is almost incontrovertible. The author of the 'Journall' was, on internal evidence, a fervent Jacobite, a Gaelic scholar, a Clanranald MacDonald, and an officer in the Jacobite army. MacDonald was all these things (Bishop Forbes always refers to him as Captain Alexander MacDonald). In addition, the author of the 'Journall' relates how he engaged the Prince in conversation, not knowing who he was, and drank a glass with him; and MacDonald in 1747 related the same incident to Bishop Forbes as having happened to himself at the same time. Several such incidents are related in the 'Journall', and with the author's comments throw considerable light upon the finer side of MacDonald's character:

> July 19 [the early dates in the 'Journall' are a week wrong throughout] ane express was dispatch'd for young Clanronald, and next day, being the 20th, Clanronald, Alexander MacDonald of Glenaladale, Aeneas MacDonald of Dalily, [that is to say, MacDonald's friend, cousin, and elder brother respectively] and *I* came to Forsy, a small village opposite to the road where the Prince's ship lay. We called for the ships boat and were immediately carryed on board, and our hearts were overjoyed to find ourselves so near our long wished for P——ce.

MacDonald went on board, and met the Prince without knowing who he was. The ensuing conversation, in which MacDonald explained to the Prince the use of the Highland garb, has often been quoted; his poem *Am Breacan Uallach* ('The Noble Plaid') supplements this description. The next personal incident occured when the Prince and his company were being entertained in Borradale's house in Arisaig:

After we had all eaten plentifully and drunk cheerfully, H.R.H. drunk the grace drink in English, which most of us understood; when it came to my turn I presumed to distinguish myself by saying audibly in Erse (or highland language) *Deoch slaint' an Riogh*; H.R.H. understanding that I had drunk the King's health made me speak the words again in Erse and said he could drink the King's health likewise in that language, repeating my words; and the company mentioning my skill in the highland language, H.R.H. said I should be his master for that language, and so was made to ask the healths of the P. and D.

MacDonald's known 'skill in the highland language' is strong corroborative evidence in favour of his authorship of the 'Journall'. 'Several of the Captain's acquaintances have told me', wrote Bishop Forbes in 1747, 'that he is by far the best Erse poet in all Scotland'. The exact degree of skill acquired by the Prince in Gaelic under his tuition is still undecided.

MacDonald next received his commission from the Prince, which flattered his pride greatly:

As the P. was setting out for Glenfinin to meet his friends according to appointment, I was detatched to Ardnamurchan to recruit, and soon returned with 50 cliver fellows who pleased the P., and upon review, His H. was pleased to honour me with the command of them, and told me I was the first officer he had made in Scotland; which complement encouraged my vanity not a little, and with our freinds vowed to the Almighty we would live and die with our noble P. though all Britain should forsake him but our little regiment alone.

'Our little regiment' is further referred to:

So all may judge how hazardous ane enterprize we [i.e. Clanranald's people] were now engaged in, being for some time quite alone, who notwithstanding resolved to follow our P. most chearfully and risque our fate with him.

In his poem to Young Clanranald, MacDonald calls him 'the first colonel that the Prince had', and in the well-known *Oran Luaidh* addressed to 'Morag' he comments on the readiness with which Young Clanranald and his clansmen had joined the Prince:

> My hero would not fail thee,
> Thy own Captain, young Clanranald,
> He joined thee before all others,
> And will again, if thou comest;
> Every man in Uist and Moidart
> And dark green Arisaig of birchwoods.
> In Canna, Eigg, and in Morar,
> The noble regiment of Clanranald!

The 'Journall' continues to describe the Rising day by day. MacDonald is noticeably ready to defend the Highlanders against charges of barbarity brought unfairly against them, and to point out the good behaviour of the Jacobite army:

> [After having entered Edinburgh] the main body drew up in the Parliament Closs, and guards were immediately placed at every gate of the city; and the inhabitants cannot in justice but acknowledge that the behaviour of our Highlanders was civil and innocent beyond what even their best friends could have expected.
>
> Now whatever notion or sentiments the low country people may entertain of our Highlanders, this day [the day of Prestonpans] there were many proofs to a diligent spectator amidst all the bloodshed (which at the first shock was unavoidable) of their humanity and mercy; for I can with the strictest truth and sincerity declare that I often heard our people call out to the soldiers if they wanted quarters, and we the officers exerted our utmost pains to protect the soldiers from their first fury, when either through their stuborness or want of language [i.e. Gaelic] they did not cry for quarters, and I observed some of our privat men run to P[ort] Seton for ale and other liquors to support the wounded. And as one proof for all, to my own particular observation, I saw a Highlander supporting a poor wounded soldier by the arms until he should ease nature, and afterwards carry him on his back into a house, and left him a sixpence at parting. In all which we followed not only the dictates of humanity but the orders of our P. in all, like the true father of his country.

'The true father of his country.' This phrase sums up MacDonald's attitude to the Stuarts. In his poem called 'A song composed in the year 1746', he calls King James VIII 'our earthly father' (*Is tu is righ 's is athair talmhaidh dhuinn*) who can be expected to treat his children – that is, his people – with a father's mercy and to give them a father's care and protection. King George, on the other hand, can feel no such consideration:

> The care and kin he shows
> Us is a raven's for his bone.
> The men are not his own,
>   And so for them he nothing cares
> Even though we fell to blows.

MacDonald also refers to the good behaviour of the army at Carlisle and at Lord Stair's house:

> Yet did not his army, tho' flushed with victory, commit any abuse, as neither was done in the least degree at Lord Stair's house at Newliston in their way to Edinburgh, tho' the Glenco men were of our number and could not have forgot the massacre of their clan soon after the Revolution and by whose orders.

The militia that served in Carlisle, and all the inhabitants of the city and neighbourhood can testify the exact discipline of our army, who payed for every thing they got, and all were protected in their libertys and propertys.

At Prestonpans another personal incident is recorded.

The P. left his guard on the march to the attack, talking earnestly to the Duke of Perth and Clanronald and giveing his last orders and injunctions; but returning to his guard, as I happened to pass near by him, he with a smile said to me in Erse, 'Greas ort, Greas ort,' that is, Make haste, make haste.

When the decision to retreat was made at Derby, MacDonald commented on it in words which sum up the feelings of all who have disagreed with and regretted the abandonment of the advance:

How far this was the properest course has been much canvassed; some thinking the intelligence from Scotland of the great numbers conveend in arms or landed from France was ane imposition and that the P. with great unwillingness consented to a retreat. One thing is certain, never was our Highlanders in higher spirits notwithstanding their long and fatiguing march; they had indeed got good quarters and plenty of provisions in their march and were well paid; so that we judged we were able to fight double our numbers of any troops that could oppose us; and would to God that we had pushed on tho' we had all been cutt to pieces, when we were in a condition for fighting and doing honour to our noble P. and the glorious cause we had taken in hand, rather than to have survived and seen that fatall day of Culloden when in want of provisions money and rest &c. we were oblidged to turn our backs and lose all our glory.

MacDonald later commends the skill and bravery of the army at Falkirk; and with regard to the fighting that took place in Ross-shire after the army had retreated to Inverness, he makes the following interesting statement:

We McDonalds were much perplex'd in the event of ane ingagement how to distinguish ourselves from our bretheren and nighbours the McDonalds of Sky, seeing we were both Highlanders and both wore heather in our bonnets, only our white cocades made some distinction.

There could be no more convincing proof of the modernity of the so-called 'clan tartans' than this chance remark.

MacDonald describes vividly the conditions of affairs before Culloden:

Our army had got no pay in money for some time past, but meal only, which the men being obliged to sell out and convert into money, it went but a short way for their other needs, at which the poor creatures grumbled exceedingly and were suspicious that we the officers had detaind it from them. To appease them we had oblidged ourselves to give them payment of all their arrears two days before the battle, which we not being able to perform made the fellows refractory and more negligent of their duty. However on Tuesday the fifteenth we lay under our arms upon the hill all day expecting the enemy, without any other provision but a sea bisket to each man...

Upon our return to the muir of Culloden, tho the P. had given orders for bringing meat and drink for us to the field, which our men not expecting, through their great want of sleep meat and drink many slipt off to take some refreshment in Inverness, Culloden and the nighbourhood, and others to three or four miles distance where they had freinds and acquaintances; and the said refreshment so lulled them asleep that designing only to take ane hours rest they were afterwards surprised and killed in their beds. By this means we wanted in the action at least one third of our best men, and of those who did engage, many had hurried back from Inverness &c. upon the alarm of the enemys approach, both gentlemen and others, as I did myself, having only taken one drink of ale to supply all my need... All these unhappy circumstances for us considered, it is no wonder the event of this day proved so fatal to us as it did. Add to this, what we of the Clan McDonalds thought ominous, we had not this day the right hand in battle as formerly and as we enjoyed in this enterprize when the event proved successfull, as at Gladsmuir and Falkirk, and which our clan maintains we had enjoyed in all our battles and struggles in behalf of our Royall family since the battle of Bannockburn, in which glorious day Robert the Bruce bestowed this honour on Angus M'Donald, Lord of the Isles, as a reward for his never to be forgotten fidelity to that brave prince in protecting him for above nine months in his country of Rachlin, Isla and Vist, as the same name has done since to his royall successor. This right we have (I say) enjoyed ever since unless when yielded by us out of favour, upon particular occasions, as was done to the Laird of McLean at the battle of Harlaw; but our sweet natured P. was prevailed on by L. and his faction to assign this honour to another on this fatall day, which right we judge they will not refuse to yeild us back again next fighting day. As to particulars of the Culloden battle I leave it to the abovementioned [i.e. Colonel Ker, Lord George Murray, and O'Neil] and other accounts well known to many.

Observe the restraint and dignity of these remarks; there is no petty fault-finding or whining reproaches. In his poems Culloden is twice mentioned:

Never let yourselves believe [the Campbells are addressed] that we yielded to you; we were caught by a strong army three times our numbers, who had the advantage of ground and of weather, on a low, hard, level moor, while numerous cavalry and cannons were furiously destroying our army; a strong, well disciplined host (against us) who were used to battle, to firing, and to slaughter.

But when Duke William met us with three times our numbers, and with a hundred disadvantages of combat, he routed us; but it is long before they would exchange blows with us once coming to combat against us in equal numbers.

After Culloden, MacDonald was on the run, presumably until the passing of the Act of Indemnity in June 1747. During this time his house was plundered by the Hanoverian soldiery, even his cat being killed. On 28th December 1747, he was in Edinburgh, and brought to Bishop Forbes at Leith the account of the Prince's wandering after Culloden which he had prepared with Young Clanranald and Glenaladale. This account is printed in *The Lyon in Mourning*, the first and last thirds of it are in MacDonald's own writing. Glenaladale in a letter received by Forbes on 4th December 1749, states that

> for my part it was merely to avoid disoblidging a young lady who desired the favour of me that I thought on setting pen to paper to relate anything of the matter, and as I was not att all well at the time, was obliged to make our friend honest Alister, Dallile's brother, my clerk, and he keept a double of what he wrott.

This 'double' may well be the slightly differing and more condensed version of the account which is printed in the *Lockhart Papers* Vol. II., p. 539, entitled 'a genuine historical journal of P. Charles' retreat from the battle of Culloden, April sixteenth, and of his many disasters in both the isles and continent till he embarked at Lochnanuagh in Arisaig, for France, the twentieth of September, 1746. Written by a Highland Officer in his army'.

'A Highland Officer in his Army' is the title by which the author of the 'Journall' calls himself, be it noted.

In this narrative, MacDonald does not write as if he had been personally present at any time; but many of the people who were most directly involved in the Prince's escape were his relations or his friends. His cousins Flora MacDonald and Glenaladale, his brother Lachlan of Dremisdale, who visited the Prince at Corrodale in South Uist, his nephews Lieutenants Alexander and Rory MacDonald, who with others kept watch on the Hanoverian forces approaching South Uist in search of the Prince, and John MacDonald who was helmsman of the boat that took the Prince and Flora MacDonald from Benbecula to Skye – from these and others MacDonald must have had plenty of first-hand information for his account, which has been of great value to chroniclers of the

'Forty-five. Here MacDonald, who himself had suffered, indicts the conduct of the Hanoverian forces in the Highlands:

> Upon which occasions, were I to be particular, such barbaritys and monstrous scenes of wickedness were perpetrated by murdering the aged, the innocent and the young, by ravishing the women weak and helpless, and destroying their habitations by fire &c. as is horrible to relate; when those who escaped their savage hands by flight were often found perishing with hunger and cold in the fields and caverns of the hills; when such things were committed wantonly and needlessly as would seem incredible to relate, and which the posterity of those sufferers never will, never can, forget, and it will become their dolefull tale to tell their children to future generations. Such was the lot of numbers in the Highlands, which in the lower and less exceptionable part of the country was mostly confined to rifling and an universall desolation by fire of all the Protestant Non-jurant places of worship in the kingdom; and the impression which all these dismal scenes have made upon my mind have forcibly drawn me away from pursuing the thread of my dear P——'s story, to which I return.

Well may MacDonald say of this at the end of his elegy on Lord Lovat:

> We are beneath oppression's heel;
> Ashamed we are, and weary.
> The remnant that remains of us
> Is scattered amidst the mountains;
> With terror filled before our foes,
> Who hunt us amidst the islands,
> They've made of us but wretched thralls.
> O Charlie, come to help us!

The year of 1746 has not been the only time that distance from the seat of government has allowed the Highlands to become the scene of an oppression that could never have been enacted in the less remote parts of Scotland.

The account closes with the Prince embarking at Loch nan Uamh for France:

> [The ship] immediately set sail the twentieth of September, and escaping all the Government's war-ships and being in her way happily favoured by fog, he arrived safely in France; and unparallell'd instance, upon a review of all the circumstances of this escape, of a very particular Providence interesting itself in his behalf. For what wise end Heaven has thus disappointed and yet preserved this noble Prince, and what future scenes the history of his life may display, time only can tell; yet something very remarkable still seems waiting him and this poor country also. May God grant a happy issue.

In one of his poems, MacDonald expressly thanks this divine Providence that had saved the Prince form his enemies.

The day after he had given Forbes this account, MacDonald returned and corrected the narratives of Aeneas MacDonald (Kinlochmoidart's brother) and of Duncan Cameron. On 9th January 1748, he called on Forbes to introduce Donald Roy MacDonald, Baleshare's brother, an accomplished Latin poet who possibly was the writer of the verses *De Auctore Testimonium* which occur at the beginning of MacDonald's book of poems, signed with the initials D.M. On 28th December 1748, MacDonald again visited Forbes, bringing with him two pieces of the eight-oared boat in which the Prince had sailed from Borrodale to Benbecula; one of these pieces is still preserved inside the back board of the fourth volume of *The Lyon in Mourning*. On 10th July 1749, Forbes wrote to Glenaladale enclosing a letter to be forwarded to MacDonald:

> After perusing the enclosed, please seal it, and (with your conveniency) deliver it to my good friend honest Allastar, to whom I heartily wish better days, for I sympathize with him in all his distresses.

The letter asks for information on the Hanoverian atrocities in Eigg and Canna, where MacDonald had intended to go; in fact, Old Clanranald appointed him Baillie of Canna. MacDonald compiled the account from the memory of the two former baillies of Eigg and Canna, and brought it to Forbes on 22nd April 1751, the year that his Gaelic poems were published in Edinburgh. He is described as Baillie of Canna on the title page of this book.

The name of his volume of poetry was, in Gaelic, *The Resurrection of the Ancient Scottish Language*, which recalls George Buchanan's description, in 1582, of his native tongue: *sermo priscorum Scottorum.* Of the twenty-six original poems by MacDonald in this book, ten are more or less violently Jacobite. The publisher concealed his name; the book was burnt by the authorities in 1752, and Simon Fraser, in the introduction to his *Airs and Melodies of the Highlands*, which was published in 1816, writes as if the issue had been totally destroyed, but about a dozen copies are known to exist. Thirteen more of his Jacobite poems, with another of doubtful authorship, are found in Gaelic MS 63 of the National Library, written from internal evidence before 1751, one poem having been composed before Cumberland had left Fort Augustus.

The dominant purpose of these poems was to spur his fellow-countrymen on to another effort, to avenge the disaster of Culloden and the disgrace of the Disclothing and Disarming Acts. The editors of the 1924 edition of MacDonald's poems say that 'When to all others the cause seemed hopeless, and a restoration had become a forlorn hope, Alastair never despaired, but still hoped and sang'.

This, however, is not accurate. MacDonald wrote no more Jacobite poetry after 1751 – and at that time, with the activities of Young Glengarry as Pickle the Spy still unknown and hardly begun, another attempt was both hoped for and expected by many others besides MacDonald:

> O Gaeltach: if thou'rt asleep
> Lie not for long in dreams;
> Bestir thyself, I beg of thee,
> Ere stolen is thy fame.
> O, waken up full mightily,
> Kindled with wrathful fire,
> And show them that thy steel's still keen
> In one more battle dire.

And of the Disclothing Act:

> He thought that thus he'd blunted
> The keenness of the Gaels so valiant,
> But he has only made them
> Still sharper than the edge of razor.
>
> He's left them full of malice,
> As ravenous as dogs a-starving.
> No draught can quench their thirst now
> Of any wine, save England's life-blood.
>
> We're still of our old nature
> As were we ere the Act was passed.
> Alike in mind and persons
> And loyalty, we will not weaken.
>
> Our blood is still our fathers'
> And ours the valour of their hearts;
> The inheritance they left us,
> Loyalty – that is our creed!

But the most virulent of his Jacobite poems are those in MS 63, which was not published until 1908 (by Professor Donald MacKinnon in the *Celtic Review*). Many of these verses are doggerel, but they give a good picture of MacDonald's mind under the stress of the terrible days that followed Culloden. Reading these poems and the 'Journall' it seems clear that the underlying principle of MacDonald's Jacobitism was the conviction that the Stuarts, as the legitimate native sovereigns of Scotland were in a mystical way identified with their country, so that, for MacDonald, a patriot's only choice was to defend his lawful sovereign against what appeared to be essentially an external menace – personified in the German Georges. All MacDonald's appeals to his countrymen are made on the basis of this identification; to him, the 'Forty-five is but one incident in a series of struggles beginning with Bannockburn (and inspired with memories of Calgacus) and continued through Scottish history with Harlaw, the campaigns of Montrose and Killiecrankie. This is the true traditionalism that inspired the Scottish Jacobites, and MacDonald's writings show how it influenced men's thoughts in the Highlands. His regard for King James as the 'true father of his country' has already been mentioned. In the same poem there quoted from MacDonald argues the Legitimist case as he sees it; George II was not the rightful king; common knowledge of his genealogy would make everyone aware of that:

> Remote and bent and weak,
> The female branch from which thou camest
> Far distant on the tree.

Moreover, the Act of Settlement which had procured him the throne was not valid, because William of Orange, at whose instance it had been passed, was himself a usurper. Religion itself was not enough to explain the perverseness of the Whigs, since Charles I whom they had martyred, had been a Protestant. Elsewhere MacDonald says:

> Of Mary and Anne two queens you created
> As a cloak that might mask your villainous treason—

a sentiment which is curiously paralleled in a poem in the Fernaig Manuscript written about 1690. In another poem MacDonald defends James VIII from attacks on his legitimacy and declares that the best blood in Europe is mingled in Prince Charles's veins. Personal admiration for the latter (in one poem called *Am fear ruadh*, or 'The auburn-haired man') is, of course, frequently expressed.

When he comes to deal with his enemies, MacDonald is equally logical. George II was a foreigner, and therefore could not be expected to feel any real concern for the welfare of his subjects. He was in fact the real leader of the country's enemies. This for MacDonald is definitely and finally proved by the execution of three

Jacobite peers and eighty-three commoners after the Rising, an incident which seems to have roused him more than any other:

> Though thou hast quenched thy thirst with the blood of our nobles,
> That wine will taste bitter at the time when it's paid for
> By the hand of thy father, thou German man-eater:
> The blood thou hast shed will yet cost thee dearly
> Ere the game is concluded that thy father began.

Hence the highly-flattering elegy on Lovat, the most important person the Whigs executed. George II's success MacDonald attributes to the fact that he could control the money, 'his own and ours too'; a conjecture for which there is something to be said. George II is called 'son of the German sow', and 'German cannibal', while hope is expressed that Cumberland will share the fate of Herod or of Nero.

But even greater bitterness is shown towards those Highland clans whose militia had followed the professional army – in particular, the Campbells, 'folk of wry mouths who were always our foemen' (*Caimbeul* = crooked mouth). Here it must be said that MacDonald had special provocation. Shortly after Culloden a Campbell poetess had composed a Gaelic lampoon in which the Jacobite army was called 'the rabble of the Rough Bounds', and personal abuse was thrown at the Prince and at Lochiel. It is the only Whig Gaelic poem the author of this article has ever heard of; apart from MacDonald's quotations, it is now lost. It provoked him to make a number of replies, in which the charges are refuted and their author is personally abused; but this leads him nearly always into an attack on the Campbells in general, 'the devilish posterity of Diarmaid O Duibhne'. They are accused of having been bought, 'caught in Mammon's net', of having 'sold honour, faith, and conscience' to George. They are taunted with not having dared to attack the Prince's army on its return from England when it was at Glasgow close to their country, of only having been brave enough to 'pick up the bones broken by the violence of the great army of red beasts'. They are called full-brothers of Judas and accused of having robbed even the blind. In one stanza of the MS 63 version of the poem called the 'Ark', MacDonald achieves an outstanding insult:

> God must all but have repented
> That he ever made that race;
> Men who betrayed their king and kingdom
> And did of gold their idol make.

Bishop Forbes says that

> As for the story of General Campbell and Campbell of Skipness, Captain
> MacDonald declared to me he did not in the least doubt the truth of it,
> for this single reason, because the Cambpells, from the head to the foot
> of them, had discovered a most avaritious, greedy temper in the matter
> of pillaging and plundering their native country.

Innumerable stanzas support this opinion. However, when
MacDonald comes down to considering individuals, as he does in
the 'Ark', a remarkable poem predicting the submergence of Argyll
in a second flood 'because of those who rose for George', MacDonald
– in charge of the Ark himself – is directed to save a third of the
persons mentioned, including the representatives of the families
of Airds, Ardsliginish, Carwhin, Inverawe and Lochnell. Nearly half
the others are to be taken on board after the brine had purged
them of their Whiggish contaminations. No one has yet troubled to
identify all the persons mentioned in this poem, but it proves that
MacDonald was not the indiscriminate hater that some of his bitterer
compositions would suggest him to be.

The publication of the small selection of his poems in 1751 marks
the end of his known Jacobite activities. The rest of his life was
obscure, and need not be dwelt on here. He died about 1770 in
Sandaig in Arisaig, and is buried by Arisaig in the cemetery of
Kilmorie. But for all the obscurity of his end, he had had his day.

What would have become of MacDonald if the Rising had been a
success is a question that invites speculation. At least it is certain
that he would not have passed so soon into obscurity. Had Charles
Edward become king there is little doubt but that both MacDonald
and his work and the language in which he wrote would be now
much better known than they are, and we should almost certainly
have had the 'greater collection of poems of the same sort ... with
a translation into English verse, and critical observations on the
nature of such writings, to render the work useful to those that do
not understand the Galic language', to which he tried, though alas
in vain, to 'bespeak, if possible, the favour of the public', in the
preface to his ill-fated volume of poetry. It is not too much to imagine
MacDonald in these circumstances becoming the Gaelic poet-
Laureate of Scotland like his namesake Iain Lom, writing stirring
verses to commemorate the glorious victory and triumphant
crowning of his Prince, recasting the national traditions and reviving
the themes of the classical Gaelic poetry. It is even possible that the
creation of a Chair of Celtic in Scotland might have been anticipated

by a hundred and thirty years, a position which MacDonald could then certainly have occupied with credit. It was not to be, however, and the abilities of this remarkable man remained wasted – wasted even more than they had been before the Prince landed in Moidart.

In that brief hour MacDonald found himself, and gave us as a consequence some of the finest modern Gaelic poetry that has been ever written, and what is certainly one of the most interesting accounts of the 'Forty-five that we possess. What else he might have done, was not to be. In a Scotland where Whiggery had triumphed, a traditionalist patriot could expect neither advancement nor esteem.

Note

In a short account like this, it has not seemed necessary to burden the text with references. The authorities consulted are as follows:

The Lockhart Papers, Vol. II (London 1817), pp. 479–510 (Aufrere, A. (1817)).

The Lyon in Mourning (Scottish History Society, Vols.I–III, 1895–6).

Prince Charlie, by Compton MacKenzie (1932).

Galick and English Vocabulary, by Alexander McDonald, Schoolmaster at Ardnamurchan (1741).

Ais-eiridh na Sean Chanoin Albannaich, le Alasdair MacDhonuill, Edinburgh 1751.

The Poems of Alexander MacDonald, edited by the Rev. A. MacDonald, Killearnan, and the Rev. A. MacDonald, Kiltarlity; Inverness, 1924 (the latest complete edition).

Transactions of the Gaelic Society of Inverness, Vol. XI (1884–85) (William Mackay's article 'Presbyterial Notices of Mac Mhaighstir Alasdair').

Gaelic MS. 63 of the National Library of Scotland.

The translations quoted are all my own. Some of them are taken unaltered from *Highland Songs of the 'Forty-five*, where a short account of Alexander MacDonald is given.

The First Printed Gaelic Vocabulary

•

Published in *Scots Magazine*, October 1937, pp. 51–7.

The first printed Scottish Gaelic Vocabulary published as a separate book is that written by Alexander MacDonald, the well-known Gaelic poet, and published in 1741. It is entitled in English 'A *Galick* and *English* Vocabulary, with an Appendix of the Terms of Divinity in the said Language. Written For the Use of the Charity-Schools, founded and endued in the *Highlands* of *Scotland*, by the Honourable, the Society for propagating Christian Knowledge, by Mr Alexander M'Donald, Schoolmaster at *Ardnamurchan* in *Argyleshire*. Edinburgh: Printed by Robert Fleming, and sold by Mris *Brown* in the Parliament-Closs. MDCCXLI.' The Vocabulary consists of vi and 194 pages, being a word list divided into ninety-eight sections under different headings.

The circumstances of the publication of this Vocabulary seem never to have been described in detail. As is well known, the SPCK in Scotland was begun in 1709 by a band of zealous Whigs in Edinburgh, with the purpose of founding schools and employing schoolmasters and catechists in the Highlands and Islands in order to supplement the parochial schools for which the local heritors were responsible under the Act of Parliament of 1696. It is easy to understand that in the not infrequent case of the heritors being opposed to the Government in politics and religion, the minimum of encouragement was often given by them to the parochial schools in these areas. The intention of the original founders of the SPCK was to remedy this deficiency. Their policy was frankly partisan, sectarian, political and intolerant.

The Society had hardly begun when the Rising of 1715 put their whole work in jeopardy. The suppression of this Rising added flames to their zeal. In a Memorial to the Court of Police issued by the General Meeting of the SPCK on 2nd June 1716, in which the usefulness of the Society to the then Government is touched on, the policy is outlined:

> Nothing can be more effectuall for reducing those countries (i.e., the Highlands and Islands) to order and making them usefull to the Commonwealth than teaching them their duty to God, their King and Countrey, and rooting out their Irish (i.e., Gaelic) language, and this has been the care of the Society so far as they could for all the schollars

are taught in English, and none are allowed to be masters of the Societie's Charitie Schools, but such as produce sufficient certificates of their piety knowledge and loyalty.

On 15th March 1723, the General Meeting of the SPCK, hoping to obtain for their use the sum of £20,000 from the Forfeited Estates that was expected to be devoted for the purpose of 'education' in the Highlands, addressed another Memorial, this time to Members of Parliament, in which the Society explains its purpose at greater length:

> Tho' many in these countries (i.e. the Highlands and Islands who have had the advantage of education[1] are persons of honour, and good affection to the Government, yet by reason of the forsaid unhappy circumstances of these places, the Reformation from popery has never effectually reached some of them, yea there remains vestiges of the old Heathenish Customs and superstitions among them, but especially popish Idolatrie and superstition continues with many, and gross ignorance and prophanitie with most of them, and this joined with their neighbourhood to, and Identitie in Language with the native Irish, makes them to be of the same mind, and to pursue the same interests, both as to Religious and Civil respects and those altogether inconsistent with the safety of our present happy Constitution, for they depend upon the Pope as head of the Church, upon a popish pretender as their lawfull sovereign, and upon foreign popish powers as the main strength of their hopes and Expectations ... If the forsaid twenty thousand pounds were made effectual and the management thereof put in right hands, the Interest of it, with what the Societie will in course of time be able to do, may go a great way towards the maintaining as many Schools, as will through the blessing of God be a most effectual mean of Extirpating the Irish Language out of Scotland, of instructing in the principles of religion and virtue and consequently civilizeing that rude Ignorant and deluded people.

The Society, however, failed to obtain possession of the £20,000, and this golden prospect was never fully realised.

The subjects taught in the SPCK schools were reading and writing of English, Arithmetic and Church music. The teaching of Latin was forbidden and the use of Gaelic entirely prohibited.

Difficulties immediately arose from the absurd language policy of the Society in the Gaelic-speaking area, which was the more stupid as there already existed Gaelic translations of the Bible, Metrical Psalms and Catechism, which could easily have been used in their Highland schools. In 1719 James Murray, schoolmaster at Struan in Atholl, wrote to the Committee saying that he was teaching

> the Children to read Ye Irish Catechism and Irish Psalms, after they can read ye Scriptures in English, and that he does this for the good of their

ignorant parents who understand not English; That ye Children, when they come home at night, may be in case to read in the Families for the Edification thereof

and asking for some Irish Psalmbooks. The Committee

ordered a Letter to be written to the said Mr James Murray shewing that the Society are resolved to give no encouragement to the Teaching to read in the Irish Language and will therefore furnish no books for that purpose.

A year later (March 1720) Mr James Robertson, minister at Balquhidder, wrote to the Committee that

the people there are very desireous to have their Children taught to read the Irish Psalm book after they can read the Bible in English, which he thinks would be a good use in families who have nothing but Irish.

The Committee replied to Mr Robertson that

the Societie have resolved that none of their schoolmasters shall teach to read Latine or Irish, but English only, and that they expect that he'll take care to see that this is observed in his Schools.

At the next meeting of the Committee a letter was ordered to be written to all schoolmasters of the Society forbidding the teaching of Irish or Latin, and ordering presbyteries and ministers in their visitations to see this carried out.

At the General Meeting of the SPCK on 1st June 1721, three ministers, Mr Murdo MacLeod, Mr Walter Ross and Mr John Mackay, appeared and presented a petition, to the effect that

through a defect of the present method of teaching in some of the Societie's schools in their Highland bounds (i.e. in the vast majority of the SPCK schools) these good ends are much frustrate, for in places where nothing of the English tongue is understood, the Children are taught to read only in English which they understand not, and are denied the benefit of expounding and translating the same by the help of their masters into their mother tongue as is the ordinary fashion and practice of the Grammar Schools and thus return home able indeed to read the Bible but understand not the plainest Historical part of what they read, and after residing in the Country where they hear nothing but Irish, in a little time they entirely forget what with much Labour and Long time they acquired, which as it proves a great disencouragement to the parents to send them to school. So the principle design of the Society in Propagating Christian knowledge is thereby obstructed.

They go on to suggest that

the teachers in their bounds be strictly enjoined, constantly to exercise their Scholars to the translation of the Catechism and Bible and what other English books they read into the Irish, and when once they come to read English, to put in their hands the translations of the Shorter Catechism and psalm book which they have in vulgar Irish (the last of which they sing in all their Churches by order of Assembly) that they may collate and compare these translations, which method as it is the only way to make them capable to understand what they read, and when they return home to instruct their Ignorant parents who understand not English. So they take it to be the only way to extirpate the Irish Language and that for the reasons following, viz.:

The exercising of the boys at School to a ready Converting of English into Irish and reading the principles of Religion in both languages as it will instruct themselves, so it will make them capable to Exercise and instruct their Ignorant parents at home, who are of themselves extreamly fond of knowledge and are sensible that their Ignorance of the English Language is their great loss, by being thereby excluded from all Commerce, Conversation and Correspondence, with the rest of the nation, and by the having of it, promise to themselves access to employments, Stations or offices that might afford them advantage, and the parents having once understood English, the Babies from the knees would receive the same as their mother tongue, which would be the only finishing Stroak to the Irish Language, and so soon as it is understood, the Minister will embrace the favourable opportunity of being relieved from the most unsupportable burden of preaching and teaching in Irish, to effectuate all which they take the method proposed in their judgement to be the only effectual way, since the boys having acquired at School a readiness of converting either language, such performances will upon their return home become the constant exercise of the whole family and the subject of their conversation, the principles of Religion.

The Committee, having considered the matter, expressed the opinion (13th July 1721) that

the Schoolmasters should be at much pains in learning the Schollars to translate the English, but not to learn them to read Irish,

being apparently in fear of the reaction that might ensue were the Highlanders taught to read Gaelic books or manuscripts. This did not end the matter. On 21st June 1722:

The Committee finding that the teaching Highland children to read English, unless at the same time they be made to understand what they read, is but lost labour. They named Messrs Alexander McLeod, Robert Stewart, Neil Mcvicar, professor Hamilton, and Baillie Thomas Dundas, as a Sub-Committee to consider this case and how the inconvenience may be cured and report.

The report of the Sub-Committee, presented on 4th April 1723, resulted in the Committee's writing a letter to the presbyteries in

Gaelic-speaking parishes on this and other questions, which is recorded in the General Meeting Minutes of 6th June 1723:

> The Committee shewed that they had had under consideration some overtures for the better improvement of the Societie's funds, Setleing parochial schools, extirpating the Irish Language, and Regulation of the Bounties bestowed on poor Schollars, and had not only communed with such ministers as have charitie schools in their parishes that were up at the Assemblie, and desired them to lay these Overtures before the Presbyteries. But had written Letters to the Presbyteries concerned to send up their opinions about these Overtures, all this the Societie approved of, and desired the Committee to prepare the forsaid overtures against the nixt General Meeting, and having heard the said Letter read, they ordered the same to be recorded. The tenor whereof follows.
>
> Edinburgh the fifth of April one thousand seven hundred and twenty three years.
>
> Reverend Sir, It is informed that in some places due care is not taken to bring the Societie's Schollars to understand in English what they learn to read, which is wrong, and therefore it is desired the Reverend Ministers in your bounds may seriously consider the matter, and propose the best remedy they can for helping it. And among other things it is thought 1mo. That as soon so the Schollars begin to read the Catechism the master should teach them to understand their Lessons by turning and causeing the Schollars to translate from English into Irish each question or Lesson, before they enter them to another, and so on through the whole course of their reading. And when the Schollars begin to write the same method be observed in their Copies.
>
> 2do. That all the Schollars be exhorted to Learn to speak English and told the advantage thereof, and that none who can speak any of it, be allowed to speak Irish, except when turning it into English, for the benefite of these who are learning the same, and that Censors be named to delate transgressors therein, and whither an English and Irish vocables may not be of use in this matter, and Schollars obliged to Learn so many words weeklie, and dispute the same every Saturday.

Two further paragraphs relate to the bounty for poor scholars and the possibility of pupils being sent 'to some Lowland School where nothing but English is spoke' after having finished their course at the SPCK schools, and the opinion of the Presbyteries upon these questions is invited.

This letter, which presumably was based on the opinions of the Sub-Committee, contains the first reference to the English-Gaelic Vocabulary which eventually was to appear in 1741.

Meanwhile, the prohibition against imparting that dangerous accomplishment, the ability to read Gaelic, was continued. On 7th May 1724, the Committee's Minutes record a letter sent to the schoolmaster at St Kilda forbidding him 'to teach any to read the

Bible in Irish but only in English', notwithstanding the fact that, in the words of the Rev. John Richardson,[2] 'it is the avowed Doctrine and Principle of all the Reformed Churches that all Men have a right to search the Scriptures, and that in order thereunto, they should be translated into all Languages ... to lock up the Scriptures and the Service of God in an unknown Tongue, what is this but in effect to forbid men to know God?' Quite clearly the SPCK had no scruples about locking up the Scriptures in an unknown tongue for the Highlanders so long as the political *gleichschaltung* of the Highlands and Islands might be promoted by such methods.

References to the proposed Gaelic vocabulary now become frequent. On 1st April 1725, the Committee

> Appointed their Clerk to look over their former minutes, and that of the General meeting, in this manner, and to Lay an account of what is done therein before Mr Alexander Macleod, Mr Neil Mcvicar, Professor Hamilton and Mr Robert Stewart with the Treasurer who are to prepare and bring in an Overture upon this head, and also to consider the best means for extirpating the Irish Language and Learning the Societie's Schollars to speak English, and about providing an English Grammar for masters, and Likewise an Irish vocables.

At the meeting of 4th May 1725, this Sub-Committee was asked to report as soon as possible. On 25th June 1725, the Committee,

> having considered the Remite of the General Meeting concerning the most ready method for extirpating the Irish Language and teaching their schollars to speak English, are of opinion, that besides the orders formerly given in this matter, That the Schoolmaster should oblige their (*sic*) Schollars every Saturday to get by turn a certain number of Irish words into English, and for their help in this, that there be written an English and Irish vocabulary, and sent to these schools where Irish is spoke, and the Committee having had diverse English and Latine vocabularies laid before them, they make choice of that Entituled the new vocabularie for the use of Schools, to which is added a Collection of the most Comon Adjectives to Verbs, the fifth edition printed by Mr James McEwing anno one thousand seven hundred and twenty, and appointed that a letter be written to the Presbytery of Lorn, entreating they may nominate one of their number to compose the said Irish vocabularie, by puting Irish in place of Latine in that above-mentioned, and Mr William Morison one of the said presbytery being now in this city, the Clerk was ordered to put the said vocables and Letter in his hand to be delivered to the said presbytery.

The General Meeting of the SPCK approved of this step on 4th November 1725, and on 6th January 1726, the Committee Minutes record a letter from the Presbytery of Lorne saying that they were 'preparing a vocabulary English and Irish according to the Societie's desire'. Thereafter there was silence on the part of the Presbytery. On 3rd August 1727, the General Meeting Minutes record that

> the Committee Reported, That the presbytery of Lorn not having yet composed the Irish vocabulary, They had written them to dispatch the same. The General Meeting remitted back to their Committee to deal with the presbytery, that they without furder delay end the foresaid vocabulary, which will be of great use to the schools.

The Committee wrote to the Presbytery again on 15th August 1727 and 2nd November 1727, sending fresh reminders. Unluckily there is a gap in the Minutes of the Presbytery of Lorne during this period, so the other side of the correspondence cannot be traced. But the reminders of the Committee entirely failed to expedite the writing of the Vocabulary, and there is no further mention of it in the Minutes of either the Committee or the General Meeting for nearly eleven years until 8th June 1738.

During this time the Committee and the General Meeting considered, in 1737, and rejected, the proposal of the Rev. David McColm, minister of Dudingston, that they should buy a copy of his projected English and Irish Dictionary (which was never published) for each of their schools, 'as tending to promote Learning' – a welcome change from 'in order to extirpate the Irish Laguage'.

On 8th June 1738, (how had the schoolmasters got on in the meantime?) the Committee

> having considered a Letter from the said Presbytery (i.e. of Mull, with which that of Lorne had been united) about an Irish Vocabulary Revised by them, orders that they be Desired to send the same hither with a subscribed attestation of their having Examined that performance with a proper Recommendation of its usefulness for the Highlands.

On 16th November 1738, there was

> produced a letter from the Presbytery of Mull of date the sixth Current with an Irish English vocabulary composed by Alexander McDonald one of the Society's Schoolmasters in their Bounds and Revised and ammended by a Select Committee of the said Presbytery, which work has been carried on pursuant to an Act and Remit of the General Meeting of the Society dated the Fourth Day of November Seventeen hundred and twenty five years to the Presbytery of Lorn the same being intended as a mean to introduce the use of the English Language more universally into their country. The said Alexander McDonald being present The Committee remitted to Mr John Walker, Mr Albert Munro, Mr John Hepburn and the Treasurer to meet to-morrow at Eleven of the Clock in this place and advise with some printers as to the expence

of printing a Competent Number of the Said Vocabulary for the benefit of the Charity Schools, what allowance should be given to the said Alexander McDonald for his trouble and Labour in the said work and Report.

Alexander MacDonald – whom Bishop Forbes in 1747 (Paton, H. (1895–6)) described as 'remarkably well skilled in the Erse, for he can both read and write the Irish language in its original character, a piece of knowledge almost quite lost in the Highlands of Scotland ... several of (his) acquaintances have told me that he is by far the best Erse poet in all Scotland' – had been a schoolmaster in the employment of the SPCK in Ardnamurchan since 1731. Later he was to be dismissed and become a Catholic and join Prince Charles's army, in which he held a commission. How and when he was commissioned to write, or rather to translate, the *Galick and English Vocabulary*, is still unknown. Much sententious praise has been lavished upon MacDonald for his originality in writing the Vocabulary and upon the SPCK for their zeal for Highland education by writers who were patently unaware that the Vocabulary was simply a translation, sometimes a clumsy and unidiomatic translation, of a Latin-English word-list, and that its composition was ordered, not to further the study of Gaelic, but with the express purpose of 'extirpating' it.

On 20th November 1738, the Sub-Committee recommended that MacDonald be paid the sum of £10, which was agreed to by the Committee and ordered by the General Meeting on 8th March 1739, at the same time that the printing of the Vocabulary was decided.

On 20th November 1740, the Committee Minutes record:

An account due to Robert Fleming for printing the Irish English Vocabulary and price of paper amounting in all to Fourty Five pounds ten shillings sterling which being produced read and inspected the Committee granted Warrant for payment thereof.

At the General Meeting of 19th March 1741, it was agreed

That an English and Irish Vocabulary prepared in consequence of a recommendation of this Society, and Revised by the Presbyterie of Mull, is printed and published for the benefite of the Charity Schools in the Highlands of this Country, as a mean for the young one's at these schools, their better understanding the English language. The Genl. Meeting Recommended to their committee to cause distribute Copys of the said Vocabulary to the several Schools in the Highlands.

Of the contents of the Vocabulary it is not necessary to say anything here. Though swarming with misprints, and in its construction actually a Latin-English Vocabulary Word-list, not a Gaelic-English one (some of the commonest Gaelic words being absent), it is a work of considerable linguistic interest, giving many words in their Scottish, as opposed to their literary or Irish form for the first time. Its re-editing in alphabetical order, with cross-references, was in the hands of the writer of this article, aided by the late Professor James Carmichael Watson. It had been hoped to produce a new edition in time to mark the bi-centenary of the original publication, but this could not be done.

The Expurgating of Mac Mhaighstir Alasdair

·

Published in *Scottish Gaelic Studies*, Vol. XII, pp. 59–76, 1971.

The importance of Alexander MacDonald (c. 1698–1770), Alasdair mac Mhaighstir Alasdair, to Scottish Gaelic literature and lexicography is fundamental. He was the compiler or rather the translator into Gaelic[3] of the first extensive printed Scottish Gaelic vocabulary, which he was commissioned to prepare for the Society for Propagating Christian Knowledge in Scotland (hereafter in this article referred to as the SPCK), and which the Society published in 1741, and he was the author of the first book of original Gaelic poetry to be published, the famous *Ais-eiridh*,[4] which appeared in 1751, and which perhaps was intended to encourage the Highlanders to support a new rising that was a possibility in that year. Alexander MacDonald wielded an immense vocabulary with remarkable vigour, and his influence is still felt today.

It is, however, notable that five of the poems in his first edition have not appeared in print since the supplement to the edition of 1839, though four editions have been printed since that date. These also omit the last stanza of his well-known poem, *Moladh Móraig* which, however, survives in one of the anthologies, *Sàr Obair nam Bàrd*, as will be described later.

Trouble about these poems, and possibly others, began early. On 4th June 1745 the Committee of the SPCK recorded in its Minutes that:

> It's represented ... that Alexr. McDonald Schoolmaster at Ardnamurchan is an offence to all Sober Well inclin'd persons as he wanders thro' the Country composing Galick songs, stuffed with obscene language. The Committee having heard the said Letter do overture to the General Meeting [of the SPCK] that they write to the Synod of Glenelg a Letter touching the above particulars in their Bounds, that they may make strict enquiry thereanent, And having heard read over the letter from the Presbytery of Mull, anent Alexr. McDonald mentioned in Minutes of the ffourth of April last [concerning his absence from his school during most of the summer of 1744, when his son was supplying for him] Resolved to consider his case at making up the Establishment for the year ensuing.

On 13th June the Committee recorded receipt of an inspection of MacDonald's school on 28th April, which had revealed that contrary to the rules of the Society the situation of the school had been altered by the minister or presbytery without the Society's authority. The final word on MacDonald and his school comes in the Committee's Minutes for 4th July 1745:

> Upon considering the serial Representations given of the conduct of Alexr. McDonald Schoolmaster at Coirvulan in the parish of Ardnamurchan, who has as is now informed left his Station, Resolved he be dismist the Society's service and ordered to be left out of next Scheme.

MacDonald was, in fact, about to return to the traditional Jacobitism of his clan, the MacDonalds of Clanranald, to whose politics and religion the SPCK was bitterly opposed. Six years later the first edition of his poems was published in Edinburgh. Some of the poems in it, as is well known, contain scathing attacks on the Hanoverians and impassioned appeals to the Highlanders to rise and free themselves from the yoke of the Whigs. The Rev. Donald MacLean in his *Typographia Scoto-Gadelica* says that in one of the dozen or so surviving copies of this book a remark is written in to the effect that the common hangman had burnt many copies of the book in Edinburgh in 1751. Simon Fraser in his *Airs and Melodies of the Highlands of Scotland and the Isles*, for which the Letter and Prospectus is dated 1st November 1815, says (p. 111) that 'the burning of MacDonell's (*sic*) collection of the jacobite songs, is an event now to be regretted, when they can no longer affect the public mind'. But no record of any official order for the book's destruction has yet been discovered.

The 1751 edition of MacDonald's poems contained thirty-two pieces of which three are translations, two others are attributed to John MacCodrum (Matheson, W. (1938)) and one that is omitted from the post-1839 editions is not mentioned in the list of contents. Later editions of MacDonald's poems were enlarged to include poems from anthologies, particularly from the Eigg Collection published by his son Ranald in 1776, from MSS, and from oral tradition (see ante pp. 134–137). At the same time the poems which various editors considered to be objectionable were dropped. It is best to describe the various editions first.

1764. This is a very rare book, of which only one copy is known to exist, that in the library of the Marquess of Bute, at Mount Stuart in Bute. It is simply a reprint of part of the preface to the first edition, and of thirteen of the poems there.[5] MacLean says in *Typographia* that 'All the *free* pieces in the First Edition are expurgated with the exception of *Mio-Mholadh*

Moraig'. But it is not a question of expurgation: this edition is a reprint of part of the 1751 edition, less than half of it in fact, not an expurgated version.

1802. This is a reprint of the 1751 edition word for word.

1834 (1835).[6] Edited by John MacKenzie. The 'free pieces' are dropped, as is the political poem called the 'Ark'; some poems are added from the Eigg Collection and from oral tradition. Extensive liberties are taken in the way of modernising the orthography and usages of the 1751 and 1802 text.

1839. MacLean says this is a reprint of the 1834 edition with the addition of a Supplement containing a Memoir and a reprint of the poems that were omitted from the 1834 edition.

1851. MacLean says this is a reprint of the 1834 edition.

1874. This was the edition prepared by D. C. MacPherson, a member of the staff of the Advocates Library, a native of Lochaber and cousin of Fr Allan McDonald. MacPherson was by the standards of his time a very competent Gaelic scholar. In his obituary in the *Celtic Magazine* his edition is referred to as 'a new, accurate and complete edition of Mac Mhaighstir Alasdair's poems' (Vol. V. p. 392). In fact, it was anything but complete: MacPherson left out all the 'free pieces', plus the last stanza of *Moladh Móraig*. In fact, his delicacy did not even allow him to print the word for the female breasts in full: on several occasions it appears as *c–chan*.

1892. This is a reprint of the edition of 1874.

1924. The edition published by the Rev. A. MacDonald, Killearn, and the Rev. A. MacDonald, Kiltarlity, at Inverness. This edition includes the poems from MS LXIII which Professor Donald MacKinnon had published in Vol. V of the *Celtic Review* in 1924. The basis of the rest of the editors' text is MacPherson's edition of 1874. All the poems are accompanied by translations. The 'free pieces' and the last stanza of *Moladh Móraig* are of course absent, but the editors at least print words like *cìochan* in full.

At this point it is as well to list the material that has been excluded from the later editions.

The last stanza of Moladh Móraig *(1751 ed. p. 25)*
This, as I have said, was allowed to remain in the 1834 edition, and also got into *Sàr Obair*, which was prepared by the same editor, John MacKenzie (and presumably has remained there ever since, later editions having been printed from stereotypes). It was dropped with

no comment whatever by D. C. MacPherson in 1874. The editors of the 1924 edition at least admit its existence: they add a note to say that 'In the Bard's 1st Edition 16 line appear which are hardly printable.'

What this verse says, in effect, is that when the author awoke, he found that it was his wife Jean who was in bed with him, and not Mórag; Jean excited him, and he made love to her. This would hardly be considered unprintable today; and it raises the interesting question whether the verses extravagantly praising Mórag, and the poem extravagantly dispraising her, are not simply based on dreams or fantasies, whereas commentators like John MacKenzie have taken it for granted that Mórag was a real person and have been scandalised by the contrast between MacDonald's praise and dispraise of her.

Mio-mholadh Móraig *(1751, p. 26; 1764, p. 14; 1802, p. 38; 1839, p.193)*
Fourteen verses of sixteen lines (as printed), same metre and air as *Moladh Móraig*. When Mac Mhaighstir Alasdair dispraises a woman, he does it thoroughly. Mórag is portrayed as a promiscuous nymphomaniac with every possible moral and physical defect. But the way that this is done discredits not only the bard's original judgment, but also his eyesight. When he says

> Ma ghabhar i mar chí,
> Tha sgeamh amuidh gle líobh;
> Ach, fa sin tha míltion
> Do dhóibhertion:

'If she is taken as she appears, there is highly polished beauty on the outside, but beneath that there are thousands of vices', and elaborates this with the simile of a beautiful tree that is affected with internal decay, he describes a human experience that is natural and likely enough. But when he goes on to abuse her outward appearance

> Cruinn aodann a mhunci
> Air crupadh ri chéile;
> A suilin ar lasadh
> Mar laisidh na 'n éilon,

'A round monky face, wrinkled together, her eyes burning like glowing coals.' The reader will ask how the bard could have been so naive as to have been infatuated with her. The poems leave the impression of being a *tour de force* in fantasy.

Oran nam Bodach *(1751, p. 123; 1802, p. 135; 1839, p. 207)*
Fifteen sixteen-line verses. Entitled in the text *Oran a rinneadh do dha bhodach árraid a bha ann an Ardnomorchuan, a chotharraich iad fein le bhi cur ri striopachas ann an aois an ceithir-fichid bliaghna. Air fonn,* Black Jock. That is, 'A song that was made to two certain old fellows in Ardnamurchan who distinguished themselves by taking to whoring at eighty years of age. To the tune of "Black Jock".' (This is the same tune MacDonald designates for his song *A Theárlaich mhic Sheumais.*)

Oran nam Bodach is a rousing ribald song, composed with a considerable amount of wit, on a subject that has always given rise to ribaldry.

> Tha cleachdadh mio-nadorr,
> 'N drasd ann a's tírs',
> Na h oigfhir nan codul,
> 'S na sean daoin' ri suiridh;

'There is an unnatural habit just now in this district, the young men are asleep and the old men are making love.'

Marbhrainn na h Aigionnaich' *(1751, p. 153; 1802, p. 165; 1839, p. 200)*
Thirteen eight-line verses. Headed in the text *Marbhrainn Máiri nian Ean Mhic-Eun, do'n gairte, an Aigionnach. Air fonn, Piobaireachd.* 'Elegy of Mary the daughter of John, son of John, called the "Aigionnach". To the tune of a pibroch.' Mock elegy on a woman who was apparently notorious in Moidart and surrounding districts. It goes straight to the point, which is an obscene one.

The Highland Society's Dictionary translates *Aigeannach* as 'Une fille de joye', giving the context of the title in MacDonald's 1802 edition. This meaning has been omitted from Dwelly's Dictionary. In the Inverness Collection of Gaelic songs (*Co-Chruinneacha Dhan, Orain, etc.,* 1821), *Oran do Bhean Chlaoth-na-Macrui leis an Aigeanagh* (*sic*) is printed (p. 123) with the following note at the end:

> This famous Poetess left few productions worthy of being preserved. This Poem is an exception, and though of the panegyric kind, is characteristic of the Authoress. Independence, originality, and ease, were the prominent features of her mind ... Had she not prostituted her genius at the shrine of immorality, she might rank next Mairi nighean Alasdair Ruaidh, and Mairerad ni Lachuin – and the Highlands might boast of three unrivalled modern Poetesses, of three Highland Clans, MacLeod, Macdonald and Maclean.

Another poem by the Aigeannach, in praise of Lachlan MacKinnon, is printed in the Gillies Collection (1786, p. 129) and with the omission of the last five verses for no apparent reason, by MacLean Sinclair in his *Gaelic Bards from 1715 to 1765*. K. N. MacDonald in his *MacDonald Bards from Mediaeval Times* (1900) refers to her as 'this strong-minded clanswoman' and says that 'her songs were principally satires or lampoons', and goes on to remark that 'the numerous stories that are afloat regarding her encounters with the King of the Jacobite Bards, I have no doubt have been very much exaggerated'. He ends by saying that 'charity bids us draw a veil over the life of one who seemingly had many enemies'. Mac Mhaighstir Alasdair was certainly one of them; perhaps if the Aigeannach's lampoons had been preserved, we might have some idea of the reason.

Moladh air deagh bhod *(1751, p. 158; 1802, p. 170; 1839, p. 205)*
Eight lines. Not included in the list of contents. 'In praise of a good "member".' There is a remarkable resemblance to a poem in the Book of the Dean of Lismore by Duncan Campbell the Good Knight, *Bod brioghmhar atá ag Donnchadh*, see E. C. Quiggin's *Poems from the Book of the Dean of Lismore* (1937), p. 77.

A suppression and substitution by editors of MacDonald's poem *An Airce* may be noted here. The first verse at the head of p. 184 in the 1751 edition reads

> Achachrossain chiunn a chrostachd,
> Ceangail air bh-d ris an luing e,
> 'S 'nuair bhio's e réicil, 's ag osnaich,
> Slaod a's teach am poca puinnseoin:
>
>> 'Achachrossan, for his perversity, tie him by his member to the ship, and when he is howling and groaning, pull in the bag of poison.'

From 1874 onwards the editions have *Ceangail air sgroig ris an luing e*, which the editors of the 1924 edition translate 'Tie Achachrossan tightly by the neck on to the ship for all his temper vile'.

Oran do'n gairir Tinneas na h Urchaid *(1751, p. 159; 1802, p. 171; 1839, p. 205)*
Eight quatrains. In the text said to be *Air fonn, Tha me-fhin suarach ma ghruaman an tsean duin'*, &c. 'To the tune of "I am indifferent about the old man's grumpiness"' (an air I have not been able to recover while recording traditional songs in Uist and Barra).

Urchaid is defined in MacDonald's own glossary to the 1751 edition as 'vexation, confusion, &c'. So the title of the song might be translated 'The Vexatious Sickness'. On the subject of the spread of venereal diseases in the Ardnamurchan district, where they may well have been brought by English miners sent to work in the lead mines at Strontian. Sir Alexander Murray of Stanhope had acquired the estate of Ardnamurchan and discovered these mines, in 1724, and after a few years attempted exploitation by a company formed by the Duke of Norfolk and others, the lease was made over to the York Building Company, who worked them until 1740 (Cameron, A. (1937)).

This poem would undoubtedly offend the spirit of the Indecent Advertisements Act of 1889; but at the same time it is an important source for the medical history of the Highlands. A medical friend informs me that Mac Mhaighstir Alasdair's description of the symptoms is an accurate one.

The 1839 Edition

This edition has an English title page 'The Poetical Works of Alexander MacDonald, the celebrated Jacobite Poet; now first collected, with a short account of the author'. 'Now first collected' implies that this is the first complete edition. In the 'Memoir' or account of the author, disapproval of the 'Satires' is expressed; but on the same page (xiii) it is stated that 'Several persons having expressed a wish to obtain the works of Macdonald complete. To supply this demand, a small impression of the supplement has been printed, with this brief and imperfect account of the author and his works.'

This supplement occupies pages 181–214. It contains the five poems described above, that had been dropped in the 1834 edition, also the Ark, printed as eight-line stanzas, and *Oran d'a Chéile Nuadh Phòsda*, printed as four-line stanzas, and perhaps dropped from the 1834 edition on the assumption that the blanks in the text had some improper significance, though it seems much more probable that they were due to stains or other illegibility in the original manuscript. The 1839 edition's supplement also contains a lampoon that is not known from any other source. This is

Oran do'n Bhana Bhard nigh'n an Notair *(pp. 204–5)*
'A Song to the Poetess, daughter of the Notary'
Five eight-line stanzas. The poem is of the same nature as *Marbhrainn na h-Aigionnaich*. The first verse makes clear the nature of the provocation that the authoress had given:

A nighean Donnchaidh duibh Nòtair,
  Bha thu gòrach nuair thòisich
Thu dhìteadh Clann Chamshroin,
  'S Clann Dòmhnaill a' chruadail;
Mur rachadh na fir ud
  A mhilleadh le luaidhe,
Gun tugadh na gillean
  Dhe [d'] chinne na cluasan.

'O daughter of black Duncan the Notary, you were foolish when you began to condemn Clan Cameron and valorous Clan Donald; if those men had not been killed by lead, they would have smitten the ears off your clansmen.'

The lady, who was a Campbell, comes in for a good deal more abuse in MS LXIII, of which more below; '*s nion usa an fher gan eibhta donnchadh glé dhudh Nótair*' 'you are the daughter to the man called very black Duncan the Notary' (*Scottish Gaelic Studies* Vol. IV, p. 109, line 60). It is clear that she had been guilty of lampooning the Highland Jacobites, and had thereby infuriated Mac Mhaighstir Alasdair.

Before discussing the denunciations that have been made of some of these poems by various editors and commentators something must be said of the expurgation of MacDonald's poems from other sources.

The Donald MacLeod Collection, 1811

This printed, for the first time, a piece entitled *Rann Cainidh, Eadar Alaistair Domhnullach, Mac Mhaighstir Alaistair, agus Aireach a bha aig Mac Illeoin Mhuille*, i.e. 'A Flyting between Alasdair MacDonald, son of Mr Alasdair, and a Herdsman of MacLean of Mull'. So far as MacDonald is concerned, it is feeble stuff, and one wonders if his part of the flyting has been lost. The poem was not included in the 1834 edition, but D. C. MacPherson printed it in his edition of 1874. It contains a line which in the MacLeod Collection (p. 246) reads

Do cheann iachdair ann sa'n rotraich

No such word as *rotrach* is to be found in the dictionaries. One can only assume that this is a misprint for *otraich* (in which the *o* can be short, cp. Dinneen) and that the line means 'Thy backside on the midden'. D. C. MacPherson could only bring himself to print *r-tr-ch* (and may thereby have expurgated a word that does not exist). The editors of the 1924 edition printed the line in full, but did not translate it, or the following one.

Gaelic MS LXIII of the National Library

The unpublished poems in this MS were printed by Professor Donald MacKinnon in Vols IV and V of the *Celtic Review* in normalised spelling in 1908. In the course of his comments he remarked that 'Several words and clauses in the MS, especially at the ends of lines, and in one or two cases at the beginning of lines, are now illegible, and have been omitted. In other cases whole lines, and even whole quatrains, are suppressed for quite a different reason. It is unfortunately the case that this truly great poet wrote and published much that ought never to have been composed, much less printed.' (*Celtic Review* Vol. 22).

In 1935 I published the complete text of MS LXIII as it stands, in Vol. IV of *Scottish Gaelic Studies*, pp. 70–137. There were no protests that I am aware of. A comparison of this with Professor MacKinnon's text and with the 1924 edition of MacDonald's poems shows that the editors of the latter carried Professor MacKinnon's suppressions a good deal further. Details are as follows. The numbering of the poems and the lines is as given in *Scottish Gaelic Studies* Vol. IV. In a good many cases a single line there is printed as two in the *Celtic Review* and the 1924 edition.

VI Shid i chulidh scha bi Nuligh *(S.G.S. IV 83)*
MacKinnon printed one verse, the fifth (out of six). (C.R. V 26).

The editors of the 1924 edition omitted the poem entirely. It is of a similar type to *Marbhrainn na h-Aigionnaich*, and is probably a lampoon on Black Notary Duncan's poetess daughter.

X Na habir na habir *(S.G.S. IV 91)*
MacKinnon suppressed four lines, 101–104 (C.R. V 120). They are also suppressed in the 1924 edition (p. 322).[7]

XI O gan digadh ar caulich garbh daoinach *(C.R. V 122)*
MacKinnon suppressed nothing here, but printed dots after *digadh* (*tigeadh*), suggesting something was illegible. There is nothing illegigible here in the MS. The opening line of this poem suggests it is meant to be sung to the tune of *O gun tigeadh mo robairneach gaolach.*

Rather surprisingly, the editors of the 1924 edition omitted this poem entirely.

XII O Thearlaich mhic Shemis *(S.G.S. IV 102)*
MacKinnon omitted the last half line of this poem, (C.R. IV 297). The editors of the 1924 edition went further and omitted the whole

of the last line and the half line preceding it, without indicating that anything had been suppressed. They also inadvertently left out line 96 (in the spelling of the MS, *Bidh a fion iad ro sherbh dhuit noir a phaighis du duais ris*, thus producing a verse which as printed (2 lines for 1 of the MS) has only 18 lines instead of 22 (1924 ed. p. 106).

XIII Sball beg míriaghuiltich lag láidir *(S.G.S. IV 105)*
MacKinnon omitted two words in line 20 (C.R. V 226) as did the editors of the 1924 edition (p. 326).

XIV Ga dé hug dhuit a bhrachdaid shalich *(S.G.S. IV 111)*
MacKinnon omitted half line 7 and the whole of line 8 (as printed in S.G.S.: C.R. V 230); half line 20; and half line 31 and the whole of line 32 (C.R. V 231). The editors of the 1924 edition omitted half line 20 and the whole of the second and eighth verses of the poem (1924 pp. 334, 336).

XVI Bha S: C: sin am a ro an triblaid ann *(S.G.S. IV 124)*
MacKinnon omitted half line 63, as does the 1924 edition (C.R. V 234; 1924 p. 354).

XVII Ha clannach ainimoil an drásda ann an Albainn *(S.G.S. IV 128)*
MacKinnon omitted lines 26, 27, 30, and half lines 31 and 32, in the third verse (C.R. V 295, 296), and half line 104 in verse 10 (C.R. V 299). The editors of the 1924 edition went much further, and omitted the whole of verses 3, 10 and 11, without any indication (verse 11 is admittedly only partly legible in the MS) (1924 pp. 338–346).

Apart from the hearsay report recorded by the Committee of the SPCK in 1745, already quoted, disapproval of Mac Mhaighstir Alasdair's 'free pieces' was first expressed in print, as far as I know, by John Reid in his *Bibliotheca Scoto-Celtica* in 1832. 'The compositions' Reid wrote 'show everything that is low, vile, and disgusting, both in sentiment and language ... "Dimoladh Moraig" "Marbh-rann na h-Aigionnach" &c are the very quintessence of indecency'. The anonymous author of the 'Memoir' which prefaces the 1839 edition wrote more reasonably 'He attacks people with little or no provocation, and pours forth torrents of the most scurrilous, filthy, and indecent abuse. If these pieces were not illuminated with frequent and splendid passages of poetry, they deserved to be buried in oblivion. It must be admitted that he lived in a rude age, when the decencies of life were little regarded.' On the same page of the book the writer announced the printing of the supplement containing these poems, which had been omitted from the 1835 (1834) edition.[8]

Reid's denunciation of these poems has been echoed by D. C. MacPherson in the preface to his edition of 1874,[9] by A. MacLean Sinclair in 1892 in *The Gaelic Bards from 1715 to 1765* (p. 129: the only poem by Mac Mhaighstir Alasdair printed in this anthology is *A Bhanarach dhonn a' Chruidh*), by Professor Donald MacKinnon when printing MS LXIII in 1908 (C.R. V 22), and by the editors of the 1924 edition. E. C. Quiggin apparently misquotes Reid in his famous article on Celtic Literature in the 1911 edition of the *Encyclopaedia Britannica* when he says that 'MacDonald is also the author of a number of poems in MS which have been called the quintessence of indecency'.

On the other hand MacDonald has been defended by John MacKenzie, who remarked in *Sàr Obair* that 'like most men of genius, who make some noise in the world, *Mac Mhaighstir Alasdair* has been much lauded on the one side by the party whose cause he espoused, and as much vilified, and in some instances, falsified, by the other party. Mr Reid, in his book *Bibliotheca Scoto-Celtica* seems to have had his information from the last mentioned source.' MacKenzie however in a note to *Moladh Móraig* referred to the *Diomoladh* as 'an instance of his disregard to truth and common decency, as well as of moral and poetical justice', which is true enough if the poems are to be taken *à pied de la lettre*. K. N. MacDonald, in *MacDonald Bards* (1900) remarked too that 'it is not surprising that a man of such conspicuous ability should have been marked out for criticism by weak-kneed, clean-shaven philistines, goody-goodies in various stages of hypocrisy, who went out of their way to collect any scandal that could be found out about him' (p. 27).

Before discussing the attitude that a modern editor might take to these poems, it must be pointed out that we are ignorant of the provocation that was given to Mac Mhaighstir Alasdair by the Aigionnach, and of the language used by the Oban poetess, daughter of Black Duncan the Notary. The editor of the Inverness Collection of 1821 refers to the Aigionnach as having 'prostituted her genius at the shrine of immorality', and K. N. MacDonald wrote that her poems were principally satires or lampoons, but none of her lampoons have been preserved, nor has the scurrilous attack on the Jacobites and the Stuart royal family made by the Oban poetess, which was something that was bound to exasperate any Highland Jacobite. Being ignorant of the lives and of language actually used by these two poetesses, who are unlikely to have minced their words, we cannot judge whether MacDonald's scathing and scatalogical attacks on them were excessive or not.[10]

Another matter that must be considered is MacDonald's own psychology. He was in some respects a strange man, and there are aspects of his career difficult to understand in the absence of the necessary information. Hitherto commentators have hardly appreciated the degree of political and sectarian tension that then existed in the Highlands and Islands, and which are revealed in unpublished sources such as the early Minutes of the SPCK in Scotland and the report of Fr Tyrie to Rome on the condition of the Highlands in 1739. For a man like Mac Mhaighstir Alasdair, son of a non-jurant Episcopalian minister and member of a Jacobite and mainly Catholic clan, which had welcomed the Irish Franciscan missionaries in the 1620s and the Vincentians in the 1650s, service for sixteen years as a schoolmaster for the SPCK, which was explicitly following then the policy of extirpating Catholicism, Episcopalianism and the Gaelic language from the Highlands and Islands, was (besides being far from commensurate with his abilities) a total negation of the principles of his clan, for which he might be expected to stand, and argues that for quite a number of years there must have been a serious breach between Mac Mhaighstir Alasdair and his chief, Clanranald. In a situation of such tension, another man might have taken to drink. Perhaps Mac Mhaighstir Alasdair sought an escape in composing scatalogical verse.

There remains to be considered what the attitude of a modern editor towards these particular poems should be. Noel Perrin, whose book *Dr Bowdler's Legacy* has inspired this article, quotes (p. 237) a statement on the question of the publication of the unexpurgated version of Pepys's diary by C. S. Lewis, which is very applicable here. Lewis pointed out that there were two questions involved, those of propriety and of morality. So far as propriety is concerned, it would be pusillanimous and unscholarly (as Lewis himself put it) for a future editor to omit these poems from a serious critical edition of MacDonald. Their lexicographical importance is immense, and they throw much light on the psychology of the author and on the times in which he lived. Their rejection from post-1839 editions has been accompanied by the acceptance of several poems of doubtful ascription and provenance such as *Màiri shùgaideach* and *Ailein, Ailein, 's fhad' an cadal*, and the total effect is to give a misleading picture of MacDonald and his poetry.

The question of morality is, would anyone who could now read these poems nowadays be corrupted by them? This, considering the present atmosphere of society, seems to be very unlikely. Translation is another matter; anyone who attempted it would need to have the expertise and vocabulary of Sir Thomas Urquhart or Sir Richard Burton to deal with verse containing such an extraordinary prolixity of symbolism and wealth of anatomical detail. The proper context for such poems is probably a reproduction of the 1751 edition with a comprehensive glossary.

Times have changed regarding what is considered unprintable. In MacDonald's own time direct political allusions or personal names were forbidden; some of the blanks even survive in the 1834 edition. Between 1840 and 1960, sexual matters were taboo. Nowadays it is references to race: children must be taught to say 'eena meena mina mo, catch a tiger by the toe'. In 1970 the most likely passage in Mac Mhaighstir Alasdair to be suppressed is the allusion to *Na Hotentots bhreuna* on page 159 of MS LXIII.[11]

Notes on Alexander MacDonald's 'Oran a' Gheamhraidh'

·

Published in *Eigse*, Vol. IX, pp. 57–60, 1958.

The last number of *Scottish Gaelic Studies* (Vol. VIII (1955), pp. 53–55) contains a note by Mr Walter J. Mays, ingeniously dating the composition of Alexander MacDonald's well-known poem to Winter from the days of the week mentioned in the opening stanza in connexion with the summer solstice. Mr Mays shows how the only possible dates that fit in with these are 1726, 1737 and 1743, and that the last is the only year that really conforms to MacDonald's data.

There is circumstantial evidence not mentioned by Mr Mays, which also points to the same conclusion. In the first place, it is well known that MacDonald's poems on Summer and Winter were written under the influence of James Thomson's poems on the Seasons. As I shall show, there are ideas in *Oran a' Gheamhraidh* which are probably derived from Thomson's poem on Autumn: but this was not published until 1730, so that 1726 is completely ruled out as a possible date for the composition of *Oran a' Gheamhraidh.*

Nor did MacDonald take up residence in Ardnamurchan until 1729; and until late in 1738 he was engaged in preparing his *Galick and English Vocabulary* for the Presbytery of Lorne which had been requested to find someone to do this work (which was that of replacing the Latin words in a Latin-English Vocabulary by Gaelic) by the SPCK in Edinburgh. It was doubtless in the course of this work, which was probably assisted by the Rev. John MacLean of Kilninian in Mull, and by Lhuyd's *Archeologica Britannica*, that MacDonald acquired the very large vocabulary which he wields in his poems. 1737 is therefore probably too early for *Oran a' Gheamhraidh* on the grounds that MacDonald was then engaged in other work; 1743 remains as the most likely date. On the other hand, references to birds singing matins and vespers have nothing to do with MacDonald's conversion to Catholicism, which certainly did not take place before 4th July 1745, the date he was dismissed by the SPCK, who had employed him as a schoolmaster since 1729, on the ground that he had abandoned his station without permission. Such expressions are almost certainly conceptions borrowed from Scots or English poetry, and owe nothing to the author's religion.

Apart from the dating of *Oran a' Gheamhraidh* certain difficulties of interpretation remain. Mr Mays prints the first stanza from a later text than the first (1751) edition, which is the authoritative source. This reads:

> Tharraig grian riogh n 'm plainéd 's na réull',
> Go *sign chancer* Diaceadaoin go beachd,
> A riaghlas comhthrom ma'n criochnaich é thriall,
> Da-mhios-déug na bliaghna ma seach;
> Ach gur he an darra, Diasathurn na dhéigh,
> A ghrianstad-shamhraidh, aondéug, an la 's faid;
> 'S a sin tiuntaidh e chúrsa go séamh,
> Go ses-ghrian a gheamhruidh gun stad.

which I would translate:

> 'The sun, the king of the planets and of the stars, approached the Sign of Cancer certainly on Wednesday, he who regulates the recurrence of the twelve months of the year, one by one, 'ere he completes his circuit; but the second Saturday afterwards is the summer solstice, the eleventh, the longest day; and then he turns his course gently and steadily towards the winter solstice.'

For *comhthrom* here compare Dinneen *comhthrom na h-aimsire seo anuraidh*, 'this time last year': is it not the idea here that the sun's journey gives each month an equal opportunity of recurring?

This translation assumes that *grian* is the antecedent of the relative clause *a riaghlas*. But the whole line strongly recalls line 24 of Thomson's poem on Autumn.

> 23. 'When the bright Virgin gives the beauteous days
> 24. And Libra weighs in equal scales the year'

So perhaps MacDonald sees the sign of Cancer as dividing the year into two equal halves, spring and summer against autumn and winter? The allusions to the signs of the Zodiac recall Thomson's poems also.

Another question that arises here is, why is *grian*, sun, without the article and made masculine (if it is the antecedent of *a riaghlas*)? Here it must be noted that there is another version of this poem on p. 38 of MS LXV of the National Library of Scotland,[12] written in quatrains, of which the first two numbered read as follows:

> Tharruing sol rí na mplanaid s na nrell
> gos an chonsort diciadain gu beachd
> ciall is comhthrom ma ncríchnuigh se thriall
> da mios deug na bliadhna ma nseach
> Sa ndara disathairne na dhiaigh
> chaidh an samhradh na deaghlach a mfad
> sin tiunndaighar cursa gu seimh
> ro theas gréine thig an geamhrad gun stad.

The words *na deaghlach* in the second line of the second quatrain are written in Roman hand above 'an d*eag*hg*h*lais' deleted.

This also has difficulties of interpretation. But it seems probable that before the poem was printed the word 'Sol' was removed from the first line and 'grian' substituted (as more intelligible to Gaelic readers) without any change being made to 'e' or 'thriall' in line 3. In any case, the sun so personified is considered masculine, *cp.* the Index to the article on Astronomy in the 1797 of *Encyclopaedia Britannica* where the sun is always referred to as 'he' and the moon as 'she'.

Hibernating Birds

The fifth stanza of *Oran a' Gheamhraidh*, referred to by Mr Mays, presents strong similarities to a passage in Thomson's poem on Autumn, lines 834 to 841. MacDonald writes in his 1751 edition, p. 45:

> Sguiridh búirdeiseach sgiathach na spéir
> D'an ceileiridh grianach car treis,
> Cha seinn iad a maidnén' go h árd,
> Na feasgurrain-chrábhach 's an phres:
> Codul cluthor go'n dean anns gach cós,
> Gabhail fasgadh ann frógamh na'n creg';
> 'S iad ri iuntrainn na'n gathanan blá,
> Bhiodh ri dealaradh o sgáileadh do theas.

MS LXV p. 39:

> 13. Togaidh buird*ea*saic*h* sgiathach na nspeur
>   da nceilar*adh* grianach car g*h*reis
>   sco sein*n* iad a matins gu hárd
>   na feispar sailm craibh*idh* na mpres
>
> 14. Codal clúm*har* gu nd*ea*n iad sga*ch* cós
>   gab*h*ail com*h*nid*h* a mfroguib*h* na ncreig
>   is iad aig caoi na ngaban*n*uib*h* tlá
>   b*h*i dearlad*h* fuig*h* sgáile do t*hea*s

The first may be translated:

> The winged burgesses of the heavens cease awhile from their sunny music, they do not sing their matins aloud, or their devout vespers in the bush: they sleep cosily in every hole, taking shelter in the crannies of the rocks, missing the warm rays which were radiating from the mask of thy heat.

Cp. Thomson, *Autumn*, lines 834–841:

> When Autumn scatters his departing gleams,
> Warn'd of approaching Winter, gather'd, play

> The swallow people, and, toss'd wide around,
> O'er the calm sky, in convolution swift,
> The feather'd eddy floats, rejoicing once
> Ere to their wintry slumbers they retire
> In clusters clung, beneath the mouldering bank,
> And where, unpierc'd by frost, the cavern sweats.

What became of swallows (and other summer migrants) in the winter time was a question hotly disputed by eighteenth-century ornithologists, and the belief that such birds hibernated in sheltered corners was only refuted towards the end of that era (see article on the Swallow in 1797 *Encyclopaedia Britannica*). The idea that such birds hibernated was a very old one, going back, according to the 1797 *Encyclopaedia* article, to Aristotle and Pliny. It is referred to by Robert Kirk, *The Secret Commonwealth*, p. 87: 'some Sort of Birds, that sleep all the Winter over, and revive in the Spring'. Fr Allan McDonald of Eriskay recorded (Campbell, J. L. (1958), p. 217) that 'the corncraik and stonechat are called *eoin shianta* on account of their disappearance in winter. The opinion is that they are dormant all winter, and that they should be so and not die makes people consider them eerie or uncanny or *sianta*.' The swallow itself is hardly known in the Outer Hebrides. Alexander MacDonald, however, seems to derive the idea rather from Thomson's poem than from Gaelic folklore (see Campbell, J. L. (1997), pp. 175–185).

'Whispering in Her Ear': Procreation Without Lust

Alexander MacDonald's elegy for his pet dove, killed by a terrier, contains the following lines (p. 152 of his first edition, 1751; all quotations here are taken from that edition or from MS LXIII of the National Library of Scotland, see S.G.S., Vol. IV):

> Bha do mhodh-siolaich air leath o chách,
> Cha togradh tu suas,
> Ach a durraghail an taca ri d' ghrágh,
> 'G cuir cogair 'n a cluais.

In the 1924 edition of his poems by the Rev. A. and the Rev. A. MacDonald, where *leth, taice, ghrádh* and *Cur cagair* are substituted (p. 18) for what the author published, these four lines are translated:

> Thy methods of courtship and making love
> Were all thine own,
> Cooing softly beside thy mate
> In a whispering tone!

– omitting any mention of her ear. These lines are omitted from the text printed by Professor W. J. Watson in *Bàrdachd Ghàidhlig* (1932 edition), where the poem is divided into four-line verses. In the 1924 edition of MacDonald poems, it is divided into two twelve-line verses and four eight-line ones.

I would translate these four lines: 'Thy method of breeding was different from the rest (i.e. of birds), you would not desire to mount, but cooing beside thy love, whispering in her ear.'

I could find no reference to this unusual habit of mating in the catalogue of folklore-motifs in my possession, and Dr Seán O Súilleabháin, formerly Registrar of the Irish Folklore Society, tells me that he does not know of any; but I think the problem is solved by an allusion in Miriam Rothschild's book, *Butterfly cooing like a Dove*, to the Blessed Virgin Mary's having conceived through a dove whispering in her ear, according to late medieval tradition (p. 124, illustrated by a reproduction of a painting by Carlo Crivelli on p. 125, and of a page from the illuminated MS *The Hastings Hours* on p. 102). But where MacDonald acquired knowledge of the tradition is still uncertain.

Since this was written, Meg Bateman then of the Department of Celtic of Aberdeen University very kindly sent a number of references to (1) the dove as a bird without lust, (2) the dove as a symbol of pure love, (3) the Virgin Mary conceiving Christ, from Irish Gaelic literature. Of these the most relevant to the passage in Mac Mhaighstir Alasdair is in the poem *Ceithre coimperta caema*, where the female dove is said to conceive when she and her mate gaze fixedly at each other; here it is said that conception by the ear, which is nobler than any other, happened to the Blessed Virgin Mary alone. See Brian O Cuiv, 'Two items from Irish apocryphal tradition', *Celtica* X: 93–4, verses 8–12.

Modh-Siolaich

This term occurs in another context in MacDonald's first edition, in his poem called 'The Ark', describing the political friends who were to be taken aboard the vessel, and the enemies who were to be left to drown, or at least to be immersed for a while in water, in a verse on p. 173:

> Thoir dhachaidh Dubhul, is Eain,
> 'S gach fear tha dliaghach dhiut [*sic*] teasraig;
> 'S do gach teughlach eile cáraid,
> Go modh-siolaich fhagail beittir.

The 1924 edition prints, p. 250:

> Thoir dhachaidh Dughall is Iain,
> 'S gach fear tha dligheach dhut teasraig;
> 'S de gach teaghlach eile càraid,
> Gu modh-siolaich fhagail beitir.

Translated:

> Let John and Dougald both be taken home,
> And all whose welfare you would fain secure;
> While out of every family take a pair,
> So that the natural increase may be pure.

Suggested:

> Bring home Dugald and John, and save every one who is dutiful to you; and out of every family (save) a pair, to leave a (politically) clean progeny.

The metre shows that *Iain* should not have been substituted for *Eain*, which presumably was disyllabic, rhyming with *fear* (? Eathain).

Notes and References to Section 6

[1]Education in Revolution principles is meant.

[2]*Proposal for the Conversion of the Popish Natives of Ireland*, p. 136.

[3]It is based on the translation of a Latin-English vocabulary called the New Vocabulary for the Use of Schools, printed by James McEwing in 1720, of which no copy has yet been traced. See J. L. Campbell, 'The First Printed Gaelic Vocabulary', *Scots Magazine*, October, 1937, and ante pp. 165–173.

[4]Throughout this article I shall adhere to the orthography of the 1751 edition when quoting from it.

[5]See *Scottish Gaelic Studies*, Vol.VI p. 43–4.

[6]The copy in my possession bears the date 1835, though 1834 seems to be the date of most copies.

[7]Why is 'Captain Duncan' the only Hanoverian named in this song? Is it possible that he is the same person as Black Duncan the Notary, father of the poetess whom MacDonald attacked, and not necessarily the same person as Captain Donnchadh of the 1751 version of the Ark (p. 175) at all?

[8]In the preface to the 1751 edition, MacDonald wrote that one of the reasons he had had for printing his book was the hope that 'publication of those poems wrote some time ago, for the amusement of a private gentleman, may afford some entertainment to those versed in this ancient and comprehensive language,' Reid speculates on the possibility that the condemned songs had been written for this purpose. The identity of the gentleman in question has not been disclosed. He may have been 'Fear Arnabidh' who wrote a poem in praise of 'Alister Mac Domhnuil' which is printed in the Eigg Collection (p. 322) and in which direct allusion is made to *Diomoladh Móraig* and *Oran nam Bodach*. The authors of *Clan Donald* say this is John MacDonald of Ardnabie who was a captain in the Glengarry Regiment in 1745 (*Clan Donald* Vol. III, p. 346). The remarkable thing is that no editor of Mac Mhaighstir Alasdair has ever quoted or discussed this poem as far as I know.

[9]The assertion by the Rev. Donald MacLean in *Typographia Scoto-Gadelica* that the preface to the 1874 edition of MacDonald's poems was written by Donald MacKinnon, later to become the first Professor of Celtic at Edinburgh University in 1882, requires confirmation. There is no mention of it in MacLean's obituary of Professor MacKinnon in Vol. X of the *Celtic Review*. D. C. MacPherson was perfectly capable of writing the preface to his own edition of the poems of Mac Mhaighstir Alasdair; he was a Lochaber man, in closer touch with Inverness-shire Jacobite traditions than MacKinnon, who was a native of Colonsay.

[10]The extent to which MacDonald may have been influenced by the language and style of contemporary Scots and English lampoonery is a matter which has not been investigated.

[11]I must express my obligation to Mr K. D. MacDonald MA of the Celtic Department of Glasgow University for information about the 1839 edition of MacDonald's poems, and to Mr D. M. Lloyd, Keeper of Printed Books at the National Library of Scotland, for photographic reproductions of the title-page, memoir, and supplement in the 1839 edition, and of the title-page and memoir in the 1851 edition.

[12]Mistakenly catalogued by Professor Donald MacKinnon as two poems. Stanzas 7 and 9 of the 1751 printed version are added in Roman hand on the lower half of p. 37.

Section 7

.

The Clearances

.

Review – Ian Grimble,
The Trial of Patrick Sellar. London, 1962

This review was published in the *Times Literary Supplement*.

In 1746 the anonymous author of a letter to the Duke of Newcastle on the subject of the prevention of any future Jacobite risings, mentioned the possibility of transporting all the rebel Highland clans to British colonies in Africa and America from their homes where, the writer alleged, they were leading 'the poor and lazy Life of mere Shepherds ... And that the now forfeited lands, on which these pernicious Drones lived, be planted and cultivated by an industrious and loyal set of People, to be sent thither in their Stead.'

The clansmen of Sutherland had, with few exceptions, been loyal to the Hanoverian cause at the time of the Forty-five, but eventually this was not to save them from the kind of fate suggested in 1746 for their enemies. In *The Trial of Patrick Sellar* Mr Grimble tells, through the accounts of eye-witnesses and the comments of contemporary and later writers, the story of this, the most notorious of the Highland Clearances. It was notorious because of the wealth and position of the landowners, the Marquis and Marchioness of Stafford, the large area of country that was the subject of their 'improvements', and because Karl Marx was to cite the Sutherland Clearances as an outstanding example of the treatment a peasant population undergoes when feudal paternalism is replaced by *laissez faire* capitalism.

Not the least nightmarish aspect of the Highland Clearances is that they were often conceived in the abstract terms of planners who had little or no feeling for human values, and then presented, in the double-talk of the time, as 'schemes of improvement'. What could be 'better' in the terms of the interests of the owners of great Highland estates (there has never been a limit to the amount of land any one individual may own in Scotland) and the Lowland factors they often employed, and the Lowland sheep-farmers to whom they were giving leases, than that the indigenous Gaelic-speaking population, then mostly engaged in cattle-rearing, should be removed from their holdings in the interior of the country at short notice and resettled along the coast to be inshore fishermen or kelp gatherers, while their vacated holdings were turned into large sheep farms? Regardless of local custom, the law as it then stood was on the side of the 'improvers'. 'Every man my good sir has a right to do the best he can for himself', wrote MacNeil of Barra to the parish priest in 1825, 'if one set of servants (tenants at will, are nothing else) won't do, the master must try others'.

Patrick Sellar, whose name is still execrated amongst Gaelic-speaking Highlanders, and his successor James Loch, acted in this spirit. Sellar had obtained the lease of the farm of Morvich on the Sutherland estates in 1810. He acted as sub-factor to William Young on these estates. In 1814, Sellar was involved in an eviction which resulted in his subsequent trial for, amongst other things, fire-raising, demolishing houses and endangering the lives of elderly and bed-ridden people. He was acquitted of these charges at Inverness on 23rd April 1816 by a jury of whose thirteen members eight were local landed proprietors. But in spite of his successor James Loch's apologia, in spite of Harriet Beecher Stowe's defence of the Sutherland family, and of the striking disinclination of Scottish Whig historians to allude to the matter – in Hume Brown's *History of Scotland*, for instance, the only references to Sutherland are in connection with the Viking invasions – the scandal of the Sutherland Clearances spread until it reached international proportions. It received striking confirmation through the posthumous publication of the Rev. Donald Sage's diary in 1889. Since that time, while the object of the Clearances has found defenders, such as Sir Robert Rait and Dr G. S. Pryde in *Scotland* (1934), the means employed have been unanimously condemned.

The Clearances earned a lasting unpopularity for the owners of Highland estates as a class. Ultimately the almost unlimited power they and their agents possessed over their crofter tenants through the right of instant eviction was broken by the Crofters' Act of 1886, which introduced into the Highlands a security of tenure that Scandinavian crofters, for instance, had known for generations. The fact that the great majority of Protestant Highlanders supported the Free Church at the time of the Disruption was directly due to the failure of the Established ministers, appointed under patronage (itself introduced in flagrant violation of the Treaty of Union) to defend the interests of their parishioners against landlord and factor at the time of the evictions.

This is an important book, important because of the deadly but dispassionate way in which Mr Grimble marshalls and presents the evidence on what has been often a matter for emotional argument. Distinguished names figure here: General Stewart of Garth, Sir Walter Scott, Donald MacLeod of *Gloomy Memories,* Hugh Miller, Harriet Beecher Stowe, Lord Napier, the Rev. Donald Sage, Professor Blackie. There is an interesting appendix of local Gaelic songs connected with the Clearances. The only thing one could wish for is a good map of Sutherland.

Letter to the New Yorker

·

Isle of Canna
Scotland
19th December 1948

Mrs Beecher Stowe

Dear Sir,

As a foreigner I was interested to read Mr Edmund Wilson's eulogy of Mrs Beecher Stowe in your number of November 27th. This in view of the fact that in *A New American History*, W. E. Woodward remarks (p. 466) of *Uncle Tom's Cabin*, 'When her book appeared in 1852, Mrs Stowe had never been in the South, had no personal knowledge of slavery, and was wholly ignorant of the negro mentality. Her novel is a well-meaning and sincere effort to depict slavery as she thought it was. It has hardly anything to do with reality.'

We Scottish Highlanders are interested in the question of Mrs Stowe's literary integrity, because (as is little known in America) Mrs Stowe's pen was employed to write an apologia for the notorious evictions which were carried out in the County of Sutherland during the early part of the nineteenth century. This effusion, and the able reply to it of Donald MacLeod, author of *Gloomy Memories* can be read in Alexander MacKenzie's *Highland Clearances*. Her apologia for the evictions had, also, 'hardly anything to do with reality'.

It has always been a source of wonder to me how a writer whose method was based so entirely upon emotional subjectivism has been taken so seriously as a social historian, 'a first rate modern social intelligence' as Mr Wilson puts it. Do first rate modern social intelligences dispense so entirely with first hand knowledge of, and the objective approach to, their subjects?

I am,

yours truly
John L. Campbell

Highland Entailed Estates

An entailed estate in the Highlands had something in common with a family business. When the heir of entail married, the usual custom was for his prospective wife/widow to surrender her right to one-third of the property and the same amount, the prospective share of their unborn children, in return for annuities secured on the rental of the estate. In return, the bride's dowry was put under trust with reversion to her husband and, after him, to her daughters (or perhaps her unmarried daughter).

The entailed estate was under the supervision of the trustees of entail, of whom at least one was likely to be a senior member of the family, and another the family lawyer. An entailed estate could not be security for the personal debts of the occupier and any borrowings for the purpose of making improvements had to be approved by the trustees of entail.

The heir would be under the strict legal obligation of paying the annuities to his widowed mother and younger sisters (? and brothers) created by his father's marriage settlement. Specific sums bequeathed to them under his father's will would be chargeable against his father's personal estate, but could be a moral obligation if that estate was insufficient to meet them.

If the occupier of an entailed estate ran up personal debts, they could not be charged against the entailed estate – the occupier could evade payment and still retain the occupancy of the entailed estate by letting himself be made bankrupt. (Up till about 1880 the rental of an entailed estate used to be sufficient security for borrowing money for improvements approved by the trustees of entail.) The only way private debts could be met in such circumstances was by disentailing the land, in which case a sale could take place after compensating the first and second heirs of entail. Morally, an occupier who evaded paying personal debts by taking refuge in personal bankruptcy and retaining the entailed land would not be well thought of.

The Clearing of Clanranald's Islands

.

Published in *The Scots Magazine*

The following letter, from Clanranald's factor to his Edinburgh law agent in 1827, was found amongst correspondence preserved in the Clanranald Papers. It speaks for itself; we have many accounts of the Highland Clearances from outside sources, but it is not often that we have the privilege of reading frank, uncensored, confidential correspondence between a proprietor's agents laying the plans for an eviction. That is what we have here.

At the time the letter was written, Clanranald, who had succeeded as a minor in 1794 to estates paying £25,000 a year rent which had been in possession of his family for 500 years, was, after a youth devoted to high life in London and the representing of an English rotten borough in Parliament, on the verge of bankruptcy. His agents were obliged to wring the uttermost farthing from the family estates, but so little did they understand contemporary developments, that we find the Factor writing of securing an income from kelp and fishing for the proprietor at a time when the market for kelp had been completely undermined by the reduction of the import duty on salt, and when the fishing industry was likewise to be left in the lurch by the Government's withdrawal of herring fishing bounties, the reduction of which had already been begun.

At the time this letter was written there had been talk of the Government assisting emigration from the Western Highlands to Canada. The letter proves how the feudal power of the Highland lairds had been exchanged, since Culloden, for an economic power just as absolute, and far more arbitrary and irresponsible; for hereditary jurisdictions could hardly have been carried on by absentees, who could, however, easily arrange evictions. It is here seriously proposed that the Government shall pay the expenses of the emigrants, but the Lairds, their factors, and the established clergy shall retain the selection of those who are to be sent away; the political, sectarian and personal implications of such a claim can be easily imagined; the neighbouring island of Barra provides a similar case. It will be seen that after making an enormous profit on kelp – which cost the proprietor under £3 a ton and was sold for about £20 a ton – a considerable proportion of the wages paid was recovered in rent; and it was proposed to extend a similar system to the fishing. Readers of the MacNeil letters in the *Book of Barra* will recollect similar proposals made for the Barra estate. The proposal to retain a sufficient excess population to keep rents up and wages down should be noted.

These projects came too late to save Clanranald. Canna was sold in 1828; Eigg shortly afterwards; and South Uist and Benbecula in 1837. But what Clanranald's agent had proposed, his successors carried out, as the allegations made against the Gordon Cathcart administration by the South Uist and Benbecula witnesses to the Crofters' Commission in 1883 show; and in 1851 these islands were the scene of one of the worst of the evictions, still well remembered in local tradition. Canna and Eigg were also 'cleared' by the succeeding proprietors. Readers of Dr Johnson's *Journey to the Western Islands of Scotland* will note with interest how this letter fulfils the Doctor's prognostications of the economic future of the Highlands.

Benbecula
25 Feby. 1827.

Alexander Martin Esq. W.S.
5 St David's Street,
Edinburgh.

My dear Sir,
The long continuance of the Easterly winds detained our Packet in Port[1] and prevented my receiving your letter of the 7th current in the ordinary time. I was anxious also to ascertain exactly the present extent and circumstances of our population here.

Our circumstance connected with the application to Government for assistance in sending over extra Population to America I beg to call your particular attention to viz. that in the event of any assistance being granted, the meeting of their Ffactors, or these gentlemen, joined with the established Clergy, be allowed to select the ffamilies to whom assistance is to be given. If the Proprietors are not allowed to exercise very considerable influence in selecting the Emigrants, assistance will be given where it is not required, the most wealthy and industrious of our population will emigrate, and we will be left with the dregs.

With regard to Clanranald's Glebe, my object is to clear *two particular districts*, particularly well calculated for pasture, where the poorest of the people and most of the subtenants reside, and where the greater part of our inferior kelp is manufactured. The price obtained for the kelp has not for some years defrayed expense, and therefore the manufacture must be abandoned in these districts. I would not at present make any material change on the other parts of the Estate.[2]

In my Report I made a gross estimate of the Population of Clanranald's estate in South Uist without going into particulars. I have now obtained an accurate amount of the population of the Estate. I find the number of families to be 894, which, calculating 6 to a family, gives a Population of 5364. Of this Population there are

1. Tacksmen holding ffarms of Clanranald rented at from £20 to £420	Families	13
2. Tenants or crofters holding crofts rented at from £4 to £13 directly from Clanranald and paying their rents entirely by kelpmaking		481
3. Subtenants holding lands by sublet from the Principal Tacksmen and employed in making Clanranald's kelp of which the Tacksmen have the manufacture on their farms		47
4. Subtenants, under principal tacksmen, not employed as kelpers, but paying their rents to the Tacksmen in cattle or otherways		160
5. Cottars and poor people who have no means of subsistence but what they derive from the Tenants their relations		<u>193</u>
	Families	894

The number of Families normally engaged in the kelp manufacture is 528. The quantity manufactured *hitherto*, may be averaged at 1300 tons, being nearly 2 $\frac{1}{2}$ tons to a ffamily. The kelp is however apportioned according to the Rents each family pays and those having large Crofts of course have the assistance of their relatives in kelp making. The price paid for manufacture is generally £2 : 12 : 6 p. Ton, but in the districts where I wish to depopulate £3 : 3 p. Ton is paid owing to the distance from a shipping Port.

You will not fail to observe the great number of subtenants on this Estate. This is a miserable system and it is particularly desirable that it should be got rid of. With a few exceptions, the Tacksmen are miserably poor: very bad ffarmers, following the old system of ffarming with very little improvement. They are very bad payers of rent and of course their Tenants cannot be in good circumstances. It is a great object for Clanranald to introduce strangers in place of these Tacksmen[3] but this can never do without getting rid of the

Population forming the settlements. I have, as you know, succeeded in letting Askernish to a stranger, a good tenant, and I think there would be little difficulty in letting the other ffarms in the same way when we quit of the old set.[4]

I cannot flatter you with the hope of any immediate rise of rent. My views are principally directed to a well paid *money rent independent of labour*.[5] At present we get only labour even from these ffarms where no kelp is manufactured. If the kelp is given up small Tenants cannot continue to pay the present rents, because the work they got enabled them to pay rents for portions of ground so small that they could pay nothing from the produce.

The *average* Rent of the Crofts held by the Small Tenants *directly* from Clanranald may be about £6 : 10 : On these Crofts the Tenant keeps 3 ponies 3 cows and two or three young cattle generally year olds *all of inferior quality*. On the higher rented crofts say £10 or £12 they keep 3 ponies and 4 or 5 cows and young cattle in proportion while on small crofts of £4 or £5 the Tenants can only keep 2 ponies and 2 cows and a young beast or two. In many instances the greater part of the stock belongs to the crofters relatives. The crofters have besides the crofts the benefit of common where their cattle are fed in summer and harvest. The circumstances of the Subtenants are of course much worse than those of the Crofters. They are generally speaking miserably poor.

On crofts averaging the rents I have mentioned the Tenant plants 7 or 8 barells of Potatoes and gathers probably 100 barells sometimes more sometimes less. He sows from a boll to a boll and a half of *Bear*[6] and raises 7, 8 or 9 Bolls. He sows also 3 or 4 Barrels of small black oats (4 barrells to the Boll) and raises 15 or 18 Barrells.

The fishing has never been much attended to on Clanranald's Estate in Uist. I have no doubt that it might be extended. I do not however suppose the fishery will ever be carried on to any considerable extent on this Estate. The arable land is all situated on the west side of the Island. The fishing Banks are situated off the east coast and at some distance. We have never encouraged settlers on the east coast, because there our best kelp is manufactured and the settlers would commit depradations on the weed by taking it for manure – I doubt if the Bounty[7] ever induces the poorer classes to *commence* the ffishing. I suspect much the Bounty in that remote quarter falls principally to the Merchant who furnishes the salt and materials and buys the ffish. It would be a great encouragement to the poorer classes to enter into and continue the ffishery if the Proprietors, or their factors, would furnish them with salt and materials at price cost including charges : buy the ffish send it to market and allow the ffisher the price obtained deducting all expense. The Landlords would be benefited by the encreasee of the value of the Lands and a well paid rent : while the fisher would be encouraged by the consciousness that he had obtained a fair price for his commodity. Speculators charge enormous profit on their ffurnishings to the ffishers and they of course buy the ffish as cheap as they can.

I am not a good Judge of the expense of sending Emigrants to America. The expense of transporting the Irish Emigrants was ridiculous. The people from this country will all go to Cape Briton, and nowhere else if they can help it. They are accustomed to live at home almost exclusively on meal and milk and potatoes. The expense therefore of sending them across the Atlantic will be much less than that of transporting the same number of people from England. I am of opinion that from 30/- to £2 would feed a full grown Highlander for the ordinary voyage to Cape Briton and I should imagine ampill might be ffreighted for about 40/- each Passenger. If you substitute molasses for the milk they are accustomed to at home, and lay in a sufficient quantity of good meal and salt for the voyage, I do not think much more will be necessary.

The population of the Sand Island of Canna is at least 200. You will see from the plan in your possession the extent of this spot. The people neither ffish nor do anything else. I cannot imagine how they live. They are most miserably poor. They make one year 9 tons and the next 15 tons of kelp which I sell for them and credit them the price. This is all the rent they ever pay. Their whole efforts would not pay the fourth part of their arrears. The evil here arises entirely from excess of population. The people were sent to the island[8] with a view to the fishing to which however they never attended. They can contribute nothing towards payment of their freight to America.

Nothing else occurs to me on this subject beyond that I have mentioned in my report. I think I have overstated the number of people it would be necessary to send from Clanranald's Long Island Estate (i.e. Uist and Benbecula), I think 2000 would be sufficient. It would be well that there was a partial demand for land beyond the supply, for reasons which it is not necessary to mention. In this view I think Col. Campbell was right in keeping a full supply though I do most assuredly agree with you in thinking he might spare a good many more than he proposes. I cannot divine how Tiree supports such a population,[9] it must be a perfect Lombardy.

You will restrict your claim for assistance to the transporting of 2000 people from this part of the Estate to this number the Inhabitants of the Sand Island are to be added.

The Island of Eigg would be the better for wanting 150 of its inhabitants. The ffarm of Cliadel in particular ought to be cleared of the small Tenants. They are in much the same state with the Sand Island people.

But if you succeed in your application to any, even the smallest extent, take care that we are to have the selection of the Emigrants, otherwise there will be a great deal of confusion amongst us. We will of course take care that only the poorer class the Subtenants and Cottars are sent off and these are assuredly unable to pay anything towards their freight. I will hope to hear from you very soon and I am

Yours truly
D. M. Shaw.

A Plea from Benbecula

·

Saved from bonfire of South Uist factorial archives when Askernish House was cleared.

My dearest Lord,

I have to tell you the oppression they are to do on us ... we are here five poor men without a boat or horse to support ourselves but we are hardly making a crop what would support us for half a year and the rest maintaining ourselves with fish and with what we would get for it now our possession is given to another man by Master William burne's[10] order ... we are saying that we will never remove from our possession[11] till this Complaint be sent before your honourable ... first because we got leases During 7 years. It is for alm we got the lots first by Doctor MacLeod's[12] order for we were unable to pay a better place ... he saw it proper to us to come to it and laid 5 shillings sterling of rent on us the first year of our lease ... Mr William Young[13] laid on us one pound sterling yearly of rent during the severe years ... the first of them we paid the rent honourably by kelp just carrying the seaweed on our back without horse very scarce of food ... besides all every one of them will be on the parochial board[14] except few because they are old men without Assistant ... but if they are left where they are they will help themselves as well as they can and they will be dilligent to pay their dues after making improvements and dykes ... they wanted us to go to worse place where we cannot get any seaweed nearer than a m.[ile].

This letter is not well written but I hope your honour will excuse me for I had no learn and we would not get any person at Uist that should write for us supposing they would kill us for fear of the factor and ground officer. We have 4 acres of moss apiece and the manure is at the end of each croft for it is so favourable for us as it is... We hope your honour will have pity on us for it is said by the factor that we will be sent away from your estate at Whitsunday because we refused to go to the bad place they want [us] to go ... We have no more to add ... this is the name of our place ... Airdneon Benbecula South Uist ...

these are the names of the crofters –

Margaret MacAnnish
Angus MacLellan
Neil MacPhie
Angus MacLean
Margt widow Charles MacAnnish

The Background of the Hebridean Clearances
•

We must think of a Hebridean laird of old family who has prospered in the days between 1770 and 1815 from the sale of kelp, made by his small tenants possibly as a condition of their tenure, at a time when landowners exercised foreshore rights and could even forbid their tenants from taking seaweed to manure their holdings. The business was extremely profitable to Hebridean landowners, and looked like being so permanently. On the strength of it money was borrowed to build a grand new mansion, to keep up with the way of living in the south. Moreover, the estate would be an entailed one; under the Deed of Entail the laird would have to make adequate settlements for his prospective widow and the younger brothers and sisters of his heir, which the heir would have to meet as legal obligations when he succeeded to the estate; they would be administered by trustees, usually Edinburgh lawyers and senior collateral relatives; there was no legal way to get out of having to pay them, unless the widowed mother and the younger brothers and sisters were prepared to renounce their interests in them.

The laird dies; the price of kelp falls owing to the development of the Leblanc process of making soda from salt, and the reduction of the duty on imported kelp, called *barilla*. The young laird who succeeds is unable to meet the financial obligations of the settlements made under the Deed of Entail and by his father's Will. The widowed mother and the younger brothers and sisters refuse to renounce their rights under the Deed of Entail. The law insists that the heir to the estate must meet them. In fact he can only do so by getting rid of the majority of his small tenants, who can be removed at a year's notice without compensation for improvements, and letting their common grazing and their arable land to a Low Country farmer.

The small tenants, speaking only the Gaelic language, have little prospect of immediate employment outside the Highlands. It is useless to apply to the Courts; these do not recognise the Gaelic language. The only solution appears to be exile to Nova Scotia. The laird can get an emigration agent to arrange this at a low charge; the agent will arrange for a ship to call to take the emigrants there. The estate will choose who is to go and who can stay; those who are to go will have no choice but to board the ship and leave Scotland for ever.

Possibly the young laird may prefer to sell the estate rather than to clear it and see the introduction of sheep. That means finding a wealthy stranger who is prepared to pay a good price for an island kingdom where he can find solitude and sport. In former times this would be usually an Englishman; today it would be more likely to be a Dutchman or an Arab. In such cases almost the whole of the native population, except for a few chosen servants would have to go; the purchaser would not want to have to depend on Gaels, difficult people speaking an impossible language – he would prefer to bring in employees from the south who would have the same way of looking at things, of thinking and of speaking, as himself.

The first alternative described here is illustrated by the case of Barra; see the correspondence printed in *Songs Remembered in Exile* (Campbell, J. L. (1990)) edited by the writer. The second is illustrated by the case of the Isle of Rum, described in this book (pp. 138–141). Scottish Whig historians, who invariably write from an urban point of view,[15] seem unable to grasp that there is nothing inevitable, God-given, or sacrosanct, about Scottish land laws, particularly about those land laws before the passing of the Crofters' Act of 1886. If they had not been so shy of making any kind of comparison between Scotland and other northern countries of Europe, they might have asked why the glens and islands of Norway, from which there was voluntary emigration to North America, were never emptied as many of the Scottish glens and islands were, and consider the difference it could have made to the Hebrides, if Scottish inshore fisheries had been protected in the way that Norwegian ones were.

Ailean Dall MacDougall

Ailean Dall lived from about 1750 to about 1830; this poem is taken from the second edition of his poems, which was published in 1829. It is headed in English 'Sung to Heroic Gaelic Metre', which means it was composed to be sung to an 'Oran Mór' ('Great Song') air.

The song expresses the bard's disgust at the depopulation of the Highlands when the country was invaded by Lowland shepherds ignorant of Gaelic, and sheep supplanted most of the cattle to whose rearing Highlanders had been devoted, as a direct consequence of the Clearances.

Ailean Dall was born in Glencoe and lived at Inverlochy. The first edition of his poems was published in 1798, edited by Ewen MacLachlan. This came to the attention of Alasdair MacDonell of Glengarry, born in 1773, an eccentric who kept up the style of a pre-1745 Highland chief with a 'tail' of personal employees; Alasdair MacDonell persuaded Ailean Dall to become his family bard, and rewarded him with a house and a small pension. The second (and authoritative) edition of Ailean Dall's poems was published in 1829, a year after Glengarry's death in January 1828 in an accidental shipwreck, and about the time of Ailean Dall's own death.

Sheep were very much disliked in the Highlands when they were introduced in large numbers to replace most of the cattle, the traditional livestock of the country. Compare Duncan Ban MacIntyre's blessing on the foxes because they hunted the sheep: 'Are these the sheep of brindled face that caused dispeace throughout the world; the land to be laid waste to us, and the rent to become dearer?'[16] and John MacLean of Inverscadale's poem on the condition of the Highlands after Culloden, ending: 'And I who had lived in Ardgour, where oft heard was the roebuck, now am in drab little Sornan mucking with sheep' (Campbell, J. L. (1990), p. 257).

In spite of Ailean Dall's invective against sheep and shepherds, and praise for Glengarry for disliking them, the fact was that Glengarry's old fashioned style of living had cost him a great deal of money, and left his estates financially embarrassed. To pay the debts, all of them except Knoydart were sold, and in 1853 Knoydart itself was cleared by Alasdair MacDonell's daughter-in-law in one of the most notorious of the Highland Clearances (see Meek, D. E. (1997)).

A Song on the Lowland Shepherds

1. An affliction has come on us in Scotland; poor people are exposed to it, they are without food, without clothing, without

211

a piece of green land; the North is destroyed. There is nothing to be seen but sheep and lambs, with Lowlanders around them on every hillside, every farmland is getting emptied, the Gaels are buried in chickweed.

2. Milk cattle are not to be seen in the glens, and rarely horses being harnessed; fulfilling the prophecy that the plough would go out of use.[17] Hunting has gone out of favour, every crooked gun is without a lock, neither roebuck nor kid is killed, and yelling of Lowlanders has banished the deer.

3. Throughout the hills there is no diversion, the marksman is under restraint, the stag is lost, every hind and year-old deer has disappeared, the greyhound will not find the red buck of the burns to put it to the low ground; in exchange for all this there is the whistling of Lowlanders in every dell.

4. No lowing is heard in the cattlefold; the white-shouldered cattle are no longer in fashion; neither song nor ditty is heard from the brown-haired maiden milking a cow. Since our herd is diminished, thirst often afflicts us; instead of our friends, we have a grey idler at the foot of every mound.

5. As if they had fallen from the tree, blind nuts are dying on the branches; old folk are so, and little children without milk; they have been thrown out of favour from the place of birth of their grandfathers. I'd prefer that the French came to behead the Lowlanders.

6. There are no more marriages nor wedding parties; poets have ceased to sing. I have often heard it said 'Cadgers are coming with baskets'. So it has happened to me, I am not invited to the fair where I used to be welcome, they'd prefer to set a dog onto cattle.

7. Every one of them who has got the upper hand, has exiled each person who would face hardship, if pursuit was to come in strength; if the Kingdom were involved in war, the Shepherds would be in want; that's the tale we'd like to hear, that they had all been put to extremities.

8. They'll get up early on the Sabbath, and meet each other, and when they get to talking, the talk is about grazing, each man asking his neighbour 'How did you leave the flock? What price did the wethers make? Did you send them to the sale?'

9. 'There was no cause for complaint this year, they made sixteen shillings and more; if you want to know, I bought the [oat] meal with the wool; the old ewes went [sold] quickly, and if I

keep the young lot, even if a third of them die, I'll get the rent out of those that survive.'

10. When one of them arises early and climbs the hill, there will come a Lowland yell from his mouth, shouting after his dogs; his shout is music I don't like; wrapped in a green plaid he carries a braxy sheep in a sack, with sheep ticks in his hair and on his body.

10. When one of them arises early and climbs the hill, there will come a Lowland yell from his mouth, shouting after his dogs; his shout is music I don't like; wrapped in a green plaid he carries a braxy sheep in a sack, with sheep ticks in his hair and on his body.

11. When he comes near us, pity whoever is on his lee side; his smell can't be pleasant when he's carrying tripes home, often he's bathed in blood from his waist to his feet; anyone who goes to have a drink with him, would have to stop up his nostrils.

12. When two or three are sitting in the inn, having settled their business, there will be seen at the head of the table a shepherd with his dog after him; he should be put in a corner, and a knee should be put on his gullet; throw him out on the midden, let him get his own smearing.

13. An unclean man is bad company for others; a man who castrates lambs with his teeth is no proper company for people. Up to his knees in sheep-dirt greedily sucking them out, if you offer him a drink, don't taste it afterwards.

14. Away with handlers of wool, if you want right company! If you get close to them, don't let your nose in! As you won't hear from them anything other than talk about skins and wool being sold, accounts of the weather, and all the time about selling lambs before they're born.

15. We will sit happily around a table, with unblemished singing and fiddling, kindly and charitable to each other; let there not be one of their tribe in our presence; drink to the health of MacKenzie, and of the fine Colonel of Glengarry, because they dislike sheep and the people who drive up the price of land.

16. Fill up your glasses, don't forget [Cameron of] Erracht, he wants us to live, and to prevent that tribe from getting the better of us. If the gentry of the Kingdom would stand as faithfully as the friends of Ailean, the tenants would not be dispersed, making them dependent on hospitality.

A Very Civil People

Notes and References to Section 7

[1]Mails for the southern Outer Islands were then carried by boat between Dunvegan and Lochmaddy.

[2]i.e. Benbecula and South Uist.

[3]It must be remembered that the tacksmen themselves would be relations of Clanranald.

[4]i.e. lease.

[5]i.e. a rent entirely in cash instead of in labour on the estate.

[6]Four-rowed barley.

[7]A subsidy, of long standing, given by the Government to assist the herring fishery. It was abolished in 1830 under the influence of laissez faire.

[8]From the main island of Canna, when one farm was cleared.

[9]4,181 in 1821; 1,716 in 1921.

[10]The then factor.

[11]i.e. their land.

[12]Factor of South Uist in the 1830s.

[13]A factor after Dr MacLeod.

[14]i.e. if they were evicted, they would have to go on parochial relief.

[15]Sir Robert Rait and G. S. Pryde in their *Scotland* in the Modern World series, printed an end map which shows SHEEP as the only economic product of the Highlands. There was no mention of CATTLE or of FISHERIES.

[16]Angus MacLeod ed., *The Songs of Duncan Ban MacIntyre*, Scottish Gaelic Texts Society 1952, p. 346.

[17]Refers to the prophecy of the Brahan Seer that the time would come when sheep would put the plough out of use and up in the rafters in the Highlands. He went on to predict that the sheep there would ultimately disappear!

List of Works Cited

Allardyce, J. (Ed.) (1895) *Historical Papers Relating to the Jacobite Period 1699–1750*, Vol. I, Aberdeen: New Spalding Club

Aufrere, A. (Ed.) (1817) *The Lockhart Papers*, Vol. II, London

Buchan, A. Rev. (1732) *A Description of St Kilda*, Edinburgh

Cameron, A. (1937) 'A Page from the Past: the Lead Mines at Strontian', *Transactions of the Gaelic Society of Inverness* Vol. XXXVIII (1937–1941) 444–452

Caimbeul, I. L. (1936) *Orain Ghaidhlig le Seonaidh Caimbeul*, Dunfermline

Campbell, J. F. (1860–2) *Popular Tales of the West Highlands*, Vols 1–4, Edinburgh

Campbell, J. L. (Ed.) (1936) *The Book of Barra*, London: George Routledge & Sons. New edition Acair Stornaway, 1998

Campbell, J. L. (1939) *Sia Sgialachdan*, privately printed, Edinburgh

Campbell, J. L. (1950) *Gaelic in Scottish Education and Life*, Edinburgh: The Saltire Society

Campbell, J. L. (1952–3) 'Leabhar-latha Mhgr. Ailein (Fr Allen McDonald's Diary – March 1898)', *Gairm* 1–2

Campbell, J. L. (1954) 'Catriana Nighean Eachainn, 'ga h-aithris le Peigi Anndra', *Gairm* 3: 58–68

Campbel, J. L. (1954) 'The MacNeils of Barra and the Irish Fransiscans', *The Innes Review* (Scottish Catholic Historical Studies) V: 33–8

Campbell, J. L. (1954) 'Dunnchadh Ciobair an Ceann Bharraidh', *Gairm* 2: 271–3

Campbell, J. L. (1955) 'Catriana daughter of Hector', *The Scots Magazine*, October

Campbell, J. L. (Ed.) (1958) *Gaelic Words and Expressions from South Uist and Eriskay*, Dublin Institute for Advanced Studies

Campbell, J. L. (1960) 'A' chiad uair a dh'fhàg mi Uibhist. Air innse le Bean Nill', *Gairm* 8: 314

Campbell, J. L. (1961) 'An darna àite dha'n deach mi. Air innse le Bean Nill', *Gairm* 9: 51

Campbell, J. L. (1961) *Tales from Barra Told by the Coddy*, 2nd edition, Edinburgh: W. & A. K. Johnson & G. W. Bacon

Campbell, J. L. (Ed.) (1975) *A Collection of Highland Rites and Customes*, D. S. Brewer: The Folklore Society

Campbell, J. L. (1984) *Canna. The Story of a Hebridean Island*, Oxford: Oxford University Press

Campbell, J. L. (1984) *Highland Songs of the Forty-Five*, revised edition, Edinburgh: Scottish Gaelic Texts Society

Campbell, J. L. (1990) *Songs Remembered in Exile*, Aberdeen: Aberdeen University Press

Campbell, J. L. (1997) 'Notes on Poems by Mac Mhaighstir Alasdair', *Scottish Gaelic Studies* Vol. 18 (1997), pp 175–185

Campbell, J. L. and Collinson, F. *Hebridean Folksongs*, Vol. I, 1969; Vol II, 1977; Vol. III, 1981, Oxford

Campbell, J. L. and Eastwick, C. (1966) 'The MacNeils of Barra in the 'Forty-Five', *The Innes Review* XVII: 82–90

Campbell, J. L. and Hall, T. H. (1968) *Strange Things: the Enquiry by the Society for Psychical Research into Second Sight in the Scottish Highlands*, London: Routledge & Kegan Paul

Campbell, J. L. and Thomson, D. (1963) *Edward Lhuyd in the Scottish Highlands 1699–1700*, Oxford

Carmichael, A. (1928–71) *Carmina Gadelica*, Vols 1–6, Edinburgh

Chapman, R. W. (Ed.) (1930) *Johnson's Journey to the Western Islands and Boswell's Journal of a Tour to the Hebrides*, Oxford University Press

Clark, J. T. (Ed.) (1900) *Macfarlane's Genealogical Collections*, Vol. I, Edinburgh: Scottish History Society

Collinson, F. (1966) *The Traditional and National Music of Scotland*, London: Routledge & Kegan Paul

Fraser, S. (Ed.) (1816) *The Airs and Melodies Peculiare to the Highlands of Scotland and the Isles*, Edinburgh

Giblin, C. (1964) *Irish Franciscan Missions to Scotland 1619–46: Documents from Roman Archives*, Dublin

Goodrich-Freer, A. (1902) *Outer Isles*, Westminster: Constable

Kirk, R. (1933) *The Secret Commonwealth of Elves, Fauns and Fairies*, Stirling: Eneas Mackay

Lang, A. (1897) *Pickle the Spy*, London: Longmans

Lhuyd, E. (1707) *Archeologia Britannica*, Oxford

Macbain, A. and Kennedy, J. (Eds) (1892–94) *Reliquiae Celticae*, Vols. I–II, Inverness

Macbean, A. Rev. (1916) 'A Memorial Concerning the Highlands', In: Blaikie, W. B. (Ed.), *Origins of the Forty-Five*, Edinburgh: Scottish History Society

MacDhonuill, Alasdair (1751) *Ais-eiridh na Sean Chanoin Albannaich ('The Resurrection of the Ancient Scottish Language')*, Edinburgh

MacDonald, A. (1741) *A Galick and English Vocabulary, Leabhar a Theagasc Ainminnin*, Edinburgh

MacDonald, A. Rev. and MacDonald, A. Rev. (1904) *The Clan Donald*, Vol. III, Inverness

Mackenzie, A. (1883) *The History of the Highland Clearances*, Inverness

Mackenzie, W. (1895) *Gaelic Incantations, Charms and Blessings of the Hebrides*, Inverness

Mackenzie, W. C. (1949) *Highlands and Isles of Scotland. A Historical Survey*, Edinburgh

MacLean Sinclair, A. Rev. (1907) 'The MacNeils of Barra', *Celtic Review* III: 216–23

MacLeod, D. (1892) *Gloomy Memories in the Highlands of Scotland*, Glasgow

MacLeod, R. C. (Ed.) (1938–9) *The Book of Dunvegan*, Vols. 1–2, Aberdeen: Third Spalding Club

MacNeil, R. L. (1923) *The Clan MacNeil*, New York

MacPhail, J. R. N. (Ed.) (1920) *Highland Papers*, Vol. II, Edinburgh: Scottish History Society

MacPhail, J. R. N. (Ed.) (1934) *Highland Papers*, Vol. IV, Edinburgh: Scottish History Society

Mactavish, D. C. (Ed.) (1943) *Minutes of the Synod of Argyll Vol. I 1639–51*, Edinburgh: Scottish History Society

Martin, M. (1698) *A Late Voyage to St Kilda*, London

Martin, M. (1716) *A Description of the Western Islands of Scotland*, 2nd edition, London

Matheson, W. (1938) *The Songs of John MacCodrum*, Edinburgh: Scottish Gaelic Texts Society

Meek, D. E. (1995) *Tuath is Tighearna. Tenants and Landlords. An Anthology of Gaelic Poetry of Social and Political Protest (1800–1890)*, Edinburgh: Scottish Gaelic Texts Society

Minutes of Evidence and Report of the Crofters' Commission (1884) Edinburgh

Mitchell, A. and Clark, J. T. (Eds) (1906–8) *Macfarlane's Geographical Collections*, Vols. I–III, Edinburgh: Scottish History Society

Morrison, A. (1967–8) 'Harris Estate Papers, 1724–54', *Transactions of the Gaelic Society of Inverness* Vol. XLV: 33–97

Murray, A. (1936) *Father Allan's Island*, Edinburgh: The Moray Press

Paton, H. (Ed.) (1895–6) *The Lyon in Mourning 1745–75*, Vols. I–III, Edinburgh: Scottish History Society

Pennant, T. (1790) *A Tour in Scotland (1769)*, 5th edition, London

Reeves, W. (1874) *Life of St Columba*, The Historians of Scotland Series, Vol. VI, Edinburgh

Rossi, M. (1964) *Il Cappellano delle Fate ('The Chaplain of the Fairies')*, Giannini: Naples

Scott, H. (Ed.) (1915–61) *Fasti Ecclesiae Scoticanae*, Vols. 1–9, Edinburgh

Seton, G. (1878) *St Kilda, Past and Present*, Edinburgh

Shaw, M. F. (1977) *Folksongs and Folklore of South Uist*, 2nd edition, Oxford

Shaw, M. F. (1993) *From the Alleghenies to the Hebrides*, Edinburgh: Canongate

Skene, W. F. (1880) *Celtic Scotland: A History of Ancient Alban*, Vol. III, Edinburgh

Smith, G. G. (Ed.) (1895) *The Book of Islay*, Edinburgh

Thomson, R. L. (Ed.) (1970) *Foirm na n-Urrnuidheadh. John Carswell's Gaelic Translation of the Book of Common Order*, Edinburgh: Scottish Gaelic Texts Society

Watson, W. J. (1926) *The History of the Celtic Place-Names of Scotland*, Edinburgh: The Royal Celtic Society